# AN INTRODUCTION TO BIOETHICS

**FOURTH EDITION**
**Revised and Updated**

*Thomas A. Shannon*
*and*
*Nicholas J. Kockler*

Paulist Press
New York/Mahwah, NJ

Cover and book design by Lynn Else

Library of Congress Cataloging-in-Publication Data

Shannon, Thomas A. (Thomas Anthony), 1940–
    An introduction to bioethics / Thomas A. Shannon and Nicholas J. Kockler. — 4th ed., rev. and updated.
        p. ; cm.
    Includes bibliographical references.
    ISBN 978-0-8091-4623-9 (alk. paper)
    1. Medical ethics. 2. Bioethics. I. Kockler, Nicholas J. II. Title. [DNLM: 1. Bioethical Issues. 2. Bioethics. 3. Ethics, Medical. WB 60 S528i 2009]
    R724.S455 2009
    174.2—dc22

                                                                    2009011699

Published by Paulist Press
997 Macarthur Boulevard
Mahwah, New Jersey 07430

www.paulistpress.com

Printed and bound in the
United States of America

# CONTENTS

To our grandson, Isaiah Pietro Pinto,
and
To our granddaughter, Daisy Catherine Pinto,
Many years of joy and peace.
—T.A.S.

To my grandparents, Ralph and Marilynn Jeglum and
Nick and Christine Kockler,
Thank you for your love, support, wisdom,
and the meaning of family.
—N.J.K.

*PART I*

# GENERAL ISSUES

*Chapter 1*

# INTRODUCTION: WHAT IS BIOETHICS?

## WHAT IS BIOETHICS?

Today the word *bioethics* is commonplace. Several newsmagazines, television shows, and Web sites have devoted special editions to topics such as stem cell technology, cloning, organ transplantation, *in vitro* fertilization, and gene therapy. Almost daily, media attention focuses on some particular problem, application, or breakthrough in science that inevitably raises as many problems as it solves.

We have become so used to these discussions and events that we forget that it was only forty years ago that the Institute of Society, Ethics and the Life Sciences—as the Hastings Center was known then—was founded.[1] In 1965, few knew of the institute, and fewer still understood what its members were talking about. But the role and value of this institute, and others that were to follow in its footsteps, were soon discovered as the major questions of abortion, population control, the allocation of resources, genetic engineering, behavior modification, and all the problems associated with dying began to press in upon us. Discoveries and applications began to outpace our ability to reflect on them, and everyone was reeling from the biological revolution.

We have seen several presidential commissions and advisory boards, an encyclopedia and its revised editions,[2] numerous journals[3] and books,[4] several societies, associations, and centers,[5] and innumerable conferences all devoted to various problems in bioethics. Courses have spread throughout undergraduate and graduate schools; even graduate programs in bioethics now exist. Bioethicists have appeared as experts in court trials, and journalists frequently cite them in media reports about various dilemmas in health care and the life sciences. Institutional review boards, which examine the ethical dimensions of human research, are present almost everywhere.[6] Many hospitals now have in-house ethicists and/or ethics committees to help evaluate a variety of ethical dilemmas that occur in the routine provision of health care.[7]

Few would have thought that such events could have happened when the first few tentative steps in the ethical examination of issues in health care were being taken in the 1960s. From these early days, commentators generated a wealth of scholarship; and although many problems seem as intractable as they did when first considered, the field has advanced considerably, and we are the beneficiaries of such scholarship.

A number of names have come into use to describe different areas of study in this field. One is *medical ethics*. This looks primarily to the study of ethics within the discipline of medicine and the medical profession. Another term is *health care ethics*, which examines all the various issues in health care, including medical and nursing ethics, as well as public policy and institutional issues. The term *organizational ethics* sometimes designates ethical discourse concerning institutional issues. When considering the ethics of caring for patients at the bedside, the terms *clinical ethics* or *clinical bioethics* are used. We will use the term *bioethics*, which is a more inclusive term.

Since bioethics examines the ethical issues at both the heart and the cutting edge of technology in health care and the life sciences, the area covered is necessarily broad. This is what makes bioethics as a field of study complex but also exciting. There is a need for many specialties and disciplines because no one field can claim the territory of life. In addition to the potential benefits and harms, we have learned that medical technologies have economic consequences, which raise questions of allocation. Reality—which is itself interdisciplinary—has taught us to be interdisciplinary in our thinking. Similarly, bioethics is teaching us the necessity of genuine interdisciplinary thinking and working. Traditional disciplines that participated in one way or another in the field of bioethics include, for example, theology, philosophy, medicine, law, and biology. One might say that bioethics is a multidisciplinary field carried out through interdisciplinary discourse.

# BIOETHICS

When we focus on the first part of the word *bioethics*—"bio"—we are thrust into the exciting, complex, and often troublesome world of medicine and the life sciences, which includes neuroscience, genetics, and molecular biology. The prefix *bio-* comes from the Greek word for life (*bios*). Several questions emerge when one thinks about applications of both biotechnology and nanotechnology. This aspect of our topic requires that we study these fields to understand the biological revolution that is occurring around us. While we need be neither experts nor even competent amateurs, we do need to be informed citizens if for no other reason than the developments in these fields have a profound impact on our lives and our society. Thus paying attention to developments in these fields is a critical first step in examining ethical dilemmas in bioethics.

# BIO*ETHICS*

The other part of the word—"ethics"—is equally important, for the developments we discuss raise serious and profound dilemmas that challenge our value system as well as the culture supporting those values. The root *ethics* comes from the Greek word *ethike* meaning the science of morals or the study of habits.

Ethics, of course, has a problematic reputation. Many regard ethics as the great naysayer and dismiss it out of hand. Others reduce ethical arguments to opinion or taste and refuse to face arguments and conflicts. Still others use carefully developed principles and/or methodologies to consider various values and to tease out hidden conflicts and complex relationships.

Let us present an overview of two methods of ethical decision making that are frequently used in bioethics. The first is a kind of ethics known as deontological ethics. The Greek word *deon* means duty, obligation, or principle. Deontological ethics is a method of decision making that begins by asking, "What are my duties?" or "What are my obligations?" The correct ethical course is to follow one's duties—regardless of where they lead one. One may refer to this as the "Damn the torpedoes, full steam ahead" school of ethics. For once duties or obligations are established, the appropriate actions are clear and must be undertaken regardless of circumstances or outcomes.

A very common example of deontological ethics is the Ten Commandments of the Judeo-Christian religious tradition. The Ten Commandments are basically a set of moral duties that tell what to do or not to do. Biblical writers present them as clear and certain moral guides that mean what they say and say what they mean. They are, after all, the Ten *Commandments*, not the Ten *Suggestions*.

The second is a kind of ethics known as teleological ethics. The Greek word *telos* means end or goal. Thus, in teleological ethics, one's moral obligations are established, not by an evaluation of obligations, but by an examination of consequences or outcomes of various actions. Thus one name for this kind of ethical theory is *consequentialism*. This method attempts to predict what will happen if one acts in various ways and to compare these various outcomes against one another. This outcomes-based evaluative process determines what is moral or the right act.

Situation ethics is probably one of the better known of the many variants of consequentialism. Popularized in the mid-1960s by Joseph Fletcher, situation ethics requires that we attend seriously to the implications of actualizing our ethical beliefs. Thus situation ethics would argue that it is not enough to do good; one must also know which of the many possible goods is better. Therefore, the basis for right action is found in the particular characteristics of the situation.

Although each of these has the strengths of the ideas on which the methods are based, they both suffer from a limitation: they each have tunnel vision when evaluating means or ends. Deontological ethics typically neglects the outcome of an act and is inattentive to substantive differences in the outcome of our actions or the way an unnuanced act can affect individuals or society. Additionally, deontological ethics typically does not take into account the situation or circumstances in which individuals find themselves. Similarly, in its zeal to attend to the outcomes of our actions, consequentialism neglects to develop a way to evaluate the various outcomes or to compare them against one another. That is, situation ethics says to do that act which produces the best or better outcome. But it has no built-in standard by which to judge or to discriminate between outcomes. Perhaps a viable ethical strategy would be to use the two theories as a dialectical way of evaluating both means and ends. In this way, the theories can be mutually corrective rather than mutually exclusive by being attentive both to our obligations and to various outcomes.

We will explore ethical theories in more detail in chapter 3.

## THE ISSUES

One can find the topics we will discuss in this book in the table of contents. As an introduction, the book will present an overview of the issues in the major problem areas of bioethics: abortion, reproductive technology, early (genetic) diagnoses, death and dying, forgoing or withdrawing treatment, euthanasia, physician-assisted suicide, genetic engineering—of plants, animals, and human beings—cell-based biotechnologies (e.g., stem cell technology, cloning, and chimera research), organ transplantation, research on human subjects, and environmental issues.

As you proceed into the book, you will notice that certain questions continue to reappear, certain terms continue to make their significance felt. Certain questions and solutions to problems will raise broader social policy questions. Specific practices call into question fundamental relationships and values. This introduction to bioethics will not examine all these topics or subjects but will frame various questions so that you will have a way of orienting yourself to these broader questions of social policy. For an in-depth examination of these and other topics, we suggest books at the end of each chapter that are relevant for that particular topic.

You will also find any number of Web sites on the Internet relating to bioethics. In November 2007, we ran a Google Web search on "bioethics," which returned about 4,610,000 hits. Of course, not all of these hits may be trustworthy, good, or reliable. There are several research tools available on the Internet and through libraries. The National Reference Center for Bioethics Literature (NRCBL) at Georgetown University offers a bibliographic search service. Users submit information about the particular topic and project on which they are working, and the NRCBL will return a bibliography of bioethics resources (articles, books, etc.) fulfilling the search criteria. The Web portal for this service is: http://bioethics.georgetown.edu. As the Internet evolves, scholars, students, and others in the field of bioethics will begin to appreciate and distinguish the good resources on the Web from the problematic ones.

To return to our first question—What is bioethics?—let us consider a few definitions. One may define bioethics generally as follows: the systematic exercise, study, and methodology of responsible agents and actions in the life sciences (e.g., biology) and healing arts (e.g., medicine). The Oxford English Dictionary defines bioethics as, "The discipline dealing with ethical questions that arise as a result of advances in medicine and biology."[8] A biologist by the name of Van Rensselaer Potter first used the term to refer "to a new field devoted to human survival and an improved quality of life, not necessarily or particularly medical in character."[9] In 1977, the philosopher Samuel Gorovitz defined bioethics as the "critical examination of the moral dimensions of decision-making in health-related contexts and in contexts involving the biological sciences."[10] This definition is still a good one for it highlights the interdisciplinary and social dimensions of bioethics. It points us in the right direction as we enter the fascinating, but complex world of bioethics.

## DISCUSSION QUESTIONS

1. Why is it necessary to have basic knowledge of both scientific and ethical issues in considering the problems encountered in bioethics?
2. What major bioethical problems have been in the media recently? What are some of their implications?

3. Why must one also consider the social or policy implications of problems in bioethics?

## NOTES

1. Albert R. Jonsen, *The Birth of Bioethics* (New York: Oxford University Press, 1998), 20–22.

2. The *Encyclopedia of Bioethics* is in its third edition. See Stephen G. Post, ed., *Encyclopedia of Bioethics*, vols. 1–5, 3rd ed. (New York: Macmillan Reference USA, 2004).

3. Several key bioethics journals include, but are not limited to, the *American Journal of Bioethics, Journal of Clinical Ethics, Hastings Center Report, Bioethics*, the *Kennedy Institute of Ethics Journal*, and the *National Catholic Bioethics Quarterly*.

4. See Jonsen, *Birth of Bioethics*, and Jennifer K. Walter and Eran P. Klein, eds., *The Story of Bioethics: From Seminal Works to Contemporary Explorations* (Washington, DC: Georgetown University Press, 2003).

5. For example, the American Society for Bioethics and Humanities, the American Society of Law, Medicine, and Ethics, the Kennedy Institute of Ethics, and the Hastings Center.

6. See the compliance rules of the Department of Health and Human Services, *Protection of Human Subjects*, 45 CFR 46 (2005), §46.112.

7. See JACHO standards for accreditation: Joint Commission on Accreditation of Healthcare Organizations, *Comprehensive Accreditation Manual for Hospitals* (Oakbrook Terrace, IL: Joint Commission on Accreditation of Healthcare Organizations, 1999).

8. Though many dispute whether bioethics should be understood as a discipline in the narrow sense. See Jonsen, *Birth of Bioethics*, 325–51. See also Daniel Callahan, "Bioethics," in *Encyclopedia of Bioethics*, 1:278–87; and idem, "Bioethics as a Discipline," *The Hastings Center Studies* 1, no. 1 (1973): 66–73.

9. Callahan, "Bioethics," 280. See also Warren T. Reich, "How Bioethics Got Its Name," *Hastings Center Report* 23, no. 6 (November 1993): S6.

10. Samuel Gorovitz, "Bioethics and Social Responsibility," *The Monist* 60 (January 1977): 3.

# BIBLIOGRAPHY

Ashley, Benedict M., Kevin O'Rourke, and Jean K. deBlois. *Health Care Ethics: A Catholic Theological Analysis.* 5th ed. Washington, DC: Georgetown University Press, 2006.

Beauchamp, Tom L., and James F. Childress. *Principles of Biomedical Ethics.* 5th ed. New York: Oxford University Press, 2001.

Beauchamp, Tom L., LeRoy Walters, Jeffrey P. Kahn, and Anna C. Mastroianni, eds. *Contemporary Issues in Bioethics.* 7th ed. Belmont, CA: Wadsworth, 2007.

Cahill, Lisa Sowle. *Theological Bioethics: Participation, Justice, and Change.* Washington, DC: Georgetown University Press, 2005.

Crigger, Bette-Jane, ed. *Cases in Bioethics: Selections from the Hastings Center Report.* 3rd ed. New York: St. Martin's Press, 1998.

Department of Health and Human Services. *Protection of Human Subjects.* 45 CFR 46. 2005. §46.112.

Fletcher, Joseph. *Morals and Medicine.* Princeton, NJ: Beacon Press, 2000.

———. *Humanhood: Essays in Biomedical Ethics.* Buffalo, NY: Prometheus Books, 1979.

Fletcher, Joseph F., and James F. Childress. *Situation Ethics: The New Morality.* Louisville, KY: Westminster John Knox Press, 1997.

Gorovitz, Samuel, et al., eds. *Moral Problems in Medicine.* 2nd ed. Englewood Cliffs, NJ: Prentice-Hall, 1983.

Harron, Frank, John Burnside, and Tom Beauchamp. *Health and Human Values: A Guide to Making Your Own Decisions.* New Haven, CT: Yale University Press, 1983.

Joint Commission on Accreditation of Healthcare Organizations. *Comprehensive Accreditation Manual for Hospitals.* Oakbrook Terrace, IL: Joint Commission on Accreditation of Healthcare Organizations, 1999.

Jokobovits, Immanuel. *Jewish Medical Ethics: A Comparative and Historical Study of the Jewish Religious Attitude of Medicine and Practice.* New York: Bloch Publishing Company, 1997.

Jonsen, Albert R. *The Birth of Bioethics*. New York: Oxford University Press, 2003.

Jonsen, Albert R., Mark Siegler, and William J. Winslade. *Clinical Ethics: A Practical Approach to Ethical Decisions in Clinical Medicine*. 6th ed. New York: McGraw-Hill, 2006.

Jonsen, Albert R., Robert M. Veatch, and LeRoy Walters, eds. *Sourcebook in Bioethics*. Washington, DC: Georgetown University Press, 1998.

Kelly, David F. *Contemporary Catholic Health Care Ethics*. Washington, DC: Georgetown University Press, 2004.

————. *Critical Care Ethics: Treatment Decisions in American Hospitals*. Eugene, OR: Wipf and Stock, 2002.

————. *The Emergence of Roman Catholic Medical Ethics in North America: An Historical-Methodological-Bibliographical Study*. 2nd ed. New York: Edwin Mellen Press, 1979.

Kelly, Gerard. *Medico-Moral Problems*. St. Louis, MO: Catholic Hospital Association, 1958.

Kuczewski, Mark G., and Rosa Lynn B. Pinkus. *An Ethics Casebook for Hospitals: Practical Approaches to Everyday Cases*. Washington, DC: Georgetown University Press, 1999.

Levine, Carol, ed. *Taking Sides: Clashing Views on Controversial Bioethical Issues*. 12th ed. Guilford, Ontario: McGraw-Hill, 2007.

Mackler, Aaron. *An Introduction to Catholic and Jewish Bioethics: A Comparative Analysis*. Washington, DC: Georgetown University Press, 2003.

————, ed. *Life and Death Responsibilities in Jewish Biomedical Ethics*. New York: Louis Finkelstein Institute, 2000.

May, William F. *The Physician's Covenant: Image of the Healer in Medical Ethics*. 2nd ed. Louisville, KY: Westminster John Knox Press, 2007.

McCormick, Richard. *How Brave a New World?: Dilemmas in Bioethics*. Washington, DC: Georgetown University Press, 1981.

Menikoff, Jerry. *Law and Bioethics: An Introduction*. Washington, DC: Georgetown University Press, 2001.

Panicola, Michael R., John Paul Slosar, Mark F. Repenshek, and David M. Belde. *An Introduction to Health Care Ethics: Theological Foundations, Contemporary Issues, and Controversial Cases*. Winona, MN: St. Mary's Press, 2007.

Pence, Gregory E. *Classic Cases in Medical Ethics: Accounts of the Cases That Shaped and Define Medical Ethics*. 5th ed. New York: McGraw-Hill, 2007.

———. *Classic Works in Medical Ethics: Core Philosophical Readings*. Boston: McGraw-Hill, 1997.

Ramsey, Paul. *The Patient as a Person: Explorations in Medical Ethics*. 2nd ed. New Haven, CT: Yale University Press, 2002.

———. *Ethics at the Edges of Life: Medical and Legal Intersections*. New Haven, CT: Yale University Press, 1978.

Reich, Warren, ed. *The Encyclopedia of Bioethics*. 2nd ed. New York: Macmillan, 1995.

Shannon, Thomas A., ed. *Bioethics: Basic Writings on the Key Ethical Questions That Surround the Major, Modern Biological Possibilities and Problems*. 4th ed. Mahwah, NJ: Paulist Press, 1993.

Shannon, Thomas A., and Joann Manfra, eds. *Law and Bioethics: Texts with Commentary on Major Court Decisions*. New York: Paulist Press, 1982.

Starr, Paul. *The Social Transformation of American Medicine: The Rise of a Sovereign Profession and the Making of a Vast Industry*. New York: Basic Books, 1982.

Veatch, Robert M. *Case Studies in Medical Ethics*. Cambridge, MA: Harvard University Press, 1977.

Verhey, Allen, and Stephen Lammers, eds. *On Moral Medicine: Theological Perspectives in Medical Ethics*. 2nd ed. Grand Rapids, MI: William B. Eerdmans, 1998.

Walter, James J., and Thomas A. Shannon. *Contemporary Issues in Bioethics: A Catholic Perspective*. Lanham, MD: Rowman & Littlefield, 2005.

Walter, Jennifer, and Eran Klein, eds. *The Story of Bioethics: From Seminal Works to Contemporary Explorations*. Washington, DC: Georgetown University Press, 2003.

*Chapter 2*

# TECHNOLOGY, NATURE, AND RESPONSIBILITY

## INTRODUCTION

Humans have always seemed to find ways of intervening in nature. The ability to make a fire and the invention of the wheel had profound impacts on the development of human society. The domestication of plants and animals allowed humans to live in ways unthought of before. The rise of modern science and the Industrial Revolution stand as markers of yet another major change in our way of life.

Our current technological revolution presents further opportunities for intervening in life on both the micro and macro levels. The technologies surrounding conception and birth, such as *in vitro* fertilization and amniocentesis, help determine when we will be born and what some of our qualities may (or may not) be. Developments in genetics led to the production of new grains that produce more bushels per acre.[1] An oil-eating bacterium has been manufactured to help clean up oil spills.[2] Although a totally implantable artificial heart is not yet a reality, various assist devices are available to serve as a transition to technology; in fact, some researchers are developing technology that makes three-dimensional tissues using inkjet technology.[3] In terms of regenerative medicine, the hope for these scientists is to one day use the technology to create fully functional replacement organs or tissues. The sequencing of the human genome by the Human Genome Project and Celera Genomics has given us the map and sequence of our genetic structure. Current research is aimed at deciphering the functions of our genes for new approaches to treating genetic diseases and preventing others.

Technology touches virtually every part of our lives; but the moral record of technology is certainly a mixed one. Clearly technology has brought benefits. Computers have given us incredible capacities for calculating and information processing. The vast amounts of information about individuals collected and stored through technology raise serious issues of privacy and confidentiality. Medical technologies provide improved diagnostic capacities, but frequently we can do little or nothing about the disease diagnosed. Other technologies have fairly negative consequences. Nuclear weapons brought us to the brink of annihilation. To protect national interests, governments continue to develop more sophisticated instruments of "interrogation." The impact of yet other technologies is mixed. Nuclear power stations provide necessary energy but problems of waste disposal have yet to be fully resolved. Birth technologies provide children but do not cure infertility. In addition, many wonder whether such technologies reduce children to commodities. Developments in biotechnology promise new cures or the end of global hunger, yet they carry threats to social justice, biodiversity, and ecological harmony.

Whatever one's judgment about a particular technology, technology is here to stay and will continue to have far-reaching effects on our lives.

# CHARACTERISTICS OF TECHNOLOGY

While specific technologies vary, technology itself has several common themes. Let us indicate some of these by following ideas proposed by Norman Faramelli in his book *Technethics*.[4] Here, we will introduce six characteristic themes of technology.

## *The Empirical or Pragmatic Spirit*

This is certainly close to the American spirit. We want to get the job done and get it done quickly. The issue is results, preferably results that we can measure.

## Functionalism

Functionalism follows from the pragmatic bent of our culture. The issue is design and performance. We are frequently more concerned about how something will work than why we should do it.

## Preoccupation with Means, Not Ends

We know that it is often easier to figure out how to solve a particular problem than to agree on which problem ought to be solved. The question of ends requires explicit value judgments for solutions. We often hope that we can finesse that difficult debate by focusing on the means—and by pretending that the means debate involves no value or ethical judgments.

## Preference for Quantity over Quality

An old song says that if you can't be with the one you love, then love the one you're with. This attitude reflects—among other things—a preference for that which is at hand, for what is available, rather than that which is better. Of course, quantitative measurements are easier to do and the phrase *the bottom line* has a nice objective, realistic ring to it. Yet for all the material goods available to us, we seem too unsatisfied, unfulfilled. Plus, knowledge of the bottom line may not give us the important information we want and need for critical decision making.

## Efficiency and Profit

The concept of standardization led to the development of interchangeable parts, which led to mass production, which led to fewer skilled laborers being needed, which led to lower wages, which led to higher profits. Now robots, which are directed by computers, perform much of this process—hence, the emergence of automation in manufacturing. Pragmatism, functionalism, and preoccupation with means and quantity all join here to promote efficiency in the service of higher profits.

## Manipulation

Concern for efficiency and quantity leads to a desire to exercise greater rational control over all phases of life. For only in this way can one increase productivity at a cost-effective level. Manipulation to achieve rational control is one thread in the manufacturing process—though the final word on the use of robots is yet to be heard. But such manipulation may be quite another thing if we begin more intensive selection of characteristics of our offspring through advanced diagnostic technologies and genetic interventions.

# WHAT IS TECHNOLOGY?

Having seen some of the characteristics of technology, let's now look to defining it. An obvious approach to technology is through hardware—the machines, the instruments, the robots. This is certainly an important part of technology, for this dimension of it clearly has a major impact on our lives.

Others, however, like French theologian Jacques Ellul see technology more as technique.[5] *Technique* is a complex of standardized means for achieving a predetermined result. Someone using technology obtains results through a deliberate and rationalized process, using many of the characteristics of technology described above. Technique is the rational organization of behavior, not hardware or output; in other words, technique is like software.

This orientation is more helpful because it allows us to see technology as a cultural phenomenon, a method of organization, an angle of vision. While the products of the technological revolution impact our lives, technology as an organizational method for both thought and social interaction profoundly affects our social reality.

Daniel Bell has also analyzed technology and has defined five essential dimensions: function, energy, fabrication, communication and control, and regulated decision making.[6]

## Function

Function is the primary element in design and relates to nature only insofar as nature is an efficient guide. As noted before, the issue is what something does and how something performs, not why we should do this.

## Energy

The technological revolution gradually demanded new power sources, and we fulfilled that need by shifting from natural sources such as wind, water, and personal strength to manufactured sources such as steam and electricity. Now that we are depleting the natural resources required for their generation, we are turning to nuclear power. Our need for power is outstripping both our resources and our capacity to generate it, and this is creating a crisis, nationally and internationally.

## Fabrication

Bell uses this word to describe the process of standardization of both parts and actions. This permits the replacement of one part or person with another so that one can achieve greater efficiency. One can use this process in manufacturing, in organizing a corporation, or in education.

## Communication and Control

Technological systems feed off information and require increasing amounts of it to keep the system going. Thus, whoever controls the communication system controls the power. Information is useless unless someone communicates it, and technology, through increasing utilization of computer networks, provides an increasingly effective and efficient method of communication and control. Of course, this has vast implications for social power because not everyone will have access to these technologies or know how to use them.

## *Decision-Making Rules*

Since function, fabrication, and communication are critical parts of the technological culture, we need to be assured that there will be coherence in their use and application. Rules of communication and decision making cannot be random or spontaneous, or the vital flow of information may be interrupted. Thus there is a need for speed and accuracy in the decision-making process, which calls for greater standardization, which leads to further decisions about what one will or will not include in decision making. This, of course, leads to a greater centralization of power and reinforces communication and control systems.

Whether understood as hardware or software, technology has profound effects on our everyday lives. Because of this, people see the need to examine technology to predict its effects and to evaluate them. Such assessments will, we hope, help us avoid many undesirable aspects or consequences of a particular technology.

One such method of evaluation is called *technological assessment*. This is a systematic study of the effects on society that may occur when a technology is introduced, expanded, or modified, with special emphasis on the impacts that are unintended, indirect, and delayed. This method attempts to evaluate a broad range of effects, including—but not limited to— environmental, social, economic, and political dimensions. Thus, a technological assessment seeks to examine as thoroughly as possible the short- and long-term consequences of a technology, its risks and benefits, its social and environmental impacts, and the cultural implications. Only by attending to all of these dimensions can one obtain a full sense of the significance of a technology.

Henk ten Have, a professor of medical ethics in the Netherlands, has argued that we must also recognize that technologies may "recast the initial problem into a new phraseology that may create new concepts; they also relocate problems and may shift responsibility for finding acceptable solutions."[7] From this perspective an assessment of technology should not only examine the implications of introducing a new technology as noted above, but also examine the impact of technical rationality on ourselves, our personal and professional relations, and our society. This technical rationality has led to a preference for compartmentalization, a diminishment or even distrust of subjectivity, and a preference for instruments and objectivity. This orientation to technological assessment follows from understanding technology as a way of thinking. The important part of a technology assessment, then, is to think of how the introduction of a technology helps us reconceptualize or reimagine who we are as well as our relation to society.

# TYPES OF TECHNOLOGY

In his study of technology, Daniel Callahan identified five types of technology.[8] The purpose of developing this classification schema was to help us see the potential of various technologies as well as understand the impact various technologies have on our lives. They are preservation technologies, improvement technologies, implementation technologies, destructive technologies, and compensatory technologies.

## Preservation Technologies

These technologies help us adapt to nature or to survive various environments so we can fit into our environment, or help us investigate our environment. Some examples of these technologies are our homes, furnaces, irrigation systems, eyeglasses, and telescopes.

## Improvement Technologies

Technologies such as these enable people to meet their felt needs or to go beyond the limits of their particular natural capabilities. As such, improvement technologies can enhance our physical dimensions or can help decorate or embellish our bodies. Examples of these are genetic engineering, prosthetics, and cosmetic surgery.

## *Implementation Technologies*

These technologies are difficult to describe because their purpose is to assist in the implementation of other technologies. One can best think of these technologies as facilitators or enhancers. Thus, the computer allows us access to other information technologies, and the telephone allows us access to information. Planned obsolescence or the changing fashion allows people to have work.

## *Destructive Technologies*

Technologies such as these are designed with one primary purpose: destruction. They may help us achieve other ends, but the purpose of these technologies is clear from their design. Such technologies may achieve their end through manipulation and control or simply by the capacity for obliteration. Examples are behavior modification technologies, weapon systems, and vacuum aspirators.

## *Compensatory Technologies*

Having developed and implemented all manner of technologies, we now need other technologies to help us deal with the effects of these technologies on our lives. Thus, we have machines to help us exercise, we have noise-canceling headphones to help drown the sounds of other technologies, and we have sensitivity training to enable us to experience the world of nature that we have removed through technology.

# UNDERSTANDINGS OF NATURE

Individuals or groups always use or apply technologies within a context. One critical context affected by our view of technology is that of nature. Here, we present three views of nature, developed by Daniel Callahan, to help understand both the arena in which technologies are often applied and some of the presuppositions we bring to them.

## Nature as Plastic

In this perspective, one sees nature as alien and removed from human beings. It is outside of us and we are separate from it. It is plastic in that humans can shape and use it in any way human beings see fit. The model assumes that the only limit to nature is the limit human beings put on it. Thus, nature is totally at the disposal of human beings.

## Nature as Sacred

This tradition finds a home in both Eastern and Western religious traditions. Taoism suggests conformity to nature so that an individual may become part of the cosmic whole of which nature is a manifestation. The medieval theologian Bonaventure, following the lead of Francis of Assisi, saw nature as the footprints of God. The natural was a reflection of the glory of God. These perspectives create an attitude of stewardship or conservation of nature. While one may intervene, such acts should be discrete, infrequent, and reverent.

## Nature as Teleological

This understanding of nature suggests that there is a purpose and logic in nature. There is an inner dynamism that leads nature to certain ends. There is a limit that prevents the violation of nature. Thus, the extent of interventions into nature is set by the dynamism of nature itself.

What we think we can do determines, in part, what we do. If, for example, we think that nature is only an object existing apart from us, we may be willing to consider more interventions than if we thought of it as being part of an organic whole that is sensitive to interventions.

Ironically, the Judeo-Christian tradition is partly responsible for the desacralization of nature. In its clear and firm rejection of idolatry and its affirmation of God's being a God *of* nature rather than a God *in* nature, that tradition helped validate the objectification of nature. While many in that tradition would not want to intervene to the same extent that others have, nonetheless the balance is a difficult one to maintain.

# RESPONSIBILITIES OF SCIENTISTS

In addition to thinking about the various meanings of technology and nature, we also need to think of the responsibilities of the scientists, for these are the individuals most directly involved in interventions into nature. James Gustafson proposed four models we can use to think about professional responsibility in this area and to evaluate the consequences of a particular position.[9]

## Total Intervention

In this position, scientists would have the right to do whatever is possible; some call this the technological imperative. The justification for this position is the inherent value of knowledge itself. This is complemented by the valuing of intellectual curiosity and the seemingly inherent human drive to solve problems. In this model the only limit is the lack of technical capacity.

## No Intervention

This blanket prohibition is based on either a view of nature as sacred and therefore inviolable or a conviction that the proposed research violates a limit imposed by nature. This model is reminiscent of the position of some Native Americans who refused to practice agriculture because to do so was to rip up the breast of their mother, the earth. Total consistency in this position would lead to the reduction of the human community to hunting-and-gathering societies. Thus, many individuals would not use this principle absolutely but would rather understand it as a strong check on the previous understanding of intervention.

## Limited Interventions

This perspective argues that scientists have no right to change the most distinctive human characteristics. This model, related to an understanding of nature as teleological, sees interventions checked by a particular limit: human nature. Thus, one *can* intervene in nature (as opposed to the second model) but human nature is the boundary, not lack of technical capacity (as in the first model).

## Directed Interventions

This model says that scientists have the right to foster the growth of valued human characteristics and to remove those that are harmful. This model suggests a high level of intervention both to control and to direct human development. The goal is quality of life, and it is served by directing human growth and removing obstacles to its fulfillment.

Clearly, nobody practices these models in a pure form, but we do find traces of them in most of us. The issue is to use these perspectives to understand better why we are intervening in nature and to ask if there are any restraints on this. In other words, one can use these models as a way to evaluate a scientist's responsibility in the development and use of technology.

# SOCIETY, SCIENCE, AND TECHNOLOGY

For those who are not bench scientists, a helpful way to think about being responsible with technology is to consider the relationships between society, science, and technology. Ian Barbour illustrates three ways to understand technology: technology as threat, technology as liberator, and technology as an instrument of power.[10] Barbour argues that technology should be seen as an instrument of power, formed by dynamic interactions between society, science, and technology itself. Because institutions yield these instruments and exercise their powers, technology serves institutional interests, which include human values (e.g., goods necessary for human beings to flourish), expansion of human knowledge (a value itself), profit, and so on. These interests interact and help shape the research, development, marketing, and use of technology across a wide array of human situations. It is within these situations that individuals and groups face the profound bioethical questions in the responsible use of these technologies.

## SUMMARY

If we look around us, it is clear that technology is here to stay. Our culture is utterly dependent on various aspects of it. We could not get through our day without technology. From clocks to microwaves to transportation systems to digital video recorders and high-definition TV, our lives, work, and entertainment are inherently tied up with technology.

Our quality of life has greatly increased because of technology. We live in greater comfort in various climates. We have abundant food and water supplies, we can communicate and travel much more efficiently, and our health has improved.

After two world wars and attacks such as the one on September 11, 2001, we have become acutely aware of how some can use technology to cause terror and suffering throughout the world. We stand in daily dread of the release of weapons that could destroy us—whether they are designed for destruction (e.g., nuclear weapons) or not (e.g., commercial aircraft). We have more information accessible to us but we know less of what it means or what to do with it. Pollution, a byproduct of our technical culture, is threatening to destroy our ecosystem. Many resources needed for daily living are in short supply or in danger of being depleted.

Thus many benefits and problems are given to us by technology. Each requires much study and examination. But it is to one application of technology—the biomedical—that we now turn for further examination.

## DISCUSSION QUESTIONS

1. What are the costs and benefits, the strengths and weaknesses, of the vast technological society that has developed in America?
2. What are some examples of unintended and delayed side effects of technology? Do you think these could have been avoided?
3. Develop lists of examples of the various types of technologies. What needs are these technologies meant to satisfy? What values are these technologies based on?
4. How has technology benefited your life? How has it complicated your life?
5. Which is more helpful for you: to think of technology as hardware or as a system? Why?

## NOTES

1. David Zilberman, Holly Ameden, and Matin Qaim, "The Impact of Agricultural Biotechnology on Yields, Risks, and Biodiversity in Low-Income Countries," *Journal of Developmental Studies* 43 (2007): 63–78.

2. Victor de Lorenzo, "Blueprint of an Oil-Eating Bacterium," *Nature Biotechnology* 24 (2006): 952–53.

3. Tao Xu, Joyce Jin, Cassie Gregory, James J. Hickman, and Thomas Boland, "Inkjet Printing of Viable Mammalian Cells," *Biomaterials* 26 (2005): 93–99.

4. Norman J. Faramelli, *Technethics* (New York: Friendship Press, 1971), 31ff.

5. Jacques Ellul, *The Technological Society* (New York: Vintage Books, 1964), 13ff.

6. Daniel Bell, faculty seminar presentation (Worchester Polytechnic Institute, 1976); see also idem, *The Coming of the Post-Industrial Society: A Venture in Social Forecasting* (New York: Basic Books, 1973).

7. Henk A. M. J. ten Have, "Medical Technology Assessment and Ethics: Ambivalent Relations," *Hastings Center Report* 25 (September–October 1995): 18.

8. Daniel Callahan, *The Tyranny of Survival* (New York: Macmillan, 1973), 55ff.

9. James Gustafson, "Basic Issues in the Biomedical Fields," *Soundings* 53 (Summer 1970): 151ff.

10. Ian G. Barbour, *Ethics in an Age of Technology: The Gifford Lectures 1989–1991*, vol. 2 (New York: HarperCollins Publishers, 1993), 3–25.

## BIBLIOGRAPHY

Barbour, Ian. *Ethics in an Age of Technology: The Gifford Lectures 1989–1991*. Volume 2. New York: HarperCollins Publishers, 1993.

———, ed. *Science and Religion*. San Francisco: Harper and Row, 1968.

Bell, Daniel. *The Coming of the Post-Industrial Society: A Venture in Social Forecasting*. New York: Basic Books, 1973.

Bronowsky, Joseph. *Science and Human Values*. San Francisco: Harper and Row, 1965.

Bross, I. D. J. "Metatechnology: A Technology for the Safe, Effective, and Economical Use of Technology." *Theoretical Medicine* 2 (1981): 145–53.

Callahan, Daniel. *The Tyranny of Survival*. New York: Macmillan, 1973.

de Lorenzo, Victor. "Blueprint of an Oil-Eating Bacterium." *Nature Biotechnology* 24 (2006): 952–53.

Diamond, Jared. *Guns, Germs, and Steel*. New York: W. W. Norton & Co., 2005.

Ehrlich, Paul R. *Human Natures*. Washington, DC: Island Press, 2000.

Ellul, Jacques. *The Technological Society*. New York: Vintage Books, 1964.

Faramelli, Norman J. *Technethics*. New York: Friendship Press, 1971.

Ferkiss, Victor C. *The Future of Technological Civilization: The Myth and the Reality.* New York: George Braziller, 1969.

Gustafson, James. "Basic Issues in the Biomedical Fields." *Soundings* 53 (Summer 1970): 151–80.

Hardin, Garrett. *Exploring New Ethics for Survival: The Voyage of Spaceship Beagle.* New York: Viking Press, 1972.

Häring, Bernhard. *Ethics of Manipulation: Issues in Medicine, Behavior Control, and Genetics.* New York: Seabury Press, 1975.

Have, Henk A. M. J. ten. "Medical Technology Assessment and Ethics: Ambivalent Relations." *The Hastings Center Report* 25 (September–October 1995): 13–19.

Kuhn, Thomas. *The Structure of Scientific Revolutions.* Chicago: University of Chicago Press, 1970.

Lappe, Marc. *Genetic Politics: The Limits of Biological Control.* New York: Simon and Schuster, 1977.

Lock, Margaret, and Deborah Gordon. *Biomedicine Reconsidered.* Dordrecht: Kluwer, 1988.

MacKay, Donald. *Human Science and Human Dignity.* Downers Grove, IL: Intervarsity Press, 1979.

Shinn, Roger. *Forced Options: Social Decisions for the 21st Century.* San Francisco: Harper and Row, 1982.

Shinn, Roger, and Paul Abrecht, eds. *Faith and Science in an Unjust World: Report of the World Council of Churches' Conference on Faith, Science, and the Future.* 2 vols. Geneva: World Council of Churches, 1981.

Xu, Tao, Joyce Jin, Cassie Gregory, James J. Hickman, and Thomas Boland. "Inkjet Printing of Viable Mammalian Cells." *Biomaterials* 26 (2005): 93–99.

Zilberman, David, Holly Ameden, and Matin Qaim. "The Impact of Agricultural Biotechnology on Yields, Risks, and Biodiversity in Low-Income Countries." *Journal of Developmental Studies* 43 (2007): 63–78.

## Chapter 3

# ETHICAL ISSUES AND THEORIES

## INTRODUCTION

In the last chapter, we saw the importance of responsibility in the research, development, and use of technology, including biomedical technology. In this chapter, we will explore ways we can judge which uses of technology, or our moral choices, are the most responsible. This examination of the criteria upon which one bases such decisions is called *ethical analysis*. Our principal goal is to prepare you for some of the discussions that will emerge in the various topics we will cover and to suggest basic frameworks for ethical analysis.

## ETHICAL ISSUES

What are ethical issues? One can think of ethical issues as the variables one considers in making a judgment or decision about which option is the best or more morally viable. Ethical issues can constitute a range of areas in the moral life—from the macro-level issues in public policy to the micro-level issues of end-of-life treatment decisions at a patient's bedside. We cannot, however, address ethical issues in a vacuum; we need an overarching framework or structure to analyze them properly. Thus, to answer the question, How do we make ethical judgments or responsible decisions? we apply ethical theories, which are informed by the various ethical issues at stake.

# ETHICAL THEORIES

In general, an ethical theory is the process by which we justify a particular decision or answer a specific normative question; a theory provides an overarching framework in which one addresses and evaluates ethical issues. Ethical theories organize complex information and competing values and interests, and help us formulate answers to questions such as What should I do? What kind of person should I be? or What is the right course of action? The main purpose of a theory is to provide consistency and coherence in our decision making. That is, an ethical theory gives us a common approach to various problems. If we have a theory, we do not have to figure out where to begin each time we meet a new problem. A theory also allows us to develop some degree of consistency in our decision making; we aim at reliable patterns of practical reason, not whimsical emotional or uncritical reactions. We will begin to see how different values relate to one another. If we are consistent and coherent in our decision making, we will have a greater degree of internal unity and integrity in our decision making. Given the complexity of problems in bioethics, these qualities are extremely worthwhile.

One can organize different kinds of ethical theories in two categories: action-based theories and character-based theories. There are two very basic sets of moral questions one can ask.[1] The first kind of questions has to do with human behavior in action: an ethics of *doing*. The second kind of questions has to do with being human itself: an ethics of *being*. Generally speaking, all ethical theories address aspects of the moral life: what it is, how to live it, and so on. Action-based ethical theories are basically oriented to answering ethical questions of the first kind—ethics of *doing*. They attempt to figure out what is the right or good thing *to do*. We already discussed two kinds of action-based theories (deontology and teleology) in chapter 1. Character-based ethical theories, in the broadest sense of the term, are basically oriented to answering ethical questions of the second kind—ethics of *being*. They attempt to figure out *who a good person is* and what such a person ought to do.

Our goal in this section is to introduce the basic structures of various ethical theories and briefly sketch some advantages and disadvantages of each. Unfortunately, we cannot provide a thorough examination of ethical theories that many moral philosophers have proffered. Instead, we have provided a list of works in the bibliography regarding moral philosophy and theology of ethical theory. Thus, this section is not exhaustive of (a) the variety of ethical theories or (b) the analyses of them.

## Action-Based Ethical Theories

Action-based ethical theories address moral questions pertaining to human behavior in action. In this regard, an ethics of doing can move in two directions: an evaluation of the *means* (the act, process, or way a human behaves) or an evaluation of the *ends* (the ends, outcomes, or consequences of the particular human behavior). On the one hand, we saw in chapter 1 that teleological ethical theories, like consequentialism, assess the values, goods, benefits, or utility in relation to the disvalues, evils, harms, or burdens in the *results* of a human action. Deontological ethical theories, on the other hand, assess the action itself by reference to particular rules, duties, or norms, which ask primarily whether the *means* constitute or violate such duties.

*Teleological Ethics.* An action-based ethical theory, like consequentialism, answers the question, What should I do? by considering the consequences of various options in a decision. That is, what is ethical is the option that brings about consequences that have the greatest number of advantages over disadvantages or that generate the greatest good for the greatest number of people. Basically, in this theory, one determines what is moral by looking to outcomes, to consequences, and to the situation.

The ethical theories of *situation ethics* and *utilitarianism* are common types of action-based, consequentialist ethical theories. We discussed situation ethics in chapter 1, but another common consequentialist theory is utilitarianism, which Jeremy Bentham and John Stuart Mill developed.[2] Utilitarianism states that what is moral maximizes "utility" in the consequences of an act—for example, the greatest good for the greatest number of people. A principle of utility specifies what constitutes "utility" or what is "useful." A consequence (or set of consequences) may have utility if (on balance) it evokes happiness, including, pleasure, health, knowledge, and so forth.

The major benefit of this kind of theory is that it looks to the actual impact of a particular decision and asks how such a decision will affect people. Consequentialism is attuned to the nuances of life and seeks to be responsive to them. The major problem of this theory is that the theory itself provides no standard by which one could measure one outcome against another. That is, while being sensitive to the circumstances, consequentialism has no basis for evaluating the relative merits or problems of one outcome against another.

*Deontological Ethics.* Deontological ethics looks to one's obligations to determine what is moral. This theory answers the question What should I do? by specifying one's obligations or moral duties. That is, the moral act is one in which one meets his or her obligations, his or her responsibilities, or fulfills his or her duties. For a deontologist, obligations and rules are primary, for only by attending to these dimensions of morality can one be sure that self-interest does not override moral obligations. The Ten Commandments, Kant's Categorical Imperative,[3] and certain forms of rights ethics are probably the most common examples of deontological ethics.

Rights ethics is a theory that resolves moral dilemmas by first determining what rights or moral claims are involved. Then one settles dilemmas in terms of a hierarchy of rights. Paramount for a person of this orientation is that the moral claims of individuals— their rights—are taken seriously. Rights may include duties, privileges, or entitlements. The duties relative to certain rights may be the duty of the subject (e.g., the right to vote implies a duty and a privilege to vote) or a duty on others (e.g., the right to privacy suggests a duty not to invade another's privacy). The ethical theory of rights is a popular one in our American culture. Consider, for example, the central role this theory plays in abortion and health care access debates.

On the one hand, the main advantage of a rights theory is that it highlights the moral centrality of the person and his or her moral claims in a situation of ethical conflict. On the other hand, this theory does not tell us how to resolve conflicts of rights between individuals. The theory makes the claims of the individual central without telling us how to resolve potential conflicts of rights.

The major benefit of deontological ethics is the clarity and certainty of its starting point. Once the rules are known, the duties determined, or the rights identified, then what is ethical is evident. The major problem is the potential insensitivity to circumstances and consequences. By looking only at duty or rights, one may miss important aspects of a problem.

## Character-Based Ethical Theories

Character-based ethical theories address moral questions dealing with who good persons are and how they ought to relate to one another. In these ways, an ethics of *being* deals with character traits (e.g., virtues and vices) as well as human relationships. Many philosophers have critiqued character-based ethics for being too subjective or relative to individuals or their particular communities. With feminism and the work of scholars such as Edmund Pellegrino and David Thomasma, Alasdair MacIntyre, Carol Gilligan, and others, however, *ethics of being* has seen a revival in recent years. We will consider briefly three kinds of character-based ethics here.

*Virtue Ethics.* Virtue ethics comes from a long line of philosophers and theologians dating at least all the way back to Ancient Greece. For example, Aristotle developed a virtue-based theory of ethics,[4] and Thomas Aquinas built upon Aristotle's work for Christianity. More recently, Alasdair MacIntyre revitalizes this approach to ethics; Edmund Pellegrino and David Thomasma apply it to the practice of medicine.[5] James Keenan asks what virtue ethics can bring to discussions of the new genetics.[6] In its basic form, virtue ethics is about making a habit of good behavior; that is, making good behavior a part of who we are. A virtue, or a vice, is a character trait that describes one's orientation to certain goods and the behaviors that seek those goods. Like all character-based theories, virtue ethics sees an intimate relationship between what we do and who we are. Thus, the virtue-related questions include, What would a virtuous physician do when faced with physician-assisted suicide? What (or who) is a virtuous physician? What does it mean to be a virtuous parent? By wanting to become a virtuous parent, should I use assisted reproductive technology or adopt?

*Relationality-Responsibility.* Another character-based ethical theory is relationality-responsibility. Charles Curran adapts this model from the work of H. Richard Niebuhr and offers it up as an alternative to consequentialist or deontological ethical models.[7] Stephen Happel and James Walter describe the relationality-responsibility model as one that places emphasis on the subject of moral experience—the human person—and that uses the thematic image of "persons as responsible" to represent moral experience.[8] Curran outlines the basic form of relationality-responsibility in this way:

> Responsibility involves (1) response to an action upon us; (2) in accord with our interpretation of what is going on; (3) with a willingness to be accountable for any reaction to our reaction; and (4) in solidarity with the continuing community of agents. I would, however, modify this model by calling on persons to initiate action as well as respond to the actions of others.[9]

*Ethics of Caring.* Lawrence Kohlberg studied human moral psychology and outlined the major stages of moral development, which culminated in a commitment to justice.[10] Carol Gilligan evaluated the research, conducted her own, and concluded something very important and challenging: men and women develop differently when it comes to their senses of morality. Her book, *In a Different Voice,* suggests that women tend to prioritize *caring* above *justice.*[11] Inspired in part by Gilligan's perspective, other scholars developed the approach to ethics known as *ethics of caring.* Ethics of caring is about a disposition to one another grounded in a transformative relationship resulting in care and one who is caring. It is arguably a character-based ethic because in this theory human relationships inform *who* one should *be.* This approach has been important in the evolution of the ethics of the healing professions, especially nursing ethics.

# CONCLUSION

As you read this book and discuss the problems contained in it, you will find yourself using one or more of these theories in trying to convince yourself or others of the correctness of a particular position. You may also find it interesting to adopt one theory to see how it works and where it will lead you. Discovering the theory with which you are most comfortable, and being attentive to the methods others are using, is a first step toward gaining clarity in the discussions and debates about complex bioethical problems.

## DISCUSSION QUESTIONS

1. What major ethical theory do you primarily use in decision making?
2. Can someone use more than one ethical theory in solving a problem? Why or why not?

## NOTES

1. See Michael R. Panicola, David M. Belde, John Paul Slosar, and Mark F. Repenshek, *An Introduction to Health Care Ethics: Theological Foundations, Contemporary Issues, and Controversial Cases* (Winona, MN: Saint Mary's Press, 2007), 22–43.

2. For example, see John Stuart Mill, *Utilitarianism*, ed. Oskar Piest (New York: Macmillan, 1957).

3. Immanuel Kant, *Groundwork for the Metaphysics of Morals*, ed. and trans. Allen W. Wood (New Haven, CT: Yale University Press, 2002).

4. Aristotle, "Nichomachean Ethics," in *The Complete Works of Aristotle: The Revised Oxford Translation*, vol. 2, ed. Jonathan Barnes, trans. W. D. Ross, rev. J. O. Urmson (Princeton, NJ: Princeton University Press, 1984), 1729–1867.

5. See Alasdair MacIntyre, *After Virtue: A Study in Moral Theory*, 2nd ed. (Notre Dame, IN: University of Notre Dame Press, 1984); Edmund Pellegrino and David Thomasma, *The Christian*

*Virtues in Medical Practice* (Washington, DC: Georgetown University Press, 1996); idem, *The Virtues in Medical Practice* (New York: Oxford University Press, 1993); and idem, *A Philosophical Basis of Medical Practice: Toward a Philosophy and Ethic of the Healing Professions* (New York: Oxford University Press, 1981).

6. James F. Keenan, "What Does Virtue Ethics Bring to Genetics?" in *Genetics, Theology, and Ethics: An Interdisciplinary Conversation*, ed. Lisa Sowle Cahill (New York: Crossroad, 2005), 97–113.

7. Charles E. Curran, *The Catholic Moral Tradition Today: A Synthesis* (Washington, DC: Georgetown University Press, 1999), 73–83; see also H. Richard Niebuhr, *The Responsible Self* (New York: HarperCollins Publishers, 1963).

8. Stephen Happel and James J. Walter, *Conversion and Discipleship: A Christian Foundation for Ethics and Doctrine* (Philadelphia: Fortress Press, 1986), 165–67. Happel and Walter go as far as to say that the relationality-responsibility model is, in fact, a virtue-dominant model.

9. Curran, *Catholic Moral Tradition*, 73.

10. Lawrence Kohlberg, *The Philosophy of Moral Development: Moral Stages and the Idea of Justice*, 1st ed. (San Francisco: Harper & Row, 1981).

11. Carol Gilligan, *In a Different Voice: Psychological Theory and Women's Development* (Cambridge, MA: Harvard University Press, 1993).

## BIBLIOGRAPHY

Aiken, Henry David. *Reason and Conduct: New Bearings in Moral Philosophy*. New York: Alfred A. Knopf, 1962.

Aristotle. "Nichomachean Ethics." In *The Complete Works of Aristotle: The Revised Oxford Translation*, vol. 2. Edited by Jonathan Barnes. Translated by W. D. Ross. Revised by J. O. Urmson. Princeton, NJ: Princeton University Press, 1984, 1729–1867.

Broad, C. D. *Five Types of Ethical Theory*. London: Routledge & Kegan Paul, 1956.

Curran, Charles E. *The Catholic Moral Tradition Today: A Synthesis.* Washington, DC: Georgetown University Press, 1999.

Gilligan, Carol. *In a Different Voice: Psychological Theory and Women's Development.* Cambridge, MA: Harvard University Press, 1993.

Gula, Richard M. *Reason Informed by Faith: Foundations of Catholic Morality.* New York: Paulist Press, 1989.

Happel, Stephen, and James J. Walter. *Conversion and Discipleship: A Christian Foundation for Ethics and Doctrine.* Minneapolis: Fortress Press, 2007.

Harrington, Daniel, and James Keenan. *Jesus and Virtue Ethics: Building Bridges between New Testament Studies and Moral Theology.* Lanham, MD: Sheed & Ward, 2002.

Jonsen, Albert R., and Stephen Toulmin. *The Abuse of Casuistry: A History of Moral Reasoning.* Berkeley: University of California Press, 1988.

Kant, Immanuel. *Groundwork for the Metaphysics of Morals.* Edited and translated by Allen W. Wood. New Haven, CT: Yale University Press, 2002.

Keenan, James F. "What Does Virtue Ethics Bring to Genetics?" In *Genetics, Theology, and Ethics: An Interdisciplinary Conversation.* Edited by Lisa Sowle Cahill. New York: Crossroad, 2005, 97–113.

Kohlberg, Lawrence. *The Philosophy of Moral Development: Moral Stages and the Idea of Justice.* 1st ed. San Francisco, CA: Harper & Row, 1981.

Lonergan, Bernard. *Collected Works of Bernard Lonergan.* Vol. 3, *Insight: A Study of Human Understanding.* Edited by Frederick E. Crowe and Robert M. Doran. Toronto: Lonergan Research Institute, 1992.

MacIntyre, Alasdair. *After Virtue: A Study in Moral Theory.* 2nd ed. Notre Dame, IN: University of Notre Dame Press, 1984.

———. *A Short History of Ethics: A History of Moral Philosophy from the Homeric Age to the Twentieth Century.* 2nd ed. Notre Dame, IN: University of Notre Dame Press, 1998.

———. *Three Rival Versions of Moral Enquiry: Encyclopedia, Genealogy, and Tradition.* Notre Dame, IN: University of Notre Dame Press, 1990.

————. *Whose Justice? Which Rationality?* Notre Dame, IN: University of Notre Dame Press, 1988.

Mahoney, John. *The Making of Moral Theology: A Study of the Roman Catholic Tradition.* New York: Clarendon Press, 1987.

Mill, John Stuart. *Utilitarianism.* Edited by Oskar Piest. New York: Macmillan, 1957.

Moore, G. E. *Ethics and "The Nature of Moral Philosophy."* Edited by William H. Shaw. New York: Clarendon Press, 2005.

————. *Principia Ethica.* Cambridge: Cambridge University Press, 1959.

Niebuhr, H. Richard. *The Responsible Self.* New York: Harper-Collins Publishers, 1963.

Panicola, Michael R., David M. Belde, John Paul Slosar, and Mark F. Repenshek. *An Introduction to Health Care Ethics: Theological Foundations, Contemporary Issues, and Controversial Cases.* Winona, MN: Saint Mary's Press, 2007.

Pellegrino, Edmund, and David Thomasma. *The Christian Virtues in Medical Practice.* Washington, DC: Georgetown University Press, 1996.

————. *A Philosophical Basis of Medical Practice: Toward a Philosophy and Ethic of the Healing Professions.* New York: Oxford University Press, 1981.

————. *The Virtues in Medical Practice.* New York: Oxford University Press, 1993.

Plato. *Republic.* In *Plato: Complete Works.* Edited by John M. Cooper. Translated by G. M. A. Grube. Revised by C. D. C. Reeve. Indianapolis, IN: Hackett Publishing Company, 1997, 971–1223.

Porter, Jean. *Natural and Divine Law: Reclaiming the Tradition for Christian Ethics.* Grand Rapids, MI: William B. Eerdmans, 1999.

Rawls, John. *A Theory of Justice.* Rev. ed. Cambridge, MA: Belknap Press, 1999.

Ross, W. D. *The Right and the Good.* Edited by Philip Stratton-Lake. Oxford: Clarendon Press, 2002.

Salzman, Todd A. *What Are They Saying about Catholic Ethical Method?* New York: Paulist Press, 2003.

Selling, Joseph A., ed. *Personalist Morals: Essays in Honor of Professor Louis Janssens.* Leuven: Leuven University Press, 1988.

Shafer-Landau, Russ. *Ethical Theory: An Anthology*. Malden, MA: Blackwell Publishing, 2007.

Traina, Cristina L. H. *Feminist Ethics and Natural Law: The End of Anathemas*. Washington, DC: Georgetown University Press, 1999.

*Chapter 4*

---

# COMMON TERMS USED IN BIOETHICS

## INTRODUCTION

Philosophers and theologians, like physicians, nurses, lawyers, and other professionals, have their own language and jargon. This chapter will introduce you to some of the basic concepts and terms used in bioethical discussions so you can join in on the conversations.

In *The Birth of Bioethics*, Albert Jonsen notes that when one sees bioethics as a discourse, there are several different contexts within which the conversations happen.[1] Bioethics discussions occur in high schools, colleges, and graduate and professional schools (e.g., nursing and medical schools). They also occur in the clinical setting with an institution's ethics committee or during clinical bioethics consultations at patients' bedsides. We also discuss bioethics in the community and hear about issues through the media.

Bioethics discourse happens when presidential candidates debate their platforms on stem cell research or when Congress develops laws prohibiting human cloning. Governments also have special commissions and councils, like the President's Council on Bioethics. Bioethics discourse happens in judicial reviews and court rulings, as in, for example, the *Cruzan* case. There are organizations—think tanks, businesses, and professional associations—who participate in bioethics discourse, too. In all of these contexts, there are common threads: the terms of bioethics serve as conceptual currency in the exchange of ideas, in the debates, and in the discussions we have. Though bioethics discourse has evolved, it still requires concepts and terms. Therefore, knowing the major concepts and terms of bioethics discourse is essential if one wishes to participate in the field of bioethics.

We divide this chapter into two parts. In the first part, we will outline some fundamental terms used in general ethical discourse. In the second part, we will elaborate on some common terms used in bioethical discourse.

# FUNDAMENTAL TERMS IN ETHICAL DISCOURSE

## *Moral Norms*

Moral norms are propositions proscribing or prescribing certain behaviors; they set standards for the moral life. There are three basic kinds of moral norms: formal norms, material norms, and virtually exceptionless material norms.[2] Formal moral norms are the more universally applicable, abstract, and general norms. An example of this is the primary precept of the natural law according to Aquinas: good is to be done and evil avoided. Who could dispute that standard? The problem is in specifying what is good and what is evil. Thus, as one gets more specific, one begins to articulate material moral norms. Material moral norms are the more narrowly applicable, concrete, and specific norms. An example of this kind of norm is the following: one should obtain informed consent of human research subjects before conducting the experiment. Virtually exceptionless material norms are material moral norms for which it is nearly impossible to think of exceptions. An example might be "it is wrong to torture children with hot irons." It is hard to think of circumstances in which torturing children would be justifiable regardless of the reasons one has or the tools one uses.

## *Principles*

Despite how common it is, the word *principle* is a fairly complex word and can mean a variety of things. We will describe three general uses of the word *principle*. In the first use, principles serve an *evaluative* function. This function helps us to find meaning in a situation and to analyze it. An example of this kind is the Principle of Double Effect. The Principle of Double Effect helps one evaluate actions that have both good effects and bad effects in order to determine which actions—if any—are morally permissible. In another use, principles perform an *axiomatic* function. That is, they help guide our behavior by describing rules of conduct (axioms); principles might proscribe certain behavior ("thou shall not murder") or prescribe other behavior ("love your neighbor"). Finally, principles operate in an *axiological* way.[3] Here, principles help us identify what is valuable and worthy, or disvaluable and harmful, and so on. The Principle of Autonomy, for example, suggests that autonomy is of significant value and should be protected: we should act in ways that minimize our intrusion in another person's autonomy.

One should not confuse the term *principles* with a popular method in bioethics: *principlism*. Principlism developed out of early discussions in bioethics (e.g., *"The Belmont Report"*[4]) and was canonized by Tom Beauchamp and James Childress in their text, *The Principles of Biomedical Ethics*.[5] Principlism seeks to determine what the right course of action is by examining, specifying, and balancing the biomedical principles at work (i.e., autonomy, beneficence, nonmaleficence, and justice).

## *Laws*

Laws are an authoritative expression of certain rules, norms, or principles. There are several different kinds of laws. For example, there is civil law, moral law, and divine or eternal law (i.e., God's law). In the Catholic tradition, the natural law is an expression of the moral law, which is related to how human beings experience the eternal law. The differences between civil law and moral law indicate that what is legally required may not be what is morally required. Furthermore, even though a civil law may not say that an action is illegal, this does not mean that the action is morally acceptable. For example, many believe that even though the law protects a woman's right to an abortion, obtaining an abortion when there is not a medical reason is immoral. In fact, some in that camp wish to change the law to reflect more closely their view of the morality of abortion. The point here is to remember that what is legal is not necessarily moral and vice versa.

# COMMON TERMS IN BIOETHICAL DISCOURSE

## *Justice*

Justice is a concept one explores to determine the relevant properties or characteristics of people or circumstances necessary for fairness.[6] Difficulties arise when determining what is fair in a particular case. Is it equal share? Is it fair if one person gets more health care and another person gets less? Justice can be understood in two basic ways: it can be either comparative or noncomparative. Comparative justice seeks to compare the needs or claims of one person or group against the same needs or claims of another person or group. Alternatively, noncomparative justice seeks fairness without comparing needs or claims of the individuals or groups after the same resource.

In bioethics, there are three basic types of justice involved: distributive, commutative, and contributive justice. To begin, *distributive justice* is perhaps the most common form of justice in bioethics discussions. Distributive justice asks What does society owe to the individual? The individual can be understood as a person or as an organization or group. Here, the common dilemmas are rationing scarce health care resources, access to health care, and so forth.

Should there be a universal health insurance program with a single payer (i.e., the federal government) in the United States? We will return to distributive justice below when we consider how we should allocate health care resources; this requires a material principle of justice. Next, *commutative justice* involves the exchange of goods (or burdens) between individuals or groups. Commutative justice asks, What does one owe another? What price is fair for over-the-counter medications? Finally, *contributive justice* involves questions of an individual's duty to society. In other words, contributive justice asks, What does an individual owe to society? What should a person or group contribute to the health care system? What amount of taxation on an individual would be fair in order for a government to pay for health care? Does a person have a duty to eat well and avoid risky behaviors such as smoking to promote a just health care system?

You might ask, however, Given all these types of justice, how do we figure out what is owed? In other words, recognizing the question is one thing, but we still have to figure out how to deal with the situation. In order to move toward resolution, and away from injustice, one uses principles of justice, which can be formal or material. A formal principle of justice is noncomparative in that it states a rule by which someone measures distributions. It proposes a standard independent of the properties (e.g., needs) of individuals. The rule does not, however, tell how we determine what qualifies as equality, inequality, or equity. That is, with respect to what standard is someone equal or unequal? What is morally relevant in our determining equality and inequality? The strength of the formal principle of justice is that it gives us a clear rule; its major deficit is that it does not specify how to apply it.

To cope with the problem of applications, philosophers devised material principles of justice. Generally speaking, a material principle of justice identifies some relevant property or criterion on the basis of which one can judge a distribution. Thus, material principles of justice are typically, though not always, comparative in that they examine needs or qualifications and on that basis determine what to do. Let us illustrate this by identifying several of these material principles of justice one can use in determining distributive fairness.

First is the noncomparative material principle of *to each an equal share*. The standard is strict quantitative equality, and one arrives at this by dividing what is to be allocated by the number of actual recipients. Second is distribution according to *individual need*. Here, one looks at specific needs of individuals and judges them. For example, this comparative material principle evaluates one's health needs against another's. Third is *social worth* criteria, which go beyond needs and evaluate the status of an individual and his or her actual or potential contributions to society. Fourth is the final form of material justice, which is distribution accord-ing to *individual effort* or *merit*. This criterion does not necessarily examine one's accomplishments but looks at what one attempted and the efforts to realize his or her goals. The higher the effort, the greater the reward.

Each of these principles has its benefits and problems, and because of this some philosophers have suggested a middle way.[7] This method of allocation emphasizes formal equality but shifts this by utilizing *equality of opportunity* rather than one of the com-parative forms of justice. This method of distribution is random-ized either through a lottery or by distribution to people as they show up.

On the one hand, the obvious benefit of this method is that it protects strongly our intuitive sense of respect for people. That is, randomization provides a formal rule of allocation that does not force us to make invidious and potentially harmful choices between people based on assumptions about social worth. Individuals maintain their dignity because they will be treated fairly by having an equality of opportunity. Finally, such a system will help maintain trust between members of the health care team and the patient. The patient is not at the mercy of biases of an institution or of individuals, but rather knows that he or she will be treated fairly.

On the other hand, this standard does not deal with some important questions. First, should there be some medical screen through which one should pass before entering the door? Second, should one's condition or likelihood of benefit be considered? That is, if a fifteen-year-old is more likely to benefit from a proce-dure than an eighty-year-old, should the eighty-year-old have an equal opportunity for treatment? Third, the mode of distribution assumes an endless supply of resources in that the only relevant criterion is equality of opportunity, not appropriateness of inter-vention.

From this discussion one can easily see not only why discus-sions of justice are important in bioethics, but also why they are among the most complex.

## Human Dignity

Human dignity is a term that is not clearly defined and it can mean many different things. The term *dignity* comes from the Latin words *dignitas* and *dignus*, which mean worth and worthy, respectively. In some ways, we use the term *human dignity* as a way to understand the value or worth of human life. Alternatively, we use human dignity to describe the moral status of individuals—whether someone or something is part of our moral community and, therefore, worthy of protection and respect.

Reflecting on human dignity, Daniel Sulmasy classifies different kinds of value.[8] Sulmasy argues that one can understand values as attributed, intrinsic, or derivative. For our purposes, it is important to highlight the first two. For example, people *attribute* dignity to others because they possess certain traits (e.g., higher brain function) or are socially useful (e.g., they have important jobs). Others argue that people have dignity by virtue of being human or by being created by God. That is, human beings have *intrinsic* dignity.

Human dignity arises in a variety of bioethical contexts. One can see human dignity in various beginning of life issues: for example, abortion, reproductive technologies, and embryonic stem cell research. One can also see human dignity in end-of-life issues like forgoing or withdrawing medical treatment, euthanasia, and physician-assisted suicide. As you can imagine, human dignity is a central concept in bioethics.

## Beneficence and Nonmaleficence

*Nonmaleficence* is the technical way of stating that we have an obligation not to harm people—one of the most traditional ethical principles of medical ethics: "First of all, do no harm." This is the basic principle derived from the Hippocratic tradition. If we are unable to benefit someone, then at least we should do them no harm.

The harm we are to avoid is typically understood as physical or mental, but harm can also include injuries to one's interests. Thus, Dr. C harms Mr. A by having Mr. A's property unjustly taken or by having his access to it restricted. Or, we can harm Ms. B by unfairly restricting her liberty of speech or action. Another example of this kind of harm is identity theft. Although there is not necessarily a physical impact on us from these latter harms, nonetheless constraining our interests does harm us.

Though the Principle of Nonmaleficence[9] clearly imposes a duty not to harm someone intentionally or directly, it is also possible to expose others to a risk of harm. For example, if we drive too fast, we may not actually harm someone, but we are clearly exposing others to the risk of harm. Thus, the duty of nonmaleficence would prohibit speeding. There are, however, other situations in which individuals are exposed to the risk of harm where the duty of nonmaleficence is not necessarily violated. A doctor giving a patient chemotherapy is exposing the patient to various risks of harm from the therapy.

*Beneficence* is the positive dimension of nonmaleficence. The Principle of Beneficence entails a duty to help others further their own interests when we can do this without risk to ourselves. Thus, the duty of beneficence argues that we have a positive obligation to regard the welfare of others, to be of assistance to others as they attempt to fulfill their plans. The duty of beneficence is based on a sense of fair play. It basically suggests that because we receive benefits from others, because others have helped us along the way, we have an obligation to return that same favor to them. Beneficence is a way of ensuring reciprocity in our relations and of passing along to others the goods we have received in the past.[10]

But this duty is not without limits. The limits include harm to one's self. Beauchamp and Childress identify a process that one can use to evaluate the risk of harm to determine the degree of one's obligation. First, the individual we are to help is at risk of significant loss or danger. Second, one can perform an act directly relevant to preventing this loss or damage. Third, one's act is likely to prevent this damage or loss. Fourth, the benefits the individual receives as a consequence of my actions (a) outweigh harms to myself and (b) present minimal risk to self. Thus, we have the necessity of making a prudential calculation about risks and benefits. Sometimes this calculation may be clear. If someone is drowning and I cannot swim, I am not obligated to go in the water to help that person, although I would be obligated to assist in other ways. At other times, the calculation may not be as clear. For example, if I'm a medic on a battlefield, do I have to cross the line of fire, or a minefield, to treat injured soldiers?

## *Autonomy*

Autonomy is a form of personal liberty of action in which the individual determines his or her course of action in accordance with a plan of his or her own choosing.[11] Autonomy involves two elements: First is the capacity to deliberate about a plan of action. One must be capable of examining alternatives and distinguishing between them. Second, one must have the capacity to put one's plan into action. Autonomy includes the ability to actualize or carry out what one has decided.

In many ways, autonomy is the all-American value. It affirms that we ought to be the master of our own fate or the captain of our ship. Autonomy mandates a strong sense of personal responsibility for our own lives. Autonomy celebrates the hardy individualism for which our country is famous. It emphasizes creativity and productivity while being the enemy of conformity. Autonomy requires that we choose who we wish to be and take responsibility for that.

In celebrating individuality and control of one's self, however, too heavy a reliance on autonomy can isolate one from the community, from one's family, and from one's friends. While ultimately one is responsible for one's self and one's actions, the community can also be involved in an individual's learning what his or her responsibilities are and can also set obligations that one needs to respect as one makes decisions. Thus, while autonomy is important, and plays a critical role in bioethics, it needs to be understood within the context of the community as well as other moral responsibilities that one may have. Moreover, many have pointed out the complexity of delivering health care in an increasingly pluralistic society. There are many different ethnic groups and religious groups that interact in the health care setting—both from professional and from patient perspectives. This situation raises the importance of cross-cultural bioethics and the challenges it poses.

One of the major issues in autonomy is known as *paternalism*. Generally speaking, paternalism involves some sort of interference with an individual's liberty of action. Typically, a reference to the person's own good justifies this interference. Paternalism may be active in that one acts on behalf of a person but not at their request. One may treat a person when they have not asked for such treatment. Or paternalism may be passive in that one refuses to help another achieve some goal they may have. For example, a physician may refuse to prescribe a tranquilizer because of her fears of its abuse by the patient.

James Childress, in his book on paternalism, identifies several types of paternalism that refine this general idea and indicate its different aspects.[12]

1. *Pure and Impure.* Pure paternalism bases its intervention into a person's life on an appeal to the welfare of that person alone. This is the classic model in which parents tell children to eat spinach because it's good for them. Impure paternalism justifies interference with another person because of the welfare of that person and the welfare of another. Thus, some argue that a parent who is also a Jehovah's Witness should have a blood transfusion not only because of the good for that person, but also for the good of his or her children.

2. *Restricted and Extended.* A restricted paternalistic intervention is one that overrides an individual's act because of some defect in the person. Thus, one may prohibit a child from doing something because of age-related or psychological incompetence. In extended paternalism, institutions or individuals restrain someone because what he or she wants to do is risky or dangerous. Thus, there are laws that mandate wearing helmets while riding motorcycles or seatbelts while in front seats of cars or when under ten years of age.

3. *Positive and Negative.* A positive paternalistic act, such as forcing a patient into a rehabilitation program, seeks to promote the person's own good. A negative paternalistic intervention, such as taking cigarettes away from someone, seeks to prevent harm.

4. *Soft and Hard.* In a soft paternalistic act, the values used to justify the intervention are the patient's values. For example, health care providers frequently remove unconscious or comatose patients from life support systems because those patients stated that preference in advance of being in that situation. In hard paternalism, the values used to justify an act are not the patient's. This is the classic case of someone else knowing what is good for you and then having you do it or having it done to you.

5. *Direct and Indirect.* In direct paternalism, the person who receives the alleged benefit is the one whose values are overridden. The motorcyclist forced to wear the helmet is the one who assumedly will benefit if there is an accident. In indirect paternalism, one person is restrained so that another individual can receive a benefit. A classic instance is child abuse, in which authorities restrain parents in some fashion to benefit the child.

The desire to help someone or provide a benefit for someone runs deep within the human spirit. Also there are the specific obligations of nonmaleficence and beneficence that we discussed earlier in this chapter. Yet people are autonomous. They know their interests and what is important to them. Respect for persons mandates a presumption against paternalistic interventions. Yet, we see harm being done that we could prevent. Can we resolve these issues?

One argument for a paternalistic intervention includes these four steps:

1. The recipient of the paternalistic act actually has some incapacity that prevents or inhibits him or her

from making a decision. The person is under undue stress, is a minor, or his or her judgment is impaired in some way.

2. There is the probability of harm unless there is an intervention. Here, one needs to determine if all harms are equal. Are physical, mental, or social harms interchangeable? Should we intervene regardless of how minor or major a harm could be?

3. There is a proportionality consideration. That is, the probable benefit of intervention outweighs the probable risk of harm from nonintervention. Here, one needs to be careful of uncritical interventions of extended paternalism.

4. The paternalistic intervention is the least restrictive, humiliating, and insulting alternative. This criterion argues that one remain as respectful of the individual as possible during the intervention.

This method will not resolve all issues connected with paternalism, but it will force individuals to recognize and justify such paternalistic interventions.[13]

Another major issue involving autonomy is *informed consent*. In fact, informed consent is, we think, one of the most critical problems in bioethics. Informed consent is a process where health care professionals and patients discuss the value implications of treatments or clarify what is important for each of them in deciding on particular treatments or treatment plans. Consent negotiations allow discussions of issues of importance for all involved parties. Informed consent is not just a signed consent form. As a process, informed consent is the knowledge of and consent to a particular form of treatment before health care providers administer that treatment. Informed consent requires that several conditions be met in the process.

First, the patient must have the *competence* (or *decision-making capacity*) to make the decision.[14] A person may possess full competence in that the person is in control of his or her life; or, someone's competence may be limited. A person may have decision-making capacities in one area but not in another. In other words, decision-making capacity is task specific. For example, someone may have the capacity to choose to color his or her hair purple, but that does not mean that person has the capacity to make an end-of-life treatment decision. An individual may not comprehend the value of money and may be restrained in its use but may be quite capable of making other decisions of daily living concerning nutrition, personal hygiene, or appointment making. Age may also suggest limited competence in that a person may be competent for some activities but not for others. Finally, and most problematically, one may be intermittently able to make decisions. That is, decision-making capacity fluctuates over time. This is especially true for patients in hospitals who receive consciousness-altering medications. Also, a person becoming senile may at times be competent, but at other times he or she may be unaware of the implications of his or her choices.

To help sort out the difficult issues of evaluating competence, experts have proposed three different standards. We will present them in order of increasing complexity. The first standard states that a person is competent when he or she has made a decision. When presented with a choice, the individual chooses an alternative. The fact of a choice is evidence of competence. The second is the capacity to give reasons for one's choice. Competence here requires some process of justification, an articulation of why one made this choice. The third standard argues not only that a person should be able to give reasons for his or her choice, but also that this choice should be a reasonable one.

Each of these standards is different and raises a variety of value judgments. What is most critical is that individuals be aware of what standard of competence they are using and recognize that it may conflict with the judgments of others.

Second, the physician must provide adequate *disclosure* of the information necessary to make an informed decision. Disclosure refers to the content of what a patient is told during the consent process. Scholars have proposed two general standards for disclosure. The first, and more traditional standard, is the professional standard. What a person is told is what professionals typically tell patients. A professional fulfills the obligation to inform patients by telling a patient what one's colleagues would tell that same patient. The obvious problem with this standard is that one's colleagues may tell a patient little or nothing. That is, the professional standard may be simply to tell a patient as little as possible about his or her condition. In this situation, one may meet the standard and fulfill the obligation, but the patient remains ignorant.

Obvious problems with that standard led to the development of the more recent standard of the reasonable person. In this perspective, the health care provider is obligated to disclose what the reasonable person would want to know. One cannot fulfill the obligation by not saying anything; the provider must communicate some information. The degree of specificity is centered outside the profession in the hypothetical reasonable person. Such a standard promotes autonomy and is protective of patients' rights. Nonetheless it remains on a general level.

This level of generality is why we think it important to go further and determine what a particular patient wants to know. Such a standard of disclosure recognizes a patient's right to be informed, but more importantly, it mediates that right with respect to the patient's desires. Some patients may want to know nothing; others may want additional reading they can do. Only by determining what a particular patient wants to know can a professional respect and protect his or her rights.

Third, the patient must demonstrate *comprehension* of the information the physician disclosed. If a patient does not understand what the doctor has told him or her, there is no way that the patient can use the information. Comprehension presents many problems and may test the patience of health care professionals. Some may assume that patients simply cannot understand the complexity of the issues. Others may assume that patients do not comprehend unless they receive a mini-course in medicine. Moreover, some may assume that there is not sufficient time to inform patients fully.

One should note several issues here. First, from the fact that someone is not *fully* informed it does not follow that he or she is not *adequately* informed. Second, health care professionals have a professional language. While that language is appropriate for peer communication, it is inappropriate for communication with patients. Thus, professionals need to translate their terms and jargon so that it will be intelligible to others. Third, comprehension typically requires time, especially when what needs to be told is not good news. Being informed does not necessitate being told everything at once. Fulfilling the condition of comprehension requires sensitivity to what a patient can take in at one time.

Finally, patients need to provide informed consent *voluntarily*. A patient's voluntariness refers to his or her ability to make a choice without being unduly pressured to make a particular choice by any specific person. Being free in making a decision means that we own the decision, that the decision is ours, that we have chosen the option. Nevertheless, it seems clear to us that no decision is ever made without some constraints or pressures. No one chooses in a vacuum or in the absence of values or experiences. The moral issue is to remove as much coercion or undue influence as possible so that the decision is the individual's and not someone else's.

Coercion and undue influence refer to two different realities. On the one hand, coercion refers to the use of an actual threat of harm or some type of forceful manipulation to influence the person to choose one alternative rather than another. Coercion may take physical, psychological, or economic forms. The nature of coercion is perhaps best captured in the widely quoted phrase from the movie *The Godfather*: "I made him an offer he couldn't refuse." This connotes the illusion of choice (made an offer) but, in effect, forecloses all options but one (the one that can't be refused). On the other hand, undue influence refers to the use of excessive rewards or irrationally persuasive techniques to short-circuit a person's decision-making process. Thus, one may use behavior modification techniques to get someone to agree with one's decision. One may offer large cash payments or the promise of benefits to induce people to participate in research that has a high risk. In either case, the appeal is not to a person's interests, rights, or values. The purpose of coercion or undue influence is to change how the patient views a choice or judgment so that the patient will do what he or she might not ordinarily have done.

## Rights

Commentators frequently use the term *rights* in ethics and bioethics. Yet the term is problematic because of its varied meanings and different connotations. This problem is evident even in the origin of the term *rights*. In the medieval ethical tradition, we do not find the term *rights*; rather, we find the term *duty*. The term *duty* referred to the reciprocal obligation members of a community had to one another. Duties were specific ways in which each helped the other realize the common good of all. In the modern tradition, beginning with the Enlightenment, rights referred to claims of the individual against the state. Rights were a means of carving out a zone of privacy or protection against the ever-increasing powers of the state. Thus, the term *rights* has two major historical origins and two different connotations.

To begin, there are at least two different kinds of rights: moral and legal. One kind of right is a *moral right*. Ethical arguments form the basis of moral rights, which exist prior to and independent of the guarantees of any institution. Frequently moral rights are rooted in the nature of the person and his or her dignity and are, therefore, understood to be universal and inalienable. Another kind of right is a *legal right*. Here, civil laws, constitutions, or political institutions of a particular country or political unit spell out legal rights. Legal rights are only those rights granted to citizens by the government. They are specific to particular cultures and are subject to social qualifications. There are two types of legal rights: positive rights and negative rights. A *positive right* is a claim to a positive action on the part of another person. A positive right entails a duty on the part of someone else to do something. For example, the right of informed consent confers an obligation on the part of a health care professional to tell the patient relevant information about the patient's diagnosis and treatment options. A *negative right* establishes an obligation for someone to refrain from action. Negative rights establish obligations of noninterference. The legal right to abortion, for example, does not secure an obligation for someone to perform an abortion, rather only that no one can interfere with a woman who is seeking an abortion.

Next, rights have different content. First, some think of rights as *privileges*, or social goods, that go beyond routine moral obligations. Second, others think of rights as a sort of *social immunity*, a protection from powers of the state. Third, some see rights as *powers* or *capacities* to act in society. Fourth, many see rights as *entitlements*. Entitlements are social responses that we see as deserved; they are derivative from being a member of a society. Finally, some see rights as *claims* or *moral demands* made on someone or on society.

One of the most difficult problems in rights theory is establishing who is the subject of a right and on what basis. Animal rights activists argue, for example, that to have rights one need only be able to feel pain or to be sentient. Others would suggest that consciousness is enough to secure rights. Still others argue that only self-consciousness can secure rights. Another suggestion is that one be able to use language. This of course presents interesting issues with respect to chimpanzees or gorillas who have been taught sign language as well as with other animals who appear to have some sophisticated form of communication. Finally, others make the argument that only persons are bearers of rights. Persons are generally understood to be moral agents with an enduring concept of self and capable of autonomous actions.

The concept of patients' rights is one whose time has come. Historically, patients have had a passive role in their treatment. Often they were told little, if anything, about what was happening. Sometimes they were not informed about their diagnosis or various treatment options. We saw this phenomenon under paternalism. The motivation for this was not malevolence or ill-will toward patients. Rather, many saw such concealment as a way of protecting patients or a way of not harming them. Why add the burden of bad or discouraging news to the already debilitating effects of the disease?

However, this practice is slowly being reversed. Consumers are becoming less afraid of experts and are informing themselves. We recognize, for instance, that expertise has its limits.[15] Many have accepted the practical philosophy that an informed patient is a more cooperative patient. More people are assuming responsibility for their health through various programs of prevention.

Finally, there have been a number of lawsuits that have forced changes in the process of informing patients of their diagnosis and prognosis.

A very important development in bioethics regarding rights is the patient rights movement. The development of the field of health care ethics and the pursuit of several rights in the courts have helped specify many rights in health care. The American Hospital Association (AHA) and the American Civil Liberties Union (ACLU) developed rights statements, too.[16] Finally, federal regulations specify some rights related to treatment and research. Let us survey some of these rights as a preview of what we will see in upcoming chapters.

*The right to information.* Probably the most critical right is the one to information. If one is ignorant of one's situation, one cannot exercise options, cannot make plans, and cannot take control. Access to and possession of information are the bases for exercising autonomy. If health care providers deny the patient relevant information, then he or she will remain a victim of paternalism.

*The right to access hospital records.* One particular expression of the right to information is the right to access one's hospital records. Thus, two questions frequently present themselves: (1) Can a patient see his or her record? and (2) Who besides the hospital or physician has access to the record? In the past, patients often were not allowed to see their records. This was part of the general practice of providing little information to patients. In addition, the records contained technical information that patients might be unlikely to understand. As the right to information and consent gained more acceptance, so did the right to access to one's records. Again, the argument is that one cannot exercise autonomy if one does not have knowledge.

The issue of who else can see records is a complex one. The Food and Drug Administration (FDA) and pharmaceutical companies have an interest in seeing patients' records to understand how new drugs work. Researchers want to examine records to understand disease patterns, causes of diseases, and differences among populations. Insurance companies want to know their clients' health status. The problems of privacy and confidentiality are thus complex and serious, especially when there are valid, competing public interest reasons for gaining access to patients' health records. In 1996, the Health Insurance Portability and Accountability Act (HIPAA) began to shape the access to, exchange of, and protection of patients' health information. HIPAA is now a major component of hospital compliance requirements and scopes out the limits to disclosing patient information.

A third problem, one whose magnitude is coming into focus, is that of electronic patients' records. As part of the shift to computers, health care professionals routinely enter patients' records on hospital computers. The primary advantage is that physicians and others involved in patient care have direct and easy access to their patients from anywhere in the hospital—or possibly anywhere else they have Internet access. A key issue is how to prevent inappropriate and unauthorized access to these records. The standard strategy of passwords to gain access to the system is fine as far as it goes. Likewise, encryption has its limits. The problem, as we so well know, is that those strategies might not go far enough. Thus, a critical problem for hospitals is devising secure strategies to safeguard patients' privacy.

*The right to privacy.* In light of the right to information, there is also a right to privacy, which is to be protected by professional confidentiality. Privacy, confidentiality, and the protection of information gained during the professional-client interchange are extremely important. If one cannot assure confidentiality, then people may not seek help, the basis of a trusting relationship may be destroyed, and a patient's position in society may be jeopardized. Such issues frequently arise in teaching hospitals, where many individuals are privy to cases because health care professionals need to discuss them with one another and because they examine patients' records as part of research protocols.

*The right to refuse treatment.* If one has the right to give informed consent to treatment, by implication one also has the right to refuse treatment. Again, such a refusal is an exercise of autonomy and a means whereby the patient exercises the right of self-determination. This right has received strong legal and ethical support. It is the right that causes the most difficulties, however. Health care professionals find it difficult to stop treating their patients for both personal and professional reasons. Families may not understand why a member does not want a particular treatment. Society may not accept a particular religion's position on medicine. Thus, the good of the individual and the good of society frequently stand in tension.

*The right to voluntary participation in research.* The right to refuse treatment is also understood as a right to voluntary participation in research. This area is the one in which the most protection of rights is expressed. There is ample ethical argumentation, legal precedent, federal regulations, and institutional support to ensure that researchers recruit potential subjects and adequately inform them before enrolling them in a research project. The primary issue here is the protection of the human research subject. The right of consent is seen as the medium between the social desire to protect individuals and the need of science to discover cures for diseases.

To some, the patients' rights movement may seem like an antimedicine or antiphysician movement. In a way, this may be correct. Many resent the status and privileges of physicians. Many harbor grudges against physicians. As in all movements, some of the motivation may be misplaced.

But, it is also clear that patients traditionally have been relegated to a passive and/or secondary role. Frequently, physicians and others involved in health care have totally removed the patient from the decision-making process. An emphasis on patients' rights seeks to correct this omission and to ensure that the values and rights of patients occupy their rightful place. This will obviously create problems and cause tension, but as both physicians and patients become used to occupying different roles, perceptions and expectations will change and tensions will decrease.

The contribution of the rights movement in medicine has been to place patients within the decision-making process. As in all other areas of life, time is necessary to learn how to exercise these rights, to redefine relationships based on these rights, and to restructure the physician-patient relationship. As long as both physicians and patients recognize that the purpose of the discussion of rights is to ensure a better ethical standard in medicine, they can enter into the discussion and practice of rights in medicine as a joint enterprise.

# CONCLUSION

Now that we have introduced you to the various ethical theories and terms used in bioethics, we will turn our attention to specific topics. We will examine topics ranging from the beginning of life (e.g., abortion) to the ending of life (e.g., euthanasia), and almost everything in between. In all of these topics, we encourage you to apply the theories and terms in this chapter as you formulate your own positions on the questions at hand.

## DISCUSSION QUESTIONS

1. Why is the concept of informed consent so important? What functions does it perform for both patient and health care professional?
2. What method of allocation of resources seems most just to you?
3. Do you think people should have the right to refuse treatment? Can you justify treating someone against their will?
4. Which do you think are more important, moral rights or legal rights?
5. Who do you think should have access to your health records?
6. When there is disagreement over how to treat a patient, whose decision should take priority?

## NOTES

1. Albert R. Jonsen, *The Birth of Bioethics* (New York: Oxford University Press, 1998), 352–76.

2. See Richard M. Gula, *Reason Informed by Faith: Foundations of Catholic Morality* (Mahwah, NJ: Paulist Press, 1989), 283–99.

3. Axiology is the study of values.

4 See National Commission for the Protection of Human Subjects of Biomedical and Behavioral Research, "The Belmont

Report," in *Source Book in Bioethics: A Documentary History*, ed. Albert R. Jonsen, Robert M. Veatch, and LeRoy Walters (Washington, DC: Georgetown University Press, 1998), 22–28.

5. See Tom L. Beauchamp and James F. Childress, *Principles of Biomedical Ethics*, 5th ed. (New York: Oxford University Press, 2001).

6. Beauchamp and Childress, *Biomedical Ethics*, 225–82.

7. For example, see Norman Daniels, *Just Health Care* (New York: Cambridge University Press, 1985).

8. Daniel P. Sulmasy, "Dignity and the Human as a Natural Kind," in *Health and Human Flourishing: Religion, Medicine, and Moral Anthropology*, ed. Carol R. Taylor and Roberto Dell'Oro (Washington, DC: Georgetown University Press, 2006), 71–87.

9. Beauchamp and Childress, *Biomedical Ethics*, 113–64.

10. Ibid., 165–224.

11. Ibid., 57–112.

12. James F. Childress, *Who Shall Decide? Paternalism in Health Care* (New York: Oxford University Press, 1982).

13. James F. Childress, *Priorities in Biomedical Ethics* (Philadelphia: Westminster Press, 1981), 27.

14. Here, we use these terms interchangeably, but we recognize that there is a difference between them. Competence tends to refer to a *legal* designation; decision-making capacity, or decisional capacity, tends to refer to a *medico-moral* reality. As a legal term, competence may reflect an overarching category of a person who can make decisions legally. Decision-making capacity is very specific to the task and time of a particular decision.

15. See Robert Veatch, "Generalization of Expertise," *The Hastings Center Studies* 1, no. 2 (1973): 29–40.

16. For a copy of the AHA's Patients' Bill of Rights, see Martin Benjamin and Joy Curtis, *Ethics in Nursing* (New York: Oxford University Press, 1981). For the ACLU position, see George Annas, *The Rights of Patients: The Basic ACLU Guide to Patient Rights*, 2nd ed. (Carbondale: Southern Illinois University Press, 1989).

# BIBLIOGRAPHY

Annas, George. *The Rights of Patients: The Basic ACLU Guide to Patient Rights*. 2nd ed. Carbondale: Southern Illinois University Press, 1989.

Ashley, Benedict M., Jean K. deBlois, and Kevin D. O'Rourke. *Health Care Ethics: A Catholic Theological Analysis*. 5th ed. Washington, DC: Georgetown University Press, 2006.

Aulisio, Mark P., Robert M. Arnold, and Stuart J. Youngner, eds. *Ethics Consultation: From Theory to Practice*. Baltimore, MD: Johns Hopkins University Press, 2003.

Beauchamp, Tom L., and James F. Childress. *Principles of Biomedical Ethics*. 5th ed. New York: Oxford University Press, 2001.

Beauchamp, Tom L., LeRoy Walters, Jeffrey P. Kahn, and Anna C. Mastroianni. *Contemporary Issues in Bioethics*. 7th ed. Belmont, CA: Thomson Wadsworth, 2007.

Benjamin, Martin, and Joy Curtis. *Ethics in Nursing*. New York: Oxford University Press, 1981.

Cahill, Lisa Sowle. *Bioethics and the Common Good: The Père Marquette Lecture in Theology, 2004*. Milwaukee, WI: Marquette University Press, 2004.

————. *Theological Bioethics: Participation, Justice, and Change*. Washington, DC: Georgetown University Press, 2005.

Cavanaugh, T. A. *Double-Effect Reasoning: Doing Good and Avoiding Evil*. New York: Oxford University Press, 2006.

Childress, James F. *Who Shall Decide? Paternalism in Health Care*. New York: Oxford University Press, 1982.

————. *Priorities in Biomedical Ethics*. Philadelphia: Westminster Press, 1981.

Daniels, Norman. *Just Health Care*. New York: Cambridge University Press, 1985.

Eckenwiler, Lisa A., and Felicia G. Cohn, eds. *The Ethics of Bioethics: Mapping the Moral Landscape*. Baltimore, MD: Johns Hopkins University Press, 2007.

Engelhardt, H. Tristram. *The Foundations of Bioethics*. 2nd ed. New York: Oxford University Press, 1996.

Farber Post, Linda, Jeffrey Blustein, and Nancy Neveloff Dubler. *Handbook for Health Care Ethics Committees*. Baltimore, MD: Johns Hopkins University Press, 2007.

Gula, Richard M. *Reason Informed by Faith: Foundations of Catholic Morality*. Mahwah, NJ: Paulist Press, 1989.

*Human Dignity and Bioethics: Essays Commissioned by the President's Council on Bioethics*. Washington, DC: President's Council on Bioethics, 2008.

Jecker, Nancy S., Albert R. Jonsen, and Robert A. Pearlman, eds. *Bioethics: An Introduction to the History, Methods, and Practice*. 2nd ed. Sudbury, MA: Jones and Bartlett Publishers, 2007.

Jonsen, Albert R. *The Birth of Bioethics*. New York: Oxford University Press, 1998.

Jonsen, Albert R., Robert M. Veatch, and LeRoy Walters, eds. *Source Book in Bioethics: A Documentary History*. Washington, DC: Georgetown University Press, 1998.

Khushf, George, ed. *Handbook of Bioethics: Taking Stock of the Field from a Philosophical Perspective*. Boston: Kluwer Academic, 2004.

Lammers, Stephen E., and Allen Verhey, eds. *On Moral Medicine: Theological Perspectives in Medical Ethics*. 2nd ed. Grand Rapids, MI: William B. Eerdmans, 1998.

Mackler, Aaron L. *Introduction to Jewish and Catholic Bioethics: A Comparative Analysis*. Washington, DC: Georgetown University Press, 2003.

————, ed. *Life and Death Responsibilities in Jewish Biomedical Ethics*. New York: Louis Finkelstein Institute, 2000.

Steinbock, Bonnie, ed. *The Oxford Handbook of Bioethics*. New York: Oxford University Press, 2007.

Taylor, Carol R., and Roberto Dell'Oro, eds. *Health and Human Flourishing: Religion, Medicine, and Moral Anthropology*. Washington, DC: Georgetown University Press, 2006.

Veatch, Robert. "Generalization of Expertise." *The Hastings Center Studies* 1, no. 2 (1973): 29–40.

Walter, James J., and Thomas A. Shannon. *Contemporary Issues in Bioethics: A Catholic Perspective*. Lanham, MD: Rowman & Littlefield Publishers, 2005.

Wilson Ross, Judith, John W. Glaser, Dorothy Rasinski-Gregory, Joan McIver Gibson, and Corrine Bayley. *Health Care Ethics Committees: The Next Generation.* Chicago: American Hospital Association Publishing, 1993.

## PART II

## ISSUES EARLY IN LIFE

## Chapter 5

# ABORTION

## INTRODUCTION

When the United States Supreme Court decided *Roe v. Wade* in 1973, few foresaw the impact it would have. In a 2006 report, *Abortion in Women's Lives*, the Guttmacher Institute reports that approximately 1.3 million abortions occurred in 2002 in the United States, though there have been some fluctuations in the rate during the last several years.[1] According to 2003 Center for Disease Control and Prevention (CDC) data, women 20–24 years old procured about 33 percent of all induced abortions for which providers adequately reported age; however, adolescents (aged 15 years or younger) had the highest abortion ratios (proportion of pregnancies that ended in induced abortion): 830 abortions per 1,000 live births.[2] In addition, protests at abortion facilities have escalated, and opponents of abortion have attacked and murdered both physicians and staff of these clinics. The social, legal, and moral debate over abortion continues to be one of the most divisive in our country's history.

This debate has only sharpened over the last few years as it continues to press on and shape electoral politics at all levels. Pro- or antiabortion debates are part of national party platform debates and, more and more frequently, a litmus test for various offices, including the presidency as well as federal and state legislative seats. Nominations for the Supreme Court are continually predicated on the candidate's position on abortion.

Religion remains an important part of the abortion debate, though in ways both strange and interesting. Catholic and Protestant women have abortions at about the same rates. Yet,

Catholics and Protestants are both as likely to disapprove of abortion. According to James Kelly, a majority of Americans "do not approve of abortion for non-medical reasons," yet fewer "than ten percent of the 1.6 million abortions obtained each year are performed for reasons of health, rape or incest."[3] Ironically, "many more Americans will describe abortion as immoral than will support laws directly prohibiting it."[4] The way Kelly, a sociologist, summarizes the findings of two public opinion polls is as follows:

> The good news was the continuing strong moral repugnance most Americans have toward abortion. The bad news was the public's rather lukewarm view of the right-to-life movement. The uncertain news was how best to translate the widespread moral disapproval rate of abortion into wise laws based on both principle and consensus.[5]

Varying issues of the abortion debate are put into sharp relief by a case in Nebraska. In 1994, "when a 15–year-old girl told her parents, her 16–year-old boy friend and his parents that she was pregnant, she and her family expected that the decision whether to continue the 23–week pregnancy would be theirs to make."[6] However, the girl's boyfriend and his parents invaded her family's house, and the girl was taken away "in the middle of the night by law-enforcement officers determined to stop her from having an abortion; she was put into foster care, and, finally, she was ordered by a judge not to abort the pregnancy."[7] The teenager eventually gave birth to a daughter and raised the child in her parents' home. The family, however, relocated because of the harassment they received.

This case brings together many elements in the abortion debate: teen sexual activity, the legal rights of the two teenagers, the legal status of a twenty-three-week-old fetus, parental rights over their children, the consent process for obtaining an abortion, the use of law enforcement officers and the judicial system to implement the law and/or perceptions of it, the question of the extent to which restraints relating to location, diet, and activities can be imposed on women during pregnancy, and perceptions about the use of violence in attempts to prevent abortions.

Regardless of the appropriateness of any resolution of this case, significant harms occurred to all parties involved, prejudices of all sorts were reinforced, lives were changed, and the social fabric of a small town was torn. In various ways and in different circumstances, personal and moral traumas continue to recur with profound personal and social consequences but with seemingly few resources for resolution.

## LEGAL DIMENSIONS

Abortion legislation has covered a lot of ground since the laws of the 1800s when the test for pregnancy was quickening and abortions were prohibited only after quickening.[8] The abortion laws that came in the mid-1800s served two functions: (1) to establish greater control over the growing field of medicine and (2) to control the kind of preparations used to procure abortions. In effect, some of these laws were poison control laws. In the late 1800s and early 1900s, there was a major shift in who was obtaining abortions. Typically, on the one hand, immigrants had the highest use of abortion. But as their lot improved, many more gave birth. On the other hand, the women of the new native Americans (i.e., descendents and relatives of the colonists and settlers) were turning to abortion as a contraceptive, and the population of this group began to decrease. Many of the abortion laws passed during this time were a consequence of a nativist backlash that feared that the immigrants would outnumber the new native Americans. Finally, the restrictive abortion legislation of the early and mid-twentieth century reflected a broad coalition of physicians, clergy, and the population who argued that abortion should be prohibited except for clearly defined and controlled medical circumstances, typically related to the health of the mother.

The legal debate on abortion continues through an ongoing challenge to nominees for membership on various courts and a constant stream of cases to test the legal right to an abortion. At least fourteen major cases have been before the Supreme Court.

While legal cases challenging *Roe v. Wade* have not succeeded in overturning it, the discussions on this right by the Supreme Court justices has grown more rancorous and rigid, and judges and legislators are drawing the right to abortion more and more narrowly.[9]

*Roe v. Wade*, decided on January 22, 1973, dramatically catalyzed the abortion debate. This case struck down a Texas statute that made it a crime to procure or attempt an abortion except on medical advice for the purpose of saving the mother's life. This decision struck down all similar legislation in all other states. Thus, the decision in *Roe v. Wade* decriminalized abortion on the grounds that the right of privacy was broad enough to include a woman's decision to terminate her pregnancy. The decision also included the statement that the fetus was not a person in the sense intended by the Constitution. Ironically, in August 1995 Norma McCorvey, the "Jane Roe" of the case, joined Operation Rescue, a militant antiabortion organization. McCorvey, however, contrary to Operation Rescue, still believes in a right to a first-trimester abortion.

The second major case was *Planned Parenthood of Central Missouri v. Danforth*, issued on July 1, 1976. This ruling declared unconstitutional two sections of Missouri abortion law. First, the state could no longer require the consent of the spouse for a first-trimester abortion. Since the state does not have this power, neither does anyone else. Second, parents or guardians of women under eighteen may not prohibit them from obtaining an abortion. Three reasons were given for this. First, as above, the state cannot grant to others what it itself does not have. Second, minors too have constitutional rights. Third, the state should not give parents the power to overrule a decision made by a young woman and her physician, for, in the judgment of the Court, this would neither strengthen family bonds nor enhance parental authority.

The third major decision was *Beal v. Doe*, issued on June 20, 1977. This decision resolved a practical point but set off other debates. In this decision, the Court held that states participating in the Medicaid program were not required to fund nontherapeutic abortions. Title 19 of the Social Security Act gives participating states broad discretionary powers in determining the extent of the medical assistance they need to provide to Medicaid recipients.

The only requirement is that the standards be reasonable and consistent with the goals of Title 19. It was argued that nontherapeutic abortions were not necessary medical services and, therefore, that a refusal to fund them is not inconsistent with the aims of Title 19.

A fourth major case, *Bellotti v. Baird*, decided on July 2, 1979, dealt with minors and abortion. The decision argued that every minor ought to have the opportunity to go to court without the prior consent of her parents. If the court determined that the minor was mature, it could authorize her to act without her parents' permission. If immature, she may show why the abortion is in her best interest, and the court can then authorize the abortion without prior permission of the parents. Also, the court may deny an abortion to a minor in the absence of parental consultation if the court judges that to be in her best interests.

Decided on July 3, 1989, the case of *Webster v. Reproductive Health Services* was critical for several reasons. First, a Missouri law that banned the use of public hospitals or clinics for the provision of abortion was upheld. Second, the center of the debate shifted from the Supreme Court to state legislatures as appropriate loci for the legal debate. Third, in light of the decision, concurrences, and dissents, there was an indication that a majority of the Supreme Court members no longer held abortion to be a fundamental constitutional right.

In the 1990 cases of *Hodgson v. Minnesota* (decided on June 25, 1990) and *Ohio v. Akron Center for Reproductive Health* (also decided on June 25, 1990), parental notification by minors was addressed again. According to *Hodgson*, the state may require that a teen notify both her parents prior to an abortion, as long as there is an alternative of a judicial hearing. In Ohio, the notification requirement was limited to one parent. According to the Guttmacher Institute, thirty-five states require some form of parental involvement in a minor's decision to procure an induced abortion.[10] Parental involvement can mean consent, notification, or both.

Decided on June 29, 1992, the case of *Planned Parenthood v. Casey* was important in that the Court affirmed the core of *Roe* but permitted some regulation of abortion by the states. While this relieved the fears of a total reversal of *Roe* that some had as a result of *Webster*, nonetheless a tendency to further restrict that right seems to be clearly established.

In 2003, Congress enacted the Partial-Birth Abortion Ban Act, which proscribes a specific method (i.e., dilation and evacuation) of abortion when certain anatomical parts of the fetus (i.e., landmarks; e.g., the head or, if breech, the navel) are outside of the mother. Though this ban includes abortions both pre-viability and post-viability, the act does not regulate the procedures most often used in first-trimester abortions. On April 18, 2007, the U.S. Supreme Court decided *Gonzalez v. Carhart*, which determined that the Partial-Birth Abortion Ban Act was not unconstitutional (as had been challenged in *Stenberg v. Carhart*). The Court held that the act did not impose an undue burden on a woman's right to abortion; the act also seems to strike a balance, argued in *Casey*, to protect the woman's right to choose and the government's interest in protecting fetal life. State laws continue to be important regarding bans on partial-birth abortions because they may impose stricter penalties and provide for local control in the prosecution of physicians.[11]

These cases set the tone for future legal debates and court decisions for the next decades. We have a different Court, and new cases are being presented to it. In addition, the age of several justices on the Supreme Court is yet another factor in the abortion debate. When they resign, who appoints their replacements, and what a newly constituted Court decides will have yet another significant impact on the abortion debate. In addition to the woman's right to choose and the government's interest in protecting the health and life of the mother and fetus, state laws address physician and hospital requirements (e.g., when must a physician perform an abortion in a hospital), gestational limits and "partial-birth" abortions, use of public funding for abortions, coverage by private insurance, refusal to participate in abortions by health care providers, mandated counseling, waiting periods prior to induced abortion, and parental involvement. The legal issues notwithstanding, the morality of abortion is not resolved through these discussions.

# ETHICAL ISSUES IN ABORTION

## *The Sanctity of Life*

A major element in the abortion debate is the concept of the sanctity of life. This phrase is a shorthand way of referring to the value of life and its inherent preciousness. Whether the value of life is external, in the sense that life is a gift from the Creator, or internal, in that the person is an inherent center of value, the concept is an important one in thinking through the abortion dilemma.

The concept of the sanctity of life is simple in its statement but complex in its explanation. The concept begins with an affirmation of the beauty and richness of biological life itself. This reflects the orientation of the Franciscan theologian Bonaventure, who affirmed that creation contained the footprints of God. That which was created mirrored its Maker and, because of that, was precious.

Furthermore, when that life is expressed in personal form, it takes on a new sense of mystery and value. On the one hand, following the thought of Pierre Teilhard de Chardin, we can say that personal life is when creation becomes conscious of itself. In the person, creation is able to be aware of itself, to experience itself, to know its source and destiny. On the other hand, the distinctively human traits of intellect and will reflect what is traditionally called the image of God within the person. That is, the capacity to understand and choose reflects qualities of the divine conferred upon us in our creation. Such is the dignity of personal life: one can determine who one is and what to do and freely commit oneself to that project.

For many, such dignity is present in all members of the human species from the moment of their first existence. All members of the human species begin with the potential to express and experience personal life. What is critical in this orientation is the capacity for such development, not the actual development itself. Such capacities are not accidental to the person, but are constitutive of the essence of that person. Thus, even though such potential may not be actualized—because of genetic disease or some intrauterine trauma—such an individual is still valued because of his or her possession of life and the essential capacities of personhood.

Thus, according to the viewpoint of sanctity of life, possession of life and distinctively human capacities confer upon individuals an inherent value and dignity. Many affirm the innocence of such individuals. Given their initial level of personal development, they are not yet morally responsible. In addition, these individuals are helpless and are dependent on others for their very existence. Such absolute innocence and dependence requires, in the judgment of many, absolute protection. Only such absolute protection can be a true expression of the appreciation of the value of life.

Finally, part of the sanctity-of-life discussion is thinking about how one relates the issue of ending life in abortion to ending life in other situations. Many secular and religious ethical theories permit or promote killing in some circumstances: for example, self-defense, defense of private property, war, or capital punishment. Here the value of life—the sanctity of life—is balanced against other important values: personal bodily integrity, the right to keep what is one's own, democracy, freedom, the security of society. The moral issue frequently is not whether we may kill, but under what circumstances killing is permitted.

Some respond to this situation by total pacifism, by prohibiting any killing or violence in any fashion in any circumstances. Others set up categories such as the just war theory that help define a narrow range of circumstances in which killing is permitted. Others declare certain kinds of killing off-limits: abortion and direct euthanasia. Each solution brings certain problems to its resolution of the moral problem of killing, but each also does its best to promote the sanctity of life.

## Who Is a Person?

A major part of the abortion debate has been the questions: Who is a person? and By what criteria can we know this? The answers to these questions obviously have a significant impact on the moral evaluation of the fetus. Daniel Callahan, in his classic study of abortion, identifies three basic orientations to personhood: the genetic school, the developmental school, and the school of social consequences.[12]

The genetic school defines a human person as any being that has a human genetic code. This orientation would argue that personhood comes with the setting of the individual's genetic code at fertilization. Further growth and development are simply spelling out the implications of the genetic code for this particular individual. A problem with this perspective is that it identifies the person with the genetic code and is open to the charge of genetic determinism.

The developmental school holds that while the establishment of the genetic code constitutes the basis for further development, some degree of development and interaction with the environment is necessary for someone to consider such a being as a full human person. This orientation suggests that one's genetic potential is not fully actualized until there has been interaction with the environment. This understanding of person includes more than the biological dimension. A problem with this perspective is trying to identify and gain consensus on what this more-than-biological dimension might be.

The third orientation is the school of social consequences, which dramatically shifts the focus of the question. This orientation departs from the biological and developmental elements and focuses on what society sees as valuable for personal existence. This school first determines what kind of persons are wanted by society and then sets the definition in accordance with that. The desires of society, expressed in public policy, take precedence over the biological or developmental aspects. A problem here is that history, both ancient and contemporary, reveals severe negative consequences for those who do not meet or fit criteria of social acceptability.

Another approach would look to what kinds of presuppositions are necessary so that one may talk of a *person*. That is, we can ask what are necessary, though perhaps not sufficient, preconditions for being a person. In this discussion, two critical biological markers play an important role.[13]

First, there is the establishment of *individuality*. While the genetic school is correct in stating that the completion of fertilization establishes genetic uniqueness—unless of course one has an identical twin—such uniqueness does not establish individuality. Up until the time the process of restriction occurs—around two or three weeks after fertilization—the cells of the developing preimplantation embryo have a twofold capacity. They possess what is called *totipotency*: the capacity for any cell of the embryo to become any part of the body.[14] In addition and related to this, a cell can be removed from the developing preimplantation embryo and have the capacity to develop into a complete organism. Equally important, the organism from which it was taken may not be harmed and itself may become a whole organism. That is, this is an organism that can be divided into parts, each of which can become a whole organism. This is a strong argument that this organism is not an individual. Therefore, it is necessary, though not sufficient, for an entity to be an individual before it can be a person. Such individuality begins at the time of restriction, when the cells of the organism become committed to becoming specific body parts.

Second, there is *neurological development*. Three stages of neural development seem important. The first occurs around the third week of development: the development of the primitive streak and the neural groove. This is the formation of the biological structure that will eventually become the neural system. Second, around the twelfth week, the embryo can begin to respond to stimuli. The neural system is developed enough to carry a signal to the brain. Finally, around the twentieth week, the entire central nervous system is integrated, and the fetus is also capable of initiating an act. At the first stage of development, the embryo is not yet capable of consciousness because the physical development of the brain has not yet occurred. Similarly, the fetus is not capable of self-consciousness at the second stage because of the lack of integration of the entire neural system. Only with the central nervous system's full integration do we have the physical conditions for what we could say are necessary, though not sufficient, presuppositions for personhood.

Yet another level of complexity comes from the growing accessibility of the fetus. Such accessibility through various monitoring devices such as amniocentesis and fetoscopy, fetal surgery, and the improvements of newborn intensive care units allow caregivers to experience the fetus as a patient. While some would argue that this is nothing new, our increased capacity to see and aid the fetus directly is a stronger basis for ascribing the status of patient than belief or ideology.

The questions then can be asked: If the fetus is a patient, might it also be a person? If this patient is not a person, then why treat—other than for the crassest of research motivations? If one experiences the fetus as being a person because of the status of being a patient, then what implications does that have for abortion? We are yet to face major dilemmas about the personhood of the fetus in light of the emergence of these new technologies and ways of seeing early human life.

## Women's Rights

The next issue involves the rights of women. Here, the issue reflects two aspects of autonomy: the reproductive liberty of women in particular and the liberty of women to have dominion over their bodies in general. In the former, one argues that women have a right to exercise their autonomy in human reproduction in any way they see fit. Thus, a woman can procure an abortion if continuing the pregnancy impinges on her reproductive liberty. Some might argue that this would be using abortion as a means of birth control, which may not be morally justifiable given other available alternatives (e.g., contraceptives, sterilization, and natural family planning). In the latter, a woman has a right to control and protect her body, even during a pregnancy. In this context, many have invoked different metaphors for viewing the fetus or embryo: a mere extension of the woman's body, an intruder, an aggressor, or a parasite. In any case, the symbolic meaning behind these tends to support a choice to procure an abortion.

## Life and Health of the Woman

Many commentators support the claim that a woman can procure an abortion for therapeutic reasons. What constitutes "therapeutic," however, is subject to much debate. Should therapeutic abortions be restricted to only those that pose an imminent and physical threat to the life or health of the woman? Should it be allowed only when there is a threat to her life? Or, should other burdens be considered? For example, mental anguish or financial distress? Although it may be rare, if a woman were to become pregnant following a sexual assault, could an abortion be seen as therapeutic if the child represents a constant reminder of the physical and emotional trauma the woman suffered?

A classic scenario to demonstrate this point, without involving the psychosocial aspects of rape, is the ectopic pregnancy. An ectopic pregnancy occurs when the developing embryo implants into the fallopian tube rather than the uterus. Thus, if the embryo continues to develop, it will rupture the fallopian tube and ultimately result in the death of the woman and the fetus. In this situation, the choices—allow the embryo to gestate or procure an abortion—present a true dilemma: neither option is really desirable (i.e., death of both embryo and woman or death of the embryo, respectively). Moralists have applied the Principle of Double Effect in these cases to justify the removal of pathological tissue (the fallopian tube) even if the death of the embryo is a foreseen consequence. Contemporary debates about this principle and its application to ectopic pregnancy involve concerns over what constitutes "pathological tissue" and therefore what is a direct or an indirect abortion. This specific debate has been renewed as other treatments have become the standard of care; physicians now treat most ectopic pregnancies without needing to remove the fallopian tube.

## Health and Viability of the Fetus

Conversely, some may argue that a "therapeutic abortion" is justifiable when the fetus has a condition that indicates it will have a poor quality of life or that its condition is "incompatible with life." Here, the abortion is more preventative than therapeutic: it prevents a person from existing with a condition. On the one hand, some claim there are clear-cut medical conditions that warrant the termination of pregnancy. An example is anencephaly, when the fetus grows without a cerebral cortex and an incomplete cranium. Often, these fetuses gestate to term alive—that is, with functional hearts and lungs—but die soon after birth. Thus, one might argue it is better for one to terminate a pregnancy than to bring a child into the world who may suffer or eventually die shortly after birth (in the process, using expensive medical resources). On the other hand, some worry that more moderate medical conditions might lead a couple or a woman to procure an abortion: for example, severe mental retardation. The worry becomes how severe the mental handicap must be to warrant an abortion. In addition, does such a decision to procure an abortion reflect a greater social problem with how one sees the already living mentally handicapped or disabled? If such abortion practices become widespread, could this lead to an erosion of right-relationships with those who are differently abled?

## The Role of Men

Although women shoulder the significant portion of the burden when it comes to pregnancy and choices for abortion, many wonder how men should respond, support, or react to the issues in abortion. What role, if any, should the man responsible for the pregnancy play in the decision-making process to procure an abortion? After all, did he not contribute to the situation too? Outside of sexual assault, men may have some legitimate say in the decision-making process. Many argue, however, that because pregnancy (and therefore abortion) involves a woman's body, the ultimate decision does and should rest with her. Nevertheless, how seriously should she consider the concerns of the man? Does excluding men from the decision-making process, or even from the conversations about the options, reflect a deeper sexism about pregnancy and childbearing that perpetuates social roles of men and women that may result in unjust distribution of burdens?

## The Role of Parents

Likewise, many argue that parents of pregnant minors should have a greater role to play in decisions regarding abortion. On the one hand, many claim that minors are too young to make such decisions (i.e., procuring abortion or carrying a pregnancy to term)—let alone the decision to give the child up for adoption or to raise the child. Even though minors may be able to have sex and get pregnant, they may not fully comprehend the significance of those acts or their consequences. Moreover, commentators worry that if minors can obtain an abortion without giving notice to their parents, then this may isolate minors and further undermine family relationships. On the other hand, some argue that forcing minors to tell their parents, even if parental consent is not required, may cause the minor to seek risky abortions from those who are not licensed or—worse—they may try to perform the abortion themselves. States vary with regard to parental involvement. Some require the consent of one or both parents before the minor can obtain the abortion. Other states do not. Some states only require that one parent be notified of the minor's intent to procure an abortion. In the end, premature sexual activity, teenage pregnancy, and the tragic situation of being ill-prepared to raise a child or of choosing abortion are enough to give parents and minor children pause and, hopefully, to engage in open and fruitful dialogue about the various aspects of human sexuality.

## Nonsurgical Abortions: The Case of Mifepristone

A critical development in the abortion debate has been the introduction of Mifepristone in the mid-1980s and its use since.[15] One major problem is what to call this: an abortion, a contraception, or—as the developers of Mifepristone preferred—a contragestation. According to the American College of Obstetricians and Gynecologists, a pregnancy occurs when the conceptus (i.e., developing embryo) implants into the uterine wall. Thus, the medical community generally views drugs that induce abortion to be those that interfere with gestation *after* implantation. Any drug that prevents implantation or fertilization is considered contraceptive. Some religious thinkers, however, hold that any drug that causes the demise of the conceptus before or after implantation is *abortifacient* (i.e., causes abortions). Any drug that prevents fertilization is *contraceptive* (i.e., prevents conception).

According to the Food and Drug Administration (FDA), Mifepristone works by blocking the hormone progesterone, which is necessary for pregnancies to continue. The drug effectively prevents or interferes with the embryo's implantation in the uterine wall, which results in the uterus reacting as it would at the end of a normal menstrual cycle. Occasionally, in smaller doses, one can use Mifepristone as an emergency contraceptive. However, the FDA approved levonorgestrel in August 2006 as an over-the-counter drug for emergency contraception.[16]

Regardless of how one describes Mifepristone, its introduction significantly changes many elements in the abortion debate: there is a shift from surgical to chemical abortions, there is a shift from abortion in clinics to physicians' offices, and there is a decrease in the cost of abortion. There is a decrease in morbidity and mortality rates in abortions. But most importantly, there will be a shift from public to private in that no one will know if the woman is going to visit a physician for a routine visit or for Mifepristone.

Another concern with the routine use of Mifepristone is that if it continues to show that it is safe, effective, and inexpensive, then it could become a primary means of birth control. That is, its availability could simply be the basis for replacing traditional means of birth control. Such a shift could lead us into thinking that abortion is a value-neutral event and could further erode the moral dimensions of the debate.

Finally, reliance on Mifepristone may shift the burden of birth control and regulation even more fully to women. If it is perceived—and the key word is *perceived*—that a pill will solve "the problem," then we suspect that even more men might disavow their responsibilities in reproductive control. Thus, reproductive control will remain a woman's issue rather than a couple's issue.

## THREE POSITIONS ON ABORTION

When all is said and done, there are three basic orientations to abortion: the conservative, the liberal, and the moderate.[17] The conservative position holds that under no circumstances may anyone perform an abortion. The religious and philosophical reasons for this include: the sanctity of life, the inviolability of innocent human life, and the fear of the social implications of a liberal abortion policy for other defenseless people such as the handicapped and the elderly.

The liberal position would allow abortion under many different circumstances. Many individuals assume a broad range of moral justifications. The liberal position tends to be more accepting of the so-called soft reasons for abortion: the quality of life of the fetus, the mental health status of the woman, her rights to bodily integrity, the welfare of the existing family, career considerations, and family planning.

The moderate position seeks a middle ground that recognizes the moral legitimacy of some abortions, but never without suffering and pain on the part of both the woman and the fetus. This position sees both the fetus and the woman as having rights and entitlements and recognizes that attempts to resolve such conflicts of rights will entail suffering and pain. Thus, while acknowledging the moral acceptability of some abortions, the moderates do so only with a sense of great tragedy and loss. Frequently, this position would limit a consideration of abortion to so-called hard indications for abortion: the health or a deformity of the fetus, risks to the life of the mother, rape, and incest.

## TWO WORLDVIEWS

Gregory Baum identifies the cause for the profound disagreements and moral conflicts presented in this chapter as rooted in radically different worldviews on nature and sexuality.[18] The first worldview sees sexuality and reproduction as part of nature. Divine providence defines sexuality as having a primarily biological function that, while being pleasurable, is intrinsically related to reproduction. Since nature is defined and watched over by the Creator, interference in that order through artificial contraception or abortion is a violation of that order. Such an orientation would typically be conservative on the abortion question.

The second orientation sees God's providence expressed, not in a static understanding of the biological order, but rather as gracious action within human history that enables people to take more responsibility for themselves and their environment. Sexuality is more than biology; it is a personal act and a human reality with many dimensions. Contraception is a means of exercising responsibility, not violating a biological order. Abortion becomes a moral possibility in this perspective.

Such differences in worldview cannot explain all differences between people. They can help reveal, however, why people disagree so much. They begin at different points, and they may be unaware of this until they are pushed back to some basic perspective. Thus, the most profound area of disagreement may be not over how to resolve a specific moral issue such as abortion, but over our assumptions about how much responsibility individuals have and whether or not the biological order can be altered. These perspectives define the context in which individuals make moral decisions and shape their understanding of moral accountability.

# ETHICAL ISSUES IN THE
# PUBLIC POLICY DEBATE

Another major problem in the abortion debate is related to the basis on which public policy is debated. The themes developed here are relevant for other policy issues (e.g., cloning and stem cell research) but come into particularly sharp focus on abortion.

Alasdair MacIntyre argues that morality is at war with itself because each moral agent reaches conclusions by valid forms of inference yet cannot agree about the correctness or appropriateness of the premises with which the argument begins. This means that we can agree on valid forms or structures of an argument, but we cannot agree on the proper or appropriate starting point.[19]

There are two major reasons for this. First, we have not inherited the social or cultural context in which we can both understand and apply a particular philosophical theory. Our use of a philosophical theory is separate from the culture that gave birth to it and nurtured it. Second, we have inherited conflicting theories of ethics and social philosophy. Ours is a culture that has many definitions, theories, and methods of ethics, few of which lead to conclusions consistent with one another. Each presents conflicting and even contrary claims with respect to what is good for human beings and how they relate to the community.

For example, the classical tradition asks the question: How might human beings together realize the common good? The modern tradition asks: How might human beings prevent themselves from interfering with one another as each goes about his or her concerns? The first question assumes that human beings can know and agree on what is good for all. The second question assumes that what is good for me might not be good for you. If people approach one another with such conflicting assumptions about human nature and the relation of human beings to society, how can policymakers and opinion leaders address major policy issues in a coherent fashion? Knowledge of such disparate points of view, while not making the debate any easier, at least helps us realize why all do not emerge at the same place.

These are some of the thematic issues that we have to face in discussing abortion. We will have to face each theme thoroughly and honestly. Plus, we will have to evaluate each theme in the light of all the other perspectives we have discussed. No matter what the decision, pain, tragedy, and a sense of loss will occur. Such is the nature of the abortion debate.

## DISCUSSION QUESTIONS

1. Is the notion of sanctity of life compatible with the taking of life?
2. Many people argue that one should be consistent in one's position on killing. That is, if one is against abortion, then one should be against war or capital punishment. Do you agree? How would you make exceptions?

3. What are the strengths and weaknesses of each of the major definitions of a person indicated in the chapter?

4. Does the argument for the moderate position on abortion work? How do you justify your response to this?

5. Do you think Mifepristone is a contraceptive or causes abortions?

## NOTES

1. Heather D. Boonstra, Rachel Benson Gold, Cory L. Richards, and Lawrence B. Finer, *Abortion in Women's Lives* (New York: Guttmacher Institute, 2006), 20; see also, Lilo T. Strauss, Sonya B. Gamble, Wilda Y. Parker, Douglas A. Cook, Suzanne B. Zane, and Saeed Hamdan, "Abortion Surveillance—United States, 2003," *Morbidity and Mortality Weekly Report* 55, November 24, 2006 (SS11): 1–32. The Kaiser Family Foundation indicates that Guttmacher and Centers for Disease Control and Prevention (CDC) data are generally considered the most reliable abortion data; the Guttmacher Institute's data are more reflective of actual abortions given the limitations on state reporting requirements to the CDC (see "Abortion in the U.S. Fact Sheet," *The Henry J. Kaiser Family Foundation*, http://www.kff.org/womenshealth/upload/Abortion-in-the-U-S-Fact-Sheet.pdf, published October 2002, accessed April 22, 2008.

2. See Strauss et al., "Abortion Surveillance." The Guttmacher Institute report suggests that more than half of abortions in the United States are to women in their twenties (Boonstra et al., *Abortion in Women's Lives*, 20).

3. James Kelly, "Abortion: What Americans *Really* Think and the Catholic Challenge," *America* 156 (November 2, 1991): 311.

4. Ibid., 314.

5. Ibid., 310.

6. Tamar Lewin, "Nebraska Abortion Case: The Issue Is Interference," *New York Times*, September 25, 1995, A8.

7. Ibid.

8. For a thorough discussion of the development of abortion legislation in America, see James C. Mohr, *Abortion in America: The Origins and the Evolution of National Policy* (New York: Oxford University Press, 1978).

9. For the text of some of these decisions, see Ian Shapiro, ed., *Abortion: The Supreme Court Decisions* (Indianapolis: Hackett Publishing Co., 1995).

10. "State Policies in Brief: An Overview of Abortion Laws," *Guttmacher Institute*, http://www.guttmacher.org/statecenter/spibs/spib_OAL.pdf, published September 1, 2007, accessed March 5, 2008.

11. "Bans on 'Partial-Birth' Abortion," *Guttmacher Institute*, http://www.guttmacher.org/statecenter/spibs/spib_BPBA.pdf, published September 1, 2007, accessed March 5, 2008.

12. Daniel Callahan, *Abortion: Law, Choice and Morality* (New York: Macmillan, 1970), 378ff.

13. For a further and more detailed discussion of this approach, see Thomas A. Shannon and Allen B. Wolter, "Reflections on the Moral Status of the Pre-embryo," *Theological Studies* 51 (1990): 603–26.

14. One should distinguish totipotency from pluripotency. As the embryo develops, certain cells (the inner cell mass) lose their totipotency yet retain significant potential in that they can develop into any cell type of an adult's body. This kind of potential is called pluripotency. We will discuss these concepts in greater detail in chapter 14.

15. In September 2000, the U.S. Food and Drug Administration approved Mifepristone (formerly known as RU 486).

16. One might consider an "emergency contraception" to be a response to a rape or sexual assault that seeks to prevent either conception or pregnancy. While Catholic hospitals do provide care to victims of sexual assault, there is some controversy over what drugs to provide given the uncertainty about whether the drug functions as a contraceptive or as an abortifacient substance.

17. James Nelson, *Human Medicine* (Minneapolis: Augsburg Publishing House, 1973), 31ff.

18. Gregory Baum, "Abortion: An Ecumenical Dilemma," *Commonweal* 99, no. 9 (November 30, 1973): 231–35.

19. Alasdair MacIntyre, "How to Identify Ethical Principles," *The Belmont Report*, Appendix, vol. 1, DHEW publication no. OSO 78–0013, 10–1–41 (Washington, DC).

## BIBLIOGRAPHY

"Abortion in the U.S. Fact Sheet." *The Henry J. Kaiser Family Foundation.* http://www.kff.org/womenshealth/upload/Abortion-in-the-U-S-Fact-Sheet.pdf. Published October 2002. Accessed April 22, 2008.

"Bans on 'Partial-Birth' Abortion," *Guttmacher Institute.* http://www.guttmacher.org/statecenter/spibs/spib_BPBA.pdf. Published September 1, 2007. Accessed March 5, 2008.

Baum, Gregory. "Abortion: An Ecumenical Dilemma." *Commonweal* 99, no. 9 (November 30, 1973): 231–35.

Boonstra, Heather D., Rachel Benson Gold, Cory L. Richards, and Lawrence B. Finer. *Abortion in Women's Lives.* New York: Guttmacher Institute, 2006.

Cahill, Lisa Sowle. *Sex, Gender, and Christian Ethics.* New York: Cambridge University Press, 1996.

Callahan, Daniel. *Abortion: Law, Choice and Morality.* New York: Macmillan, 1970.

Dellapenna, Joseph W. *Dispelling the Myths of Abortion History.* Durham, NC: Carolina Academic Press, 2006.

Hendershott, Anne B. *The Politics of Abortion.* New York: Encounter Books, 2006.

Kelly, James. "Abortion: What Americans *Really* Think and the Catholic Challenge." *America* 165, no. 13 (November 2, 1991): 310–16.

Lewin, Tamar. "Nebraska Abortion Case: The Issue Is Interference." *New York Times.* September 25, 1995. A8.

MacIntyre, Alasdair. "How to Identify Ethical Principles," *The Belmont Report*, Appendix. Vol. 1. Department of Health, Education, and Welfare Publication Number OSO 78–0013, 10–1–41. Washington, DC.

McBride, Dorothy E. *Abortion in the United States: A Reference Handbook.* Santa Barbara, CA: ABC-CLIO, 2008.

Mohr, James C. *Abortion in America: The Origins and the Evolution of National Policy.* New York: Oxford University Press, 1978.

Nelson, James. *Human Medicine.* Minneapolis: Augsburg Publishing House, 1973.

Shannon, Thomas A., and Allen B. Wolter. "Reflections on the Moral Status of the Pre-embryo." *Theological Studies* 51 (1990): 603–26.

Shapiro, Ian, ed. *Abortion: The Supreme Court Decisions.* Indianapolis: Hackett Publishing Co., 1995.

"State Policies in Brief: An Overview of Abortion Laws." *Guttmacher Institute.* http://www.guttmacher.org/statecenter/spibs/spib_OAL.pdf. Published September 1, 2007. Accessed March 5, 2008.

Strauss, Lilo T., Sonya B. Gamble, Wilda Y. Parker, Douglas A. Cook, Suzanne B. Zane, and Saeed Hamdan. "Abortion Surveillance—United States, 2003." *Morbidity and Mortality Weekly Report* 55, November 24, 2006 (SS11): 1–32.

## Chapter 6

# REPRODUCTIVE TECHNOLOGIES

## INTRODUCTION

One of the many wondrous experiences of human life is giving birth to a child. While most of the "facts of life" are known—and frequently graphically discussed and displayed in various media—the reality of a newborn still presents a moment of awe and mystery. This reality is all the more reason why the inability to reproduce is such a tragedy and a heartbreaking experience for many individuals.

In the past, the basic options for infertility were either to accept one's fate and go on with life or to adopt. Many chose this latter option, and adoption fulfills most of their heart's desires. For others, however, there is still a desire "to have a child of one's own." As satisfying as adoption is for many, for others a critical part of having a child is conception, pregnancy, and giving birth. That part of the "having a child of one's own" remained an unfulfilled hope until 1978 when Mr. and Mrs. Brown gave birth to the first child conceived outside the human body. The British team of Steptow and Edwards had been working on this procedure for years, and finally all the elements came together and resulted in a baby girl. This technique—*in vitro* fertilization—changed human reproduction forever.

In this chapter, we discuss the ethics of reproductive technologies. In particular, we focus on technologies aimed at controlling reproduction with the intended outcome of the birth of offspring. Other reproductive technologies might include those devices or substances aimed at controlling fertility in order to prevent the birth of offspring (e.g., contraception and sterilization).

Nevertheless, the technologies we will focus on here are generally understood collectively as assisted reproductive technologies or ARTs. They include an array of techniques and medications, arrangements and procedures, all designed to help an individual or a couple reproduce and "have a child of one's own."

## WHY ASSISTED REPRODUCTIVE TECHNOLOGY?

There are several reasons why one would seek assisted reproductive technology. One reason might be that one is or both individuals in a couple are infertile. In addition, there may be a genetic risk involved in a couple's decision to procreate. This risk may come from one or both individuals being carriers of a specific disease-related gene. Alternatively, one or both individuals may actually have a genetic disease. (We will discuss issues of genetic diagnosis and risk in the next chapter.) Lastly, some people seek assisted reproductive technology not to reproduce per se but to be compensated for "donating" their gametes or their wombs.

## ASSISTED REPRODUCTIVE TECHNOLOGY

There are a large number of methods of artificial reproduction. Many are variants of standard methods. Here the basic ones will be described.

First, there are methods aimed at the manipulation of the woman's menstrual cycle in order to procure eggs (oocytes) and/or to prepare her reproductive system for pregnancy. Thus, through medications and careful observation of the reproductive system, clinicians can coordinate her menstrual cycle with an assisted reproductive technology.[1]

Second, there are methods designed for manipulation of the eggs and sperm (gametes) and embryos outside of the human body. These methods include the retrieval of both male and female gametes, preparation of those gametes or embryos, and cryopreservation of either gametes or embryos.

As mentioned above, one manipulates a woman's menstrual cycle in order to obtain multiple oocytes at one time. This begins with the use of oral contraceptives and includes a process of hyperstimulating her ovaries. Specialists call this technique *superovulation.* Some woman can choose an optional unstimulated ART cycle instead of superovulation. In addition to the use of specific cocktails of hormone-related drugs, one utilizes either an aspiration technique with a needle (more common) or a laparoscopic technique to obtain the oocytes. Both procedures use general anesthesia.

Next, one prepares the gametes or embryos through specific laboratory techniques. These techniques include *micromanipulation*, which are procedures at the cellular level. These include gamete selection procedures. For example, one can use a special process for separating X-carrying sperm from Y-carrying sperm for sex selection. Another set of micromanipulation techniques are those of *assisted fertilization*. The procedures of *in vitro* fertilization or IVF (fertilizing ova in a laboratory, literally "within glass" fertilization) and *intracytoplasmic sperm injection* or ICSI (fertilization by using a laser to puncture a hole in the protective layer of the egg, the zona pellucida, and injecting a single sperm cell or spermatozoon) are forms of assisted fertilization. There are also forms of micromanipulation called *assisted hatching*, which are basically techniques to help the fertilized ovum develop into a zygote and shed the zona pellucida. Finally, one screens the developing preimplantation embryos and scores them based on health and likelihood of surviving transfer into the woman.

During this preparation phase, several new possibilities exist for one to manipulate the genetic makeup of the offspring. Presently, one can perform a *preimplantation genetic diagnosis* or PGD in order to test for disease-related genes or chromosomal abnormalities (e.g., an extra chromosome as in Down Syndrome). One can also use PGD to screen for the genetic sex of the embryo. Based on the criteria one uses, one selects the desirable embryos and transfers them to the woman or stores them. Many scientists are currently developing techniques called gene transfer, which are the procedures used in gene therapy. While the latter technology is still experimental, proponents hope one day to be able to correct the genetic structure of embryos without having to destroy them.

Another experimental procedure that might one day be used as an ART is somatic cell nuclear transfer cloning or SCNT cloning. This form of cloning accounts for both assisted fertilization (by triggering an embryonic-like state after the transfer of a somatic cell's nucleus) and genetic manipulation (by duplicating the genome of an adult). Many argue that SCNT should only be used in embryonic stem cell research; others argue that this can help some couples have children that are genetically related to one member of the couple. Yet others argue that such techniques should not be used at all with human cells. We will discuss these issues in greater detail in chapter 14.

The last method of manipulating gametes or embryos outside of the human body is the cryopreservation of gametes or embryos. By freezing gametes or embryos in this way, one can limit the number of times one needs to retrieve oocytes and/or sperm. Thus, for example, a woman only needs to undergo superovulation once and avoids the increased risks associated with it. Plus, frozen embryos can be thawed and transferred during future ART attempts, or researchers can obtain them, with proper consent, and use them in stem cell research. Alternatively, gametes and embryos that are not used may be destroyed.

Third, there is a set of methods of ART aimed at the migration of gametes or embryos into a woman's body. One method transfers the male semen into a woman; this is called *artificial insemination*. Artificial insemination can occur with a husband's semen (artificial insemination by husband, AIH) or with a donor's semen (artificial insemination by donor, AID). This is the oldest method of artificial reproduction; one performs the artificial insemination with either a syringe or a catheter. Another method that transfers gametes, instead of embryos, is called *gamete intrafallopian transfer* or GIFT. In GIFT, both oocytes and sperm are transferred to a woman's fallopian tube in the hope that a sperm cell will fertilize the egg and result in a pregnancy. With AIH, AID, and GIFT, fertilization *and* implantation occur in the woman's body.

Another set of methods aims at transferring preimplantation embryos. One method is *in vitro* fertilization with embryo transfer or IVF-ET. Here, one performs IVF (as described above) and transfers the embryos to the woman's uterus. Another method is *zygote intrafallopian transfer* or ZIFT. Here, once the zygote is formed in the laboratory, one transfers it to the woman's fallopian tube. Also, in *tubal embryo transfer* or TET, one transfers embryos to the fallopian tube. In both ZIFT and TET, those participating in the ART cycle hope that a zygote or preimplantation embryo descends into the woman's uterus and implants into the uterine wall (this is what usually occurs following natural fertilization in the fallopian tube). In IVF-ET, ZIFT, and TET, fertilization occurs outside the woman's body whereas implantation occurs inside the woman's body.

Fourth, gestational surrogacy is a technique where another woman carries the pregnancy to term.[2] In the basic model of surrogacy, the intending (to be nurturer) woman is unable to bear a child. The husband or couple then contracts with another woman—the gestational surrogate—to inseminate her artificially or use other ARTs. She then carries the fetus to term and relinquishes the newborn to the couple. This is the standard model of gestational surrogacy for which the gestational surrogate receives a fee, which can range from $22,000 to $25,000 on average.[3] Other models, referred to as altruistic surrogacy, are possible. For example, there have been cases in which a woman's mother or sister received an embryo from the egg and sperm of the intending couple and carried the pregnancy to term. There also have been reports of friends helping each other in this way.

## ETHICAL ISSUES IN IVF-ET

In 2005, there were approximately 134,260 ART cycles reported to the Centers for Disease Control and Prevention (CDC).[4] The most common form of ART is *in vitro* fertilization with embryo transfer; IVF accounted for greater than 99 percent of the treatment types. We will briefly discuss several issues of IVF-ET because it is so common and it raises several issues that are also observed in other ARTs.

## *Potential Benefits of IVF-ET*

The most significant benefit of IVF-ET is the potential to have genetically related children. Several issues emerge, however, when one considers how to measure success in applying ARTs. Should one measure success by the number of pregnancies? One might think this is a rather straightforward question and procedure. Yet, one can consider pregnancy from two perspectives. The first perspective determines pregnancy by chemical indicators; a woman is pregnant when a blood sample demonstrates a rise in certain hormones. The second perspective determines pregnancy by clinical indicators; a woman is pregnant when the embryo implants in the uterine wall.[5] Moreover, another problem with measuring success by pregnancy alone is that not every pregnancy leads to live birth: the actual benefit might not be realized.

Another option is to measure success by the number of pregnancies and live births. In fact, the CDC identifies three measures: pregnancy, birth of one or more living infants, and birth of a single living infant.[6] Furthermore, the Fertility Clinic Success Rate and Certification Act of 1992 defines specific statistics that clinics should report to the CDC. According to the CDC, the percentage of ART cycles that resulted in pregnancy for women under the age of thirty-five in 2005 was 43.1 percent.[7] In addition, the percentage of ART cycles that resulted in live births for women under the age of thirty-five in 2005 was 37.3 percent.[8] One should note the following: 32.9 percent of pregnancies were twins and 4.4 percent of pregnancies were triplets or more; and the average number of embryos transferred for women in this age bracket was 2.4 embryos.

These statistics may seem staggering, especially given the early problems of ART. In 1993, two authors noted, "Human in vitro fertilization (IVF) is surprisingly unsuccessful. In the United States, the overall birth rate per IVF treatment cycle is 14% from 16,405 oocyte retrievals."[9] This means that fertility clinical staff collected 16,405 *eggs* and attempted to fertilize them. In 2005, for women under the age of thirty-five alone, 41,302 *cycles* were performed; on average, an initial cycle includes multiple oocytes and 2.4 transferred embryos.[10] Furthermore, the percentage of ART cycles that resulted in live births for women under thirty-five years was 37.3 percent. For all age groups, the CDC indicates that there were 38,910 live births, which accounts for about 29 percent of ART cycles reported to the CDC.[11] To be fair, one has to recall that the normal probability of becoming pregnant in one menstrual cycle (i.e., fecundability) is 20–25 percent.[12] Several factors account for the increased success of this maturing technology: better control of reproductive hormones, use of adjuncts, high rate of oocyte retrieval, consistently good fertilization, improved culture techniques, better embryo transfer techniques, enhanced implantation through assisted hatching, and other techniques.[13] George Annas is still correct, however, when he says: "I've often said that the one thing these clinics ought to do is tell patients at the beginning, 'You will probably not have a child.'"[14]

## Reproductive Liberty

The ability to have genetically related children is a precious ability, and many commentators warn that there should be very little interference on that ability from the government, which might want to impose regulations on ART. Thus, the idea of one's reproductive liberty—the freedom to reproduce in any way one can—is another issue at stake in the ethics of ART. There are, however, several reasons why a government would want to regulate ART. For example, a government may want to protect children and future generations if the technology poses significant risks of harm; another reason might be if ARTs are unjustly distributed throughout society.

## Commodification of Human Reproduction: Selling Gametes

Some ethicists object to ART on the grounds that it undermines the dignity of human beings and human reproduction because it promotes the commodification of human biological material. In particular, commentators warn against compensation for gametes, that such compensation may cloud the consent process in which women agree to significant risk, and that such compensation means that egg or sperm donation is not really a donation at all but rather a commercial transaction. Additionally, opponents argue, this process of commodification reduces the meaning of reproduction and strips it of its personal dimensions—it leads to objectifying reproduction and objectifying children, too.

## Financial Costs

The President's Council on Bioethics notes that, in 2004, assisted reproduction was an approximately $4 billion enterprise that served about one in every six infertile couples in the United States.[15] Although some states mandate that insurance carriers provide fertility services, including IVF, insurance companies limit such required services either by paying for only a certain number of cycles or by imposing a lifetime cap on payments for fertility services. Thus, the individual or individuals need to assume a significant portion of the costs for ART. The council's report on reproduction indicates that at one clinic the initial consult is $370, one IVF cycle with never-frozen embryos is $9,345, an additional transfer of frozen embryos is $4,000, PGD is $4,000, ICSI is $2,000, and preconception sperm selection is also $2,000. Thus, one cycle of ART with elective testing would cost a couple approximately $17,715.[16] More recently, assisted reproduction programs have introduced risk-sharing or refund practices. Individuals seeking ART pay a higher price initially, but if the treatment is unsuccessful the clinic will refund 90 to 100 percent. The American Society for Reproductive Medicine Ethics Committee concludes that such practices are in principle ethically acceptable, but they do raise significant concerns over exploitation.[17]

## Health Risks

Health risks of ART can affect two groups directly: the woman and the fetus or child (or fetuses or children). To begin, superovulation involves hyperstimulating the woman's ovaries with drugs to obtain a large number of eggs. Traditionally, these eggs are then harvested through a needle or laparoscopy, which involves general anesthesia. Superovulation may carry risks of unbalancing the natural cycles of reproductive hormones. The hormone used to stimulate the eggs can cause the ovary to rupture. In addition, general anesthesia carries morbidity and mortality risks with it. There is also a danger of ectopic pregnancy in which the zygote or embryo implants in the fallopian tube instead of the uterus.

Another risk of IVF-ET that one needs to address is the possibility of multiple pregnancies. Because clinics transfer between two and four embryos on average, there is the possibility of multiple pregnancies. Multiple pregnancies present potential problems for the mother in terms of the impact on her reproductive system and overall health, as well as discomfort during pregnancy and delivery.

The problem of multiple pregnancies also poses potential risks to the fetuses and newborns. These complications include premature birth and low birth weight. Because of this and other complications, physicians may offer a solution to the problem called *fetal reduction*. Fetal reduction is a process involving selective abortion of certain fetuses *in utero*. That is, one can abort a number of the multiple pregnancies so that one or two fetuses will be more likely to survive in a healthier state. Thus, couples who are infertile and have been desperate to have a child now face the possibility of aborting their dream. This may not have been an option they considered, and if they have strong feelings about the morality of abortion, the couple may be in a very difficult position. Even if such an option is morally acceptable to them, individuals involved will still be troubled because the procedure so contradicts their dreams and the purpose of using ARTs.

Some have also claimed that there is a slightly higher risk of congenital abnormalities; however, this claim is controversial.[18] For example, in patients who use ICSI, there may be a risk of imprinting disorders, such as Angelman syndrome and Beckwith-Wiedemann syndrome.

## Family Implications: Concepts of Parenthood

The new capabilities of ART radically redefine parenthood. Both women and men have new ways to becoming a parent. For a woman, there are seven options of motherhood:

1. the genetic, who is the source of the egg;
2. the gestational, who carries the pregnancy;
3. the nurturing, who raises the child;
4. the genetic-gestational, who is the source of the egg and carries the pregnancy but does not raise the child;
5. the genetic-nurturing, who is the source of the egg and raises the child but does not carry the pregnancy;
6. the gestational-nurturing, who carries the pregnancy and raises the child but does not provide the egg; and
7. the whole mother, who is the source of the egg, carries the pregnancy, and raises the child.

For a man, there are three options of fatherhood:

1. the genetic, who is the source of the sperm;
2. the nurturing, who raises the child; and
3. the whole father, who provides sperm and raises the child.

To put these options into perspective, it is possible, in considering the variety of ART currently available, that a child could have five different parents: a sperm donor, an egg donor, a gestational surrogate, the nurturing mother, and the nurturing father.

Other possibilities also affect how one understands parenthood. Posthumous recovery of gametes creates the possibility of becoming a parent after one dies. Cryopreservation of embryos also raises the question of parenthood after divorce or death (of one or both members of a couple).

Historically, adoption raised similar questions because the adopting parents had no relation whatsoever to the child they adopted. These new possibilities based on technical interventions, however, clearly complicate the question of parenthood, especially when the process involves other individuals such as sperm or egg vendors[19] or a gestational surrogate. These possibilities have given rise to strenuous debates over whether nature, nurture, or some combination of these should be the basis for the new definition of parenthood, especially with respect to social policy.

## Unknown Reprogenetic Risks for Offspring

A particular social risk of ART, especially with the use of donor gametes, is the reprogenetic risks that are unknown to offspring. This kind of risk means that, when these children reach adulthood and select a mate, they may unwittingly choose a half-sister or half-brother. While the risk of meeting and selecting a half-sibling in this way is relatively low, it is still a risk nonetheless. If someone *repro*duces with a half-sibling, there is a greater chance of a *genetic* disease being expressed in the next generation of offspring (thus, it is a *reprogenetic* risk).

## Disposition of Spare Embryos

Finally, IVF-ET and other ARTs raise the question of what to do with spare or "leftover" embryos. The President's Council on Bioethics report indicates that there are five options for handling untransferred embryos:[20]

1. The embryo(s) could remain in cryostorage and transferred to the woman later;
2. The woman or couple could donate the embryo(s) to another person or couple;
3. The woman or couple could consent to scientists using the embryo(s) in stem cell research;
4. The embryo(s) could remain in cryostorage indefinitely; or
5. The embryo(s) could be thawed and destroyed.

# ETHICAL ISSUES IN GESTATIONAL SURROGACY

According to the CDC, only 1 percent of ART cycles used a gestational surrogate.[21] Although relatively rare, there are several issues in gestational surrogacy. Given the difference between IVF-ET and gestational surrogacy, we will now consider five issues in gestational surrogacy.

## Objectification of Women

Individuals frequently select gestational surrogates on the basis of their appearance, mental and physical health, and fertility. In other words, individuals value gestational surrogates for their reproductive capacity. Critics argue that such selection methods are open to the possibility of seeing the woman as an object or a means to an end. Furthermore, these methods reinforce the social stereotyping of women in the role of mother. Thus, there is the danger of compromising their human dignity.

## Commodification of Human Reproduction: Baby Selling or Womb Renting

One of the most controversial aspects of surrogacy is whether it is selling a baby or renting one's womb. The woman signs a contract and bears the child; she then receives the money and gives the baby over to the other party in the contract. Some argue that this is the standard account of buying and selling. Others argue that the fee the woman receives is a fee for a service, and the fees might include other costs such as travel expenses, maternity clothes, prenatal care, and others. Similar to the critique of selling gametes, opponents argue that it might undermine the integrity of the family or the dignity of human reproduction in a family context. Such a commodification, some have argued, perpetuates or reinforces the objectification of women.

## Financial Costs

Having a child with a gestational surrogate can cost $45,000 to $70,000.[22] This includes agency fees to find a surrogate, attorney fees to craft the contract, and the surrogate's fees. These figures do not include the financial costs of using other ART. The typical fee for a surrogacy contract is $22,000 to $25,000. Over nine months, this works out to about $2.25 per hour, which is considerably less than the minimum wage. Also, the fee remains the same regardless of the time the surrogate invests in becoming pregnant. Mary Beth Whitehead, the surrogate in the most famous surrogacy case, was artificially inseminated nine times before she became pregnant.

## Family Implications: Pressures on Families

Gestational surrogacy, as mentioned above, expands the motherhood options available to women. This form of parenting—gestational surrogacy—may put pressures on members of families. It might put pressure on the gestational surrogate's family (e.g., her husband, if she has one, and her children, if she has any). Gestational surrogacy might also put pressure on the intending family. For example, a husband of a gestational surrogate— who is desirable because he is a sign of both stability and financial support during the pregnancy—is frequently a forgotten party. While he must assent to the surrogacy, his wife is pregnant with the child of another man. Furthermore, there will literally be a third human being between the surrogate and her husband during the course of the pregnancy. There is also a legal issue here. If a husband consents to having his wife artificially inseminated with the sperm of another man, the resulting child is legally considered to be the husband's, not the sperm donor's. Moreover, perhaps the biggest concern is the bond that is formed between an unborn baby and the gestational mother; gestational surrogacy contracts reflect this concern when they describe significant penalties for failing to relinquish the child over to the intending family. Courts use a variety of standards to decide a dispute over parental rights or custody; existing statutes, which vary from state to state, may not be adequate. Courts look to the best interests of the child, the rights of birth mothers, the genetic link between the child and its genetic parents, and the intent of the couple who desired to enter into a surrogacy contract in order to become parents.[23]

## Women's Rights

In spite of these and other problems associated with surrogacy, many argue that to deny women this opportunity is to deny them the opportunity to act as full adults in society. To deny them this capacity is to treat women paternalistically by implicitly arguing that they cannot make their own decisions. Also, many feel that if one compromises this reproductive liberty or right, it will provide an opening that others can use to restrict abortion. Thus, many who may have some reservations about surrogacy support it to prevent even more undesirable public policy consequences.

# CONCLUSION

There have been three major sexual revolutions in this country. The first, which occurred in the 1950s, was the introduction of the oral contraceptive. "The Pill," as it came to be known, effectively separated sex from reproduction; one could be quite certain that engaging in sexual intercourse did not lead to reproduction. The second revolution was the introduction of *in vitro* fertilization in 1978. This led to the separation of reproduction from sex; now one could reproduce without engaging in sexual intercourse. Finally, gestational surrogacy was introduced in the 1980s. This marked the separation of sex from reproduction, reproduction from sex, and both sex and reproduction from the traditional family model. While health risks, financial costs and commodification, reproductive liberty and regulation, and other issues continue to press on us, one hopes that individuals and professionals address these issues as they navigate the separation of sex, reproduction, and the traditional family model.

# DISCUSSION QUESTIONS

1. Do you think that nature (i.e., a biological relationship) or nurture (i.e., intended social relationship) should determine parenthood?
2. Do you think the fertility industry should be regulated? If so, by whom: the federal government, state governments, professional societies or associations, or an independent agency?
3. Should insurance plans cover the costs of infertility treatment using ART?

4. Do you think IVF-ET presents too many risks for the woman?

5. Do you think gestational surrogacy is baby selling?

6. Should gestational surrogate motherhood be prohibited?

## NOTES

1. According to the Society for Assisted Reproductive Technology, an ART cycle involves several steps over a four- to six-week period. For example, in preparation for an embryo transfer and prior to oocyte retrieval, a woman begins taking oral contraceptives in the month prior to the ART cycle.

2. See Peter R. Brinsden, "Gestational Surrogacy," *Human Reproduction Update* 9, no. 5 (September 2003): 483–91.

3. Molly M. Ginty, "How Much Did These Babies Cost?" *Redbook*, July 2004, 136–41.

4. Department of Health and Human Services and the Centers for Disease Control and Prevention, "2005 Assisted Reproductive Technology Success Rates: National Summary and Fertility Clinic Reports," October 2007, http://www.cdc.gov/ART/ART2005/508PDF/2005ART508Cover_National.pdf, accessed December 12, 2007, 13 (hereafter, CDC 2005 ART Report). See also Society of Assisted Reproductive Technology (SART), "Clinic Summary Report: All SART Member Clinics," *National Summary Data*, https://www.sartcorsonline.com/rptCSR_PublicMultYear.aspx?ClinicPKID=0, accessed December 7, 2007. SART includes over 392 member practices, which represents over 85 percent of ART clinics in the United States.

5. Two things are extremely important to note about this. First, depending on which criterion one uses to define success, one can get different numbers of success in achieving a pregnancy. That is, if one measures pregnancy by the chemical definition, one might get a higher number than if using the clinical definition. Second, neither of these definitions is useful as a predictor of whether this particular embryo will be born.

6. CDC 2005 ART Report, 6.

7. Ibid., 85.

8. A multiple-infant birth is counted as one live birth.

9. Robert M. L. Winston and Alan H. Handyside, "New Challenges in Human In Vitro Fertilization," *Science*, May 14, 1993, 932–36.

10. CDC 2005 ART Report, 85.

11. Ibid., 13.

12. Wendy Y. Chang, Sanjay K. Agarwal, and Ricardo Azziz, "Diagnostic Evaluation and Treatment of the Infertile Couple," in *Essential Reproductive Medicine*, ed. Bruce R. Carr, Richard E. Blackwell, and Ricardo Azziz (New York: McGraw-Hill, 2005), 359.

13. David R. Meldrum, "Assisted Reproductive Technology: Clinical Aspects," in Carr et al., *Essential Reproductive Medicine*, 536.

14. Trip Gabriel, "High-Tech Pregnancies Test Hope's Limit," *New York Times*, January 7, 1996, A10.

15. President's Council on Bioethics, *Reproduction and Responsibility: The Regulation of New Biotechnologies* (Washington, DC: President's Council on Bioethics, 2004), 153.

16. Ibid.

17. American Society for Reproductive Medicine (ASRM) Ethics Committee, "Risk-Sharing or Refund Programs in Assisted Reproduction," *Ethical Considerations of Assisted Reproductive Technology: American Society for Reproductive Medicine Ethics Committee Reports and Statements*, http://www.asrm.org/Media/Ethics/sharedrisk.pdf, released September 1998, reviewed June 2006, accessed December 12, 2007, 1.

18. Catherine M. DeUgarte, Alan H. DeCherney, and Alan S. Penzias, "Assisted Reproductive Technologies: In Vitro Fertilization and Related Techniques," in *Current Diagnosis and Treatment, Obstetrics and Gynecology*, ed. Alan H. DeCherney, Lauren Nathan, T. Murphy Goodwin, and Neri Laufer (New York: McGraw-Hill, 2007), 950–51.

19. Technically, these individuals are not donors because they receive a fee for their services. In 2000, a man typically received between $60 and $70 for a sperm sample, and a woman received from $3,500 to $12,000 for her eggs. See President's Council Report 2004, 148.

20. Ibid., 34.

21. CDC 2005 ART Report, 85.

22. Ginty, "How Much Did These Babies Cost?" 136–41.

23. American College of Obstetricians and Gynecologists (ACOG), "Surrogate Motherhood," *Ethics in Obstetrics and Gynecology*, 2nd ed., http://www.acog.org/from_home/publications/ethics/ethics050.pdf, accessed December 10, 2007.

## BIBLIOGRAPHY

Alpern, Kenneth D., ed. *The Ethics of Reproductive Technology*. New York: Oxford University Press, 1992.

American College of Obstetricians and Gynecologists. "Surrogate Motherhood." *Ethics in Obstetrics and Gynecology*. 2nd ed. http://www.acog.org/from_home/publications/ethics/ethics 050.pdf. Accessed December 10, 2007.

American Society for Reproductive Medicine Ethics Committee. "Risk-Sharing or Refund Programs in Assisted Reproduction." *Ethical Considerations of Assisted Reproductive Technology: American Society for Reproductive Medicine Ethics Committee Reports and Statements*. http://www.asrm.org/Media/Ethics/sharedrisk.pdf. Released September 1998. Reviewed June 2006. Accessed December 12, 2007.

Brinsden, Peter R. "Gestational Surrogacy." *Human Reproduction Update* 9, no. 5 (September 2003): 483–91.

Carr, Bruce R., Richard E. Blackwell, and Ricardo Azziz, eds. *Essential Reproductive Medicine*. New York: McGraw-Hill, 2005.

DeCherney, Alan H., Lauren Nathan, T. Murphy Goodwin, and Neri Laufer, eds. *Current Diagnosis and Treatment, Obstetrics and Gynecology*. New York: McGraw-Hill, 2007.

Department of Health and Human Services and the Centers for Disease Control and Prevention. "2005 Assisted Reproductive Technology Success Rates: National Summary and Fertility Clinic Reports." http://www.cdc.gov/ART/ART2005/508PDF/2005ART508Cover_National.pdf. Published October 2007. Accessed December 12, 2007.

Gabriel, Trip. "High-Tech Pregnancies Test Hope's Limit." *New York Times*. January 7, 1996. A10.

Ginty, Molly M. "How Much Did These Babies Cost?" *Redbook*, July 2004, 136–41.

Gosden, Roger. *Designing Babies: The Brave New World of Reproductive Technology*. New York: W. H. Freeman, 1999.

Gunning, Jennifer, and Helen Szoke, eds. *The Regulation of Assisted Reproductive Technology*. Burlington, VT: Ashgate, 2003.

Peters, Philip G., Jr. *How Safe Is Safe Enough? Obligations to the Children of Reproductive Technology*. New York: Oxford University Press, 2004.

President's Council on Bioethics. *Reproduction and Responsibility: The Regulation of New Biotechnologies*. Washington, DC: President's Council on Bioethics, 2004.

Ryan, Maura A. *Ethics and Economics of Assisted Reproduction: The Cost of Longing*. Washington, DC: Georgetown University Press, 2001.

Shenfield, Françoise, and Claude Sureau, eds. *Contemporary Ethical Dilemmas in Assisted Reproduction*. Boca Raton, FL: Informa Healthcare, 2006.

Society of Assisted Reproductive Technology. "Clinic Summary Report: All SART Member Clinics." *National Summary Data*. https://www.sartcorsonline.com/rptCSR_PublicMultYear.aspx?ClinicPKID=0. Accessed December 7, 2007.

Winston, Robert M. L., and Alan H. Handyside. "New Challenges in Human In Vitro Fertilization." *Science*. May 14, 1993, 932–36.

## Chapter 7

# EARLY DIAGNOSIS OF GENETIC ANOMALIES

## INTRODUCTION

In 2003, the Human Genome Project (HGP) came to completion earlier than scheduled. The HGP produced a map of the human genome, which includes data on the location, nucleotide sequence, and identity of genes. Although we have much to learn, especially about the functions of genes and the genetic material between them, current major applications of the data include genetic screening and testing programs, such as preimplantation genetic diagnosis, prenatal diagnosis, and predictive genetic testing. Knowing the sequence of a disease-related gene is one thing; knowing how it works and treating the disease are different. Unfortunately, at present, it is impossible to cure such diseases.

In this chapter, we will focus on two standpoints: that of the patient or client (i.e., the individual or couple *receiving* diagnostic information) and that of the professional (the individual *providing* diagnostic information). For the patient or client, this means receiving information before pregnancy, during pregnancy, or after birth. It is at these times that clients make important decisions. For example, a couple may forgo having a child naturally if there is too great a risk for transmitting a genetic disease; instead, they may opt for adoption. For the professional, care must be taken in providing complex genetic and risk information to her client so that the professional does not bias the decision-making process.

In genetic medicine and counseling, genetic information is useful for a variety of decisions and medical conditions. For example, a genetic counselor may become involved in the treatment of cancer, because if a patient has a specific gene-related cancer, he or she may respond to certain chemotherapies better than others. Another clinical application of genetics is pharmacogenomics in which clinicians use a patient's genotype to determine which drugs will most likely benefit the patient and then prescribe them. While there are important issues and questions involved in integrating genetic information in different medical specialties, we will focus on the use of genetic information for reproductive decision making, a subfield called *reprogenetics*. That is, we will explore the influence and issues such information has on deciding whether to have biologically related children, continuing with a pregnancy in light of a genetic diagnosis, and deciding what to do with a diagnosis of a late-onset condition (e.g., Huntington's disease or breast cancer) early in a fetus's or child's life. Thus, our emphasis in this chapter will be on the ethical issues raised in early diagnosis.[1] Although our focus will be on the ethical issues, we recognize that any discussion of genetics and ethics tends to be very difficult because the material involves highly technical and scientific language on a subject that changes almost every day.

## THREE KINDS OF EARLY DIAGNOSIS

Diagnosis is a process of knowing the cause of symptoms and identifying disease states. Etymologically, the word comes from the Greek roots meaning "to discern" and "to distinguish" and "to learn," "to know," or "to perceive." Early diagnosis can mean a clinician has made a judgment about the presence of, absence of, or potential (i.e., predisposition) for a disease early in the development of human life or early with respect to the onset of a particular disease state.

Not everyone, however, is tested for a genetically related disease. Here, we need to make an important distinction: there is a difference between genetic *screening* and genetic *testing* (for diagnosis). James Hodge, citing Lawrence Gostin, states, "*Genetic screening* refers to programs designed to identify persons in a subpopulation whose genotypes suggest that they or their offspring are at higher risk for a genetic disease or condition."[2] In other words, health care professionals decide who should be tested for genetic diseases and other conditions by applying screening criteria to identify those individuals or groups who are at higher risk for them. Not all screening criteria require knowledge of genotypes. One example of such a screening criterion is maternal age: if a pregnant woman is thirty-five years old or older, the fetus she is carrying is at higher risk for Down syndrome. Thus, the criterion of age is used to determine if an individual should go through further testing to determine the presence of a particular disease (e.g., Down syndrome, or Trisomy 21—an extra copy of chromosome 21). In contrast, Hodge writes, "*Genetic testing* refers to medical procedures that determine the presence or absence of a disease, condition, or marker in individual patients."[3]

There are two general methods of early diagnosis: clinical and molecular/genetic. On the one hand, clinical diagnosis involves the collection, processing, and interpretation of data gleaned from clinical observation and examination. For example, clinical prenatal diagnosis can use ultrasound technology or pedigree analysis (a family's genetic history). On the other hand, genetic diagnosis involves the collection, processing, and interpretation of data obtained from specific genetic (molecular) technologies such as polymerase chain reaction (PCR), karyotyping, and fluorescence *in situ* hybridization (FISH) analysis. Polymerase chain reaction is a way to amplify and to measure the amount of genetic information in a particular biological sample usually coupled with a variety of testing known as *blotting*. Given the size and relative concentration of one's DNA in a blood sample, PCR enables technicians and clinicians to identify specific sequences and measure their presence. Karyotyping involves manipulating the cells and their genetic material in a way that results in a visual display (called a karyotype) of chromosomes, which are ordered according to length. Fluorescence *in situ* hybridization analysis is a faster way to detect specific chromosomal abnormalities than karyotyping. FISH involves the use of special (fluorescent) DNA molecules called probes to search for and bind to specific parts of targeted chromosomes. When these molecules bind to the DNA of the chromosomes, the fluorescent part of the probe emits a signal that is read by a computer. Lastly, we call one of the new and exciting technologies *microarray* or *DNA chip* technology. This technology uses short segments of genetic material on a computer chip that transmits signals to a computer when the complementary sequences bind to the segments after the chips are exposed to a biological sample. Each signal indicates that the corresponding sequence is present in the sample. Currently scientists use microarrays primarily for research; but as microarray technology matures, it will gain wider use in the clinical setting. Laboratory technicians receive biological samples from patients or clients through blood sampling, amniocentesis, chorionic villus sampling, fetal tissue sampling, maternal serum sampling (including alpha-fetoprotein testing and multiple marker screening), and other techniques.

When in combination with themselves or other technologies, these methods shape three different kinds of early diagnosis: preimplantation genetic diagnosis, prenatal diagnosis, and predictive genetic diagnosis. In bioethics literature, these may come under slightly different names (e.g., prenatal diagnosis may be prenatal genetic testing). We will now discuss each of these forms of early diagnosis.

## Preimplantation Genetic Diagnosis

As we saw in the last chapter, assisted reproductive technology (ART) has ushered in opportunities never before possible in human reproduction. One such opportunity is the ability to choose which embryos one would like to implant in the woman's uterus. The process of preimplantation genetic diagnosis (PGD) informs this decision making. PGD occurs through genetic testing of embryonic cell(s) obtained from embryos produced through IVF, selection of embryos presenting with desirable characteristics (or lacking undesirable characteristics, like a disease-causing gene), and transfer of those embryos into the woman's uterus (to complete the ART cycle). Clinicians obtain the embryonic cells through an embryo biopsy, which occurs on about day three of the cleavage stage (seven to eight cells total in the embryo). To perform the biopsy, technicians use a laser to create a hole in the shell of the embryo and then remove one or two cells with a microscopic-sized pipette. The main indication for using PGD is unsuccessful infertility treatment where there is no identifiable cause in either the female or male partner. Clinicians, however, may recommend PGD for couples where the female partner is of advanced reproductive age, couples who have three or more unsuccessful IVF cycles, and couples who have had unexplained spontaneous miscarriages. PGD may also be used to avoid transferring embryos whose genotypes suggest a predisposition for a genetic disease or a gene for an actual disease.

In choosing which embryos are to be transferred, clinicians first screen them with FISH analysis. Here, clinicians are principally concerned about chromosomes associated with spontaneous abortions. For couples who are at higher risk of having a child with a particular disease or condition, some embryos may then be tested using DNA analysis (e.g., with PCR, etc.) for the one partner's or both partners' known mutations causing the specific condition. In principle, one can use PGD to screen and test (and then select) for disease prevention and for desirable traits (e.g., sex and other phenotypes where scientists know the corresponding genotypes).[4]

## Prenatal Diagnosis

Since 1966, scientists have been able to assess the chromosomal constitution of fetuses from cultured cells obtained from amniotic fluid.[5] Today, clinicians are able to look for hundreds of conditions with a myriad of screening programs and diagnostic tests. Prenatal screening, as mentioned above, involves the application of particular criteria to identify higher risk individuals or groups. Clinicians use prenatal diagnostic testing in order to determine the presence of or potential for particular disease-related conditions *before the pregnancy is carried to term and the child is delivered*. The principal indications for prenatal diagnosis include advanced maternal age, previous child with a new chromosome abnormality, presence of structural chromosomal abnormality in one of the parents, family history of a genetic disorder that may be diagnosed by biochemical or DNA analysis, family history of an X-linked disorder for which there is no specific prenatal diagnostic test, risk of neural tube defect, and detection of fetal abnormalities by maternal serum screening and fetal ultrasound.

Prenatal diagnosis provides information for couples so they can better prepare for whatever condition the child might have (or develop) or so they can decide to terminate the pregnancy with an abortion. These choices are quite profound and often very difficult. For some disorders, a simple change in diet may address any issues resulting from a disease-causing genotype. Children born with phenylketonuria (PKU), for example, may continue to grow and live productive lives with a slight change in their diet early in life (i.e., removing the amino acid phenylalanine). In contrast, children born with the gene causing Huntington's disease may live productive lives until they reach their forties or fifties, at which time Huntington's disease begins its onset of a slow, degenerative neurological condition. Additionally, some genetic disorders, such as Tay-Sachs, may cause a significant amount of pain and suffering early in a child's life and may lead to death fairly quickly (possibly within the first year of life).

## Predictive Genetic Diagnosis

Predictive genetic diagnosis is a form of diagnostic testing in which a patient has not yet developed symptoms for a particular disease but may have the disease-related or disease-causing genotype. Clinicians can perform predictive genetic testing on children as well as adults. Predictive genetic diagnosis in children may pose significant issues. For example, should the child be tested at all? If so, when should the child be told he or she has a genetic disease if the results are positive? There are several psychosocial issues, too. Sometimes families may believe a child to have a genetic disease even before the child is tested. Such a family dynamic is called preselection, which may lead to significant stigmatization of the child.

A more general form of predictive genetic testing can also reveal carriers of disease-related alleles. Thus, while these persons may not develop the disease itself, they are carriers of the genes that may cause the disease in their offspring. Some such individuals may seek this test if they plan to have children. If a potential parent is a carrier, predicting the likelihood of that parent passing a disease-causing gene to his or her offspring (and the likelihood of the offspring receiving the disease-causing genotype from both parents) may determine whether that couple will pursue natural reproduction, assisted reproduction, adoption, or remain childless. According to Joseph Fletcher, using genetic information in this context is one way in which humankind can achieve genetic control and end "reproductive roulette."[6]

# ETHICAL ISSUES IN GENETIC COUNSELING

According to the American Board of Genetic Counseling, "Genetic counseling is the process of helping people understand and adapt to the medical, psychological and familial implications of genetic contributions to disease."[7] This process includes (1) an interpretation of family and medical histories to gauge the probability of disease occurrence or recurrence; (2) an education regarding the patterns of inheritance, testing, management, disease prevention, available resources, and research; and (3) a promotion of informed choices and adaptations to the risk or condition.

In January 1992, the National Society of Genetic Counselors adopted a code of ethics, which was since revised in 2004 and 2006.[8] Within this code, as well as in the bioethics literature, several ethical issues arise in the context of genetic counseling. When a genetic counselor develops a professional relationship with a client (or clients), he or she must deal with several values, principles, and norms. The following issues reflect the complexity and challenging nature of the process of genetic counseling.

## Value Neutrality

Genetic counselors aim to be value neutral in their professional conduct and communication of genetic information to clients. Counselors intend to provide facts in a manner that does not bias their clients' decision-making processes. These facts include the diagnostic and prognostic implications of genetic testing. The value that genetic counselors are seeking to protect is patient or client autonomy. Many scholars argue, however, that the provision of such information is inherently value laden and that the distinction between fact and value may be difficult to determine.[9] This is particularly the case since these conversations occur in the context of disease and illness, which clients and counselors already understand as negative.

## Nondirectiveness

Closely related to value neutrality is the notion of nondirectiveness. Again, genetic counselors seek to be nondirective in their professional-client relationships in order to protect client autonomy. Nondirectiveness requires a counselor to be sensitive to which facts he or she presents, how those data are communicated to clients, and the variety of ways clients may interpret the data and integrate them into health and reproductive decision making.

## Risk Assessment

One area where value neutrality and nondirectiveness challenge the professional ethos of genetic counselors is that of risk assessment.[10] Risk assessment is an interpretive and value-laden process of collecting, interpreting, and presenting data in a manner that supports rational decision making. Yet, what does a 25 percent chance of having a child with Huntington's disease mean for a particular couple? Some research suggests that even how one states the probabilities makes a difference in how clients understand the information. For example, a "twenty-five percent" or a "25%" chance is understood differently than a "1-out-of-4" chance. Moreover, presenting the converse (i.e., a 75 percent chance of *not* having the disease) may bias the decision making. Therefore, risk assessment includes issues of both content (the actual risk) and process (how the risk is communicated) in genetic counseling.

## Privacy and Confidentiality

Like other health care providers, genetic counselors seek to protect their clients' privacy and confidentiality. Occasionally, circumstances may suggest that breeching this confidentiality is justifiable. For example, if genetic testing reveals that a family member has or is at significant risk of having a genetic disease, a counselor may wish to inform her clients' family members. Nevertheless, protecting privacy and confidentiality is a major professional principle, which is related to minimizing discrimination and stigmatization and is a way to protect client autonomy by reducing the likelihood of obstacles to that autonomy.

## Genetic Essentialism and Genetic Determinism

Genetic essentialism and genetic determinism are two notions that reflect aspects of one's worldview regarding genetic causation. Genetic counselors seek to clarify genetic information (i.e., the "genetic contributions to disease"), which gives a context and framework for understanding genetics and gene-related diseases. In both genetic essentialism and genetic determinism, there is a form of reductionism at work: in some way, everything is reduced to genes and genetic causes. In genetic essentialism, one's essence is equated with one's genes or genotype ("I am my genome"). In genetic determinism, the causes of everything may be attributed to one's genes. This may range from the causes of diseases and poor health conditions to the causes of behavior (especially criminal behavior). Genetic essentialism tends to minimize the role of other aspects of being human; genetic determinism tends to minimize human responsibility ("it's not my fault, it's my genes") and other factors (including environmental factors) contributing to one's particular situation. Genetic essentialism and genetic determinism may reinforce judgments leading to discrimination and stigmatization. Therefore, the genetic counselor plays an important role in addressing the causes of many social injustices related to genetic information.

# ETHICAL ISSUES IN EARLY DIAGNOSIS

The issues in early diagnosis go beyond the context of genetic counseling and touch individuals and couples at various stages in human life: before pregnancy, during pregnancy, and after birth. Needless to say, the issues one encounters in genetic counseling are related to ethical issues that may be outside of the counselor-client relationship. The following are issues one may come across in the consideration of early diagnosis and the knowledge that may result.

## Destruction of Embryos or Fetuses

Following both preimplantation genetic diagnosis and prenatal diagnosis, an individual may choose to destroy embryos or fetuses, respectively. Thus, the dignity and sanctity of early human life are jeopardized and cast against the possibility of the burdensome, painful existence of children with genetic diseases. On the one hand, many believe one cannot use such genetic information if it will lead to the destruction of embryos or fetuses (i.e., discarding embryos or aborting fetuses, respectively). On the other hand, many believe it is irresponsible to bring a child into existence if that child will suffer tremendously and his or her entire existence will be subsumed in a fight for survival (see "A Wrongful Life" below). Here, one may invoke the perspective that such children may never have a quality of life. Furthermore, one of the reasons why genetic counselors seek to be value neutral and nondirective is to avoid biasing a decision for or against abortion: such a decision should rest with the client herself (or clients themselves).

## Risks of Harm

On the one hand, certain forms of testing carry a significant risk of harm, especially to the unborn. Even if a couple's intent is never to abort a fetus, the invasiveness of amniocentesis and chorionic villus sampling (CVS) presents a risk of fetal loss or fetal malformation. Clinicians typically perform CVS earlier in the first trimester (as early as week ten) whereas amniocentesis is usually performed in the middle of the second trimester (around week fifteen). Traditional amniocentesis and CVS possess comparable risks of harm to the fetus (approximately 0.5 percent chance of losing a pregnancy). Clinicians have attempted to perform amniocentesis earlier (at about weeks eleven to thirteen), but some research suggests that this increases the risks for fetal loss and malformation.[11]

Because traditional amniocentesis occurs at a time when the fetus is nearing viability and after women may experience quickening, clinicians have sought to develop tests for earlier in pregnancy. However, CVS, though done earlier in the pregnancy, is still an invasive procedure. Thus, alternative diagnostic methods were developed recently such as maternal serum sampling, which seeks trace amounts of fetal blood that have crossed over into the maternal blood circulation. Drawing a blood sample from the mother-to-be is less invasive than an amniocentesis, and it carries significantly less risk to the fetus itself.

On the other hand, there may be tremendous anxiety and worry associated with pregnancy. By performing tests, clinicians may be able to offer a certain degree of reassurance. While this reassurance may be accompanied with sadness (e.g., if the diagnosis is positive), it may well reduce the anxiety and stress in the woman and/or couple.

## Eugenics

Using genetic information to benefit individuals, groups, or society is not a new idea. Yet the history of using this kind of information demonstrates the more ethically problematic aspects of human history. Generally, eugenics refers to the application of genetic information to improve human heredity or to benefit human society. Historically, this occurred with the breeding techniques and husbandry. Many critics of the "new genetics" (i.e., contemporary uses of genetic information and techniques for clinical or reproductive decision making), however, suggest that there are eugenic motives at work.[12] For example, some argue that PGD selection is a form of eugenics because it "improves the stock" in the next generation. Buchanan et al. write, "Even the brightest aspirations of the new genetics are from time to time dimmed by the shadow of eugenics. The very term has been in such bad odor since the era of Nazi 'racial hygiene' that few people today wish to be associated with eugenics."[13]

## Diagnostic-Therapeutic Gap

One major problem with early diagnosis is called the *diagnostic-therapeutic gap*. The diagnostic-therapeutic gap refers to the ability of clinicians to diagnose a particular disease-state and the inability of clinicians to treat that particular disease-state. For example, while clinicians may be able to diagnose Huntington's disease, many who are at risk for it may not want to know they will eventually experience the slow, degenerative neurological condition associated with it, which ultimately will lead to their death.[14] Presently, such a diagnosis would be a prediction of a premature and painful death as there is no curative treatment available for Huntington's disease. At best, clinicians may be able to manage a patient's symptoms and provide palliative care.

## Objectification of Children

A particular problem arising out of greater control over the next generation's genotypes is an objectification of children. By subjecting embryos or fetuses to decisions that may be based on parental desires (e.g., for blond hair, for a boy instead of a girl, or for some other trait), parents may be objectifying children in a way that undermines their uniqueness and dignity as human beings. In this sense, children become the objects of parental desire. The ability to select particular traits in the next generation, however, may not simply be a matter of objectification. Some proponents claim that this is a way to prevent genetic disease; therefore, this process is better understood in the context of public health. Others may claim, however, that some traits (e.g., hair color or eye color or sex) may not be important for public health.[15] Many opponents are concerned about having market dynamics drive the inheritance pattern of human society: only those who can afford to buy the so-called best, most desired genes are more likely to have them in their children. Objectification may also reflect and reinforce elements of genetic essentialism and genetic determinism.

## Right to an Open Future

Related to the problem of the objectification of children is the notion that children have a right to an open future, which may be threatened or diminished as a result of controlling genetic information in human reproduction through early diagnosis. In citing Joel Feinberg, Buchanan et al. describe the right to an open future in this way:

> The idea is that parents have a responsibility to help their children during their growth to adulthood to develop capacities for practical judgment and auton-omous choice, and to develop as well at least a reason-able range of the skills and capacities necessary to provide them the choice of a reasonable array of differ-ent life plans available to members of their society.[16]

Through the application of genetic information, however, parents may not embody such a responsibility and may preclude the development of certain life plans, skills, or capacities in their children. For example, parents may choose to select traits for their child that increase her athletic abilities so that the child can grow up and secure college tuition through an athletic scholarship. The right to an open future, however, would mean that the child should have the freedom to choose whether she wants to be an athlete or an accountant or to pursue some other occupation. Selecting traits in this way further objectifies children, under-mines their developmental processes, supports the notion of genetic determinism, and creates the possibility of rejection or stigmatization if children resist their parents' plans for them.

## Discrimination and Stigmatization

Discrimination and stigmatization are problems that go beyond the genetic counseling relationship. A major factor in minimizing discrimination and stigmatization, however, is the protection of patient or client privacy and the maintenance of their confidentiality. Discrimination and stigmatization are two issues genetic counselors want to minimize in the provision of genetic data. In this context, discrimination refers to the unjust treatment of persons with a particular genotype. Discrimination may become manifest in employers basing their hiring decisions on genotypes; it may also be witnessed in unfairly restricting an individual's access to health care. Health insurance agencies are interested in knowing whether patients have any preexisting conditions, which include gene-related diseases. However, should insurance agencies be informed of a genetic diagnosis? Would it matter if the person was a carrier but did not have the particular disease?

Similarly, stigmatization refers to a psychosocial element of interpersonal relationships where one person projects or presumes a particular negative judgment on the abilities or worth of an individual solely on the basis of his or her genotype. Even if someone is a carrier for a condition, he or she may feel stigmatized *as if* he or she had the genetic condition. The psychosocial problems associated with stigmatization can persist even after the counseling context. Such stigmatization may remain in his or her family relationships, in his or her community, and it may ultimately erode his or her sense of belonging and self-worth.

A growing problem with discrimination and stigmatization related to privacy and confidentiality comes out of the development of storing biological samples in special banks called biobanks. Often this is done for research purposes; other times a person may wish to store particular samples or biological material (e.g., preimplantation embryos). In addition, law enforcement professionals now store some persons' genetic information in forensic DNA databases, which they use to identify criminals with a DNA match. Nevertheless, if research is conducted on such biological material, what ensures that the identity of the research subject is protected if the information obtained in research might reveal a significant health problem? What would prevent that person's information from falling into the wrong hands? Protecting patient or client privacy and confidentiality—in genetic counseling or biobanking—is a way to protect his or her autonomy since such information may be unjustly used to restrict access to jobs, health care, education, and so on.

On May 1, 2008, the House of Representatives passed the Genetic Information Nondiscrimination Act (GINA) by a vote of 414 to 1. One day before National DNA Day, on April 24, 2008, the Senate passed the same bill by a vote of 95 to 0. Legislators designed GINA to protect individuals against genetic discrimination in seeking health insurance coverage and employment. Because of these protections, policymakers hope that more Americans will take advantage of genetic testing as part of their health care.

## A Wrongful Life

Finally, early diagnosis gives rise to the concept of a wrongful life. Legally, wrongful life claims can be quite complex,[17] but the basic idea is that someone believes that a harm could have been prevented if the person suffering that harm had never been born. Here, parents may claim that the harm results from negligence of a physician, health care professional, or institution (e.g., a failure to inform them of a particular genetic diagnosis) because having the appropriate information would have led to either a decision not to conceive or to abort the fetus. Buchanan et al. write,

> The special feature of these cases that distinguishes them from other negligence cases and that has vexed many of the courts confronting them is that the disease or condition is claimed to be so harmful and irremediable that it makes the child's life not worth living. Thus the wrong done to the child is having been brought into existence or given life in this condition.[18]

Framing wrongful life claims in terms of a right, Buchanan et al. state, "The right in question is the right of the child who does exist with a life not worth living not to have been brought into existence with such a life."[19] One can levy such a claim, in principle, against parents, too, *if* they had prior knowledge of such harmful or burdensome conditions in their child-to-be. The notion of a wrongful life is causing health care providers and parents alike to consider the meaning of responsibility in human reproduction and parenthood: if we have access to certain information, to what extent are we obligated to use it in making reproductive choices?

## CONCLUSION

Early diagnosis is a very critical set of technologies because they give us significant information about embryos, fetuses, and newborns. Consequently, we now have a range of choices that we never had before. These choices are frequently problematic. People who previously would not have considered abortion may now find themselves considering it because of the presence of a severe genetic disease. Individuals may also find it difficult to understand or deal with an ambiguous diagnosis; that is, the test may reveal an abnormality, but no one may know what consequences, if any, it has. Finally, as our knowledge of genetics progresses, couples may learn that the fetus either has a predisposition for a disease or has a disease such as breast cancer or Huntington's disease that will not show up until the individual is in his or her forties or fifties. How does one respond to such information?

But the information is there. Until scientists can develop therapies for genetic diseases, many pregnancies will be tentative and couples will be forced into decisions that they may not want to make. While the various technologies of early diagnosis provide many benefits, they may also serve as case studies for the complex and frequently unintended consequences of the applications of technology.

## DISCUSSION QUESTIONS

1. What is the problem that prenatal diagnosis is intended to solve?

2. Does preimplantation genetic diagnosis resolve any of the problems surrounding traditional forms of prenatal diagnosis?

3. Should prenatal diagnosis be a routine part of prenatal health care? Why or why not?

4. Some refer to prenatal diagnosis as a "search-and-destroy mission." Others argue that it allows many fetuses to live that might otherwise have been aborted because their health condition was unknown. Which do you think is a more accurate description of prenatal diagnosis?

5. Do you think selecting against certain characteristics through abortion is a form of eugenics or genetic engineering?

6. Is it possible for a genetic counselor to be value neutral and nondirective?

7. Is it morally justifiable for parents to select traits in their children that give them a competitive advantage over others? For example, in athletics? In musical performance? In mathematics? Would it make a difference if such a selection were freely available to everyone or to only those who could afford it?

8. Do health care insurance companies have a right to genetic diagnoses?

## NOTES

1. We use the term *early diagnosis* to demonstrate that not all forms of early diagnosis require genetic technology per se.

2. James G. Hodge, "Genetic Testing and Screening: IV. Public Health Context," in *Encyclopedia of Bioethics*, vol. 2, ed. Stephen G. Post, 3rd ed. (New York: Macmillan Reference USA, 2004), 1016.

3. Ibid., 1017.

4. David Cram and Adrianne Pope, "Preimplantation Genetic Diagnosis: Current and Future Perspectives," *Journal of Law and Medicine* 15, no. 36 (2007): 36–44.

5. Robert L. Nussbaum, Roderick R. McInnes, and Huntington F. Willard, *Genetics in Medicine*, 6th ed. (Philadelphia: W. B. Saunders, 2001), 359–74 (chapter 18, "Prenatal Diagnosis").

6. Joseph Fletcher, *The Ethics of Genetic Control: Ending Reproductive Roulette* (Buffalo, NY: Prometheus Books, 1988).

7. American Board of Genetic Counseling, "What Is Genetic Counseling?" http://www.abgc.net/english/View.asp?x=1683, accessed December 7, 2007. See also *Journal of Genetic Counseling* 15 (April 2006).

8. National Society of Genetic Counselors, "Code of Ethics," http://www.nsgc.org/about/codeEthics.cfm, accessed February 11, 2008.

9. For example, see Karen Grandstrand Gervais, "Objectivity, Value Neutrality, and Nondirectiveness in Genetic Counseling," in *Prescribing Our Future: Ethical Challenges in Genetic Counseling*, ed. Dianne M. Bartels, Bonnie S. LeRoy, and Arthur L. Caplan (New York: Aldine De Gruyter, 1993), 119–30.

10. For example, see Susan Michie and Theresa Marteau, "Genetic Counseling: Some Issues of Theory and Practice," in *The Troubled Helix: Social and Psychological Implications of the New Human Genetics*, ed. Theresa Marteau and Martin Richards (New York: Cambridge University Press, 1996), 104–22.

11. Nancy Press and Kiley Ariail, "Genetic Testing and Screening: I. Reproductive Genetic Testing," in Post, *Encyclopedia of Bioethics*, 2:996–1004.

12. For example, see Allen Buchanan, Dan W. Brock, Norman Daniels, and Daniel Wikler, *From Chance to Choice: Genetics and Justice* (New York: Cambridge University Press, 2000), 9–10, 27–60, and 258–303.

13. Ibid., 9. See also Robert Proctor, *Racial Hygiene: Medicine under the Nazis* (Cambridge, MA: Harvard University Press, 1988).

14. See Sue Wright, Julia Madigan, and Anonymous, "Daily Life and the New Genetics: Some Personal Stories—1.2 Huntington's Disease," in Marteau and Richards, *The Troubled Helix*, 4–26.

15. One exception to this may be X-linked genetic diseases.

16. Buchanan et al., *From Chance to Choice*, 170.

17. Ibid., 232–42.

18. Ibid., 233.
19. Ibid., 236.

# BIBLIOGRAPHY

American Board of Genetic Counseling. "What Is Genetic Counseling?" http://www.abgc.net/english/View.asp?x=1683. Accessed December 7, 2007.

Bartels, Dianne M., Bonnie S. LeRoy, and Arthur L. Caplan, eds. *Prescribing Our Future: Ethical Challenges in Genetic Counseling.* New York: Aldine De Gruyter, 1993.

Buchanan, Allen, Dan W. Brock, Norman Daniels, and Daniel Wikler. *From Chance to Choice: Genetics and Justice.* New York: Cambridge University Press, 2000.

Cram, David, and Adrianne Pope. "Preimplantation Genetic Diagnosis: Current and Future Perspectives." *Journal of Law and Medicine* 15, no. 36 (2007): 36–44.

Fletcher, Joseph. *The Ethics of Genetic Control: Ending Reproductive Roulette.* Buffalo, NY: Prometheus Books, 1988.

Marteau, Theresa, and Martin Richards, eds. *The Troubled Helix: Social and Psychological Implications of the New Human Genetics.* New York: Cambridge University Press, 1996.

National Society of Genetic Counselors. "Code of Ethics," http://www.nsgc.org/about/codeEthics.cfm. Accessed February 11, 2008.

Nussbaum, Robert L., Roderick R. McInnes, and Huntington F. Willard. *Genetics in Medicine.* 6th ed. Philadelphia: W. B. Saunders, 2001.

Peters, Ted. *Playing God? Genetic Determinism and Human Freedom.* 2nd ed. New York: Routledge, 2003.

Post, Stephen G., ed. *Encyclopedia of Bioethics.* Vol. 2. 3rd ed. New York: Macmillan Reference USA, 2004.

Proctor, Robert. *Racial Hygiene: Medicine under the Nazis.* Cambridge, MA: Harvard University Press, 1988.

*PART III*

---

# ISSUES AT THE END OF LIFE

---

## Chapter 8

# DEFINITIONS OF DEATH

## INTRODUCTION

One of the most critical moments in the life of a person is the end of that life. But ironically, much confusion surrounds that moment with respect to both its significance and its occurrence. On the one hand, Philippe Ariès had described the medieval ritual of death in which the one dying took formal leave of his or her loved ones and the community. On the other hand, the moment of death was frequently uncertain. For example, there is a nineteenth-century American literature reflecting the fear of being buried alive. Various technical interventions such as breathing tubes or bells were attached to the interiors of coffins so that someone mistakenly buried alive could signal others. The morgue originally was a place to observe bodies to ensure that the individual was in fact dead.

Several realities softened the way many people experienced these problems. First, few medicines were available to help people overcome illnesses; death typically came quickly after the onset of an illness. Second, no technical interventions were present to prolong life. Third, since the life span was short—forty years would have been considered a ripe old age even a hundred years ago—people were more accepting of death as a fact of life. Thus, when people became ill they died, and typically they died within a community context that accepted their dying.

Perhaps the major way to show the difference between an earlier age and today is found in a petition from the litany of saints: "From a sudden and unprovided death, deliver us, O Lord." Historically, to die without taking a formal leave, without participating in reconciliation, without putting one's affairs in order, and without acknowledging the end was a personal and communal tragedy. The worst death was sudden or accidental, perhaps dying in an accident by the roadside while on a trip. This included being alone without family, friends, and religious ritual to soothe the transition between this life and what was to follow. Today, however, most would want a sudden and rapid death, preferably a death that would catch one unaware of its arrival. While people surely would want to have their affairs in order, most seem to want a rapid end because of our modern fear of a lingering, out of control death. Daniel Callahan, in his book *The Troubled Dream of Life*,[1] describes the premodern death as a tame death, one mediated by the comforts of family and community. He characterizes modern death as a wild death, a death in which dying is out of control because we have surrendered the process of dying to technology and institutions.

Several factors led to the shift from tame death to wild death. First, our life span has increased dramatically in the last several generations. People can now expect to live until their mid-seventies or even longer.[2] Thus, we are candidates for diseases that may not have afflicted our ancestors simply because they did not live long enough to contract them. Second, public sanitation, clean drinking water, and modern medicine have succeeded in eliminating many of the diseases that would routinely destroy whole populations. Third, and perhaps most critically, our generation has the technical capacity to intervene and prolong the dying process with various life-support systems.

The use of respirators and other life-support systems poses significant problems with respect to defining and recognizing death. These technical interventions mask or hide the traditional criteria used in recognizing death for the past several generations: spontaneous cessation of breathing and heartbeat. That is, if the absence of breathing and heartbeat is the sign of death, how do these criteria apply when one is on a respirator? When a respirator is breathing for an individual, in what sense, if any, can one say that person is alive? Can one consider that person to be dead? Thus, the need for an examination of the definition of death and its diagnostic criteria is pressed upon us.

# FOUR APPROACHES

The framework developed by Robert Veatch for examining various definitions of death is still useful.[3] The framework helps us identify significant issues, makes us aware of the consequences of a particular definition, and aids us in being precise in evaluating various criteria for validating the definition. Here, it is important to keep in mind the philosophical difference between a definition and its criteria. A definition of death is an ontological concept: it pertains to *what death is*. In contrast, criteria for death are epistemological concepts: they relate *ways in which we know* whether that death exists or not. In other words, a definition of death describes the reality of death while the criteria for death describe the knowledge (or how we might come to know) that death.

## Cardiopulmonary Death

This definition reflects the traditional understanding of life and death: a person is dead when his or her heart and lungs stop (i.e., cessation of cardiopulmonary functions). Since breath and blood are the vital "stuff" of life, their absence marks the presence of death. In this way, when the vital signs are absent, one recognizes that death has occurred. That is, a clinician diagnoses death when there is no evidence that the person is breathing or the heart is beating. The use of the respirator and other life-support technologies, however, clouds this traditional definition. Who (or what) is responsible for the vital signs: the person or the technology?

## Metaphysical Death

The second definition emerges from a philosophical and religious perspective: a person is dead when his or her soul separates from his or her body. This definition, based on the philosophy of Aristotle, understands the person as a unity of body and soul, or matter and form. The soul (form) animates the body (matter) creating the unique entity that we know as the person. Death occurs when these two elements separate; death is the dissolution of the union of body and soul. The main problem with this definition is how to test whether the union is dissolved. That is, we lack diagnostic criteria for this definition because, empirically, it is impossible for a clinician to measure the extent to which a person's soul is present. Some commentators talk about the loss of an "integrative unity" in the dying process, but this is extremely difficult to measure using biomedical science.

## Whole Brain Death

Veatch's third and fourth definitions—whole brain death and neocortical death—respond to the dilemmas of defining death posed by technical interventions into the dying process. Thus, as mentioned, a respirator can mask the inability to breathe spontaneously. Also, a person in an irreversible coma or a permanent vegetative state (also called a state of post-coma unresponsiveness) can have his or her physical life extended by use of various life-support systems. The intensive care unit (ICU) is a symbol of the tremendous success of modern medicine because many lives that would have been lost are routinely saved. But it is also a symbol of the dilemmas of modern medicine in that often the best that technology can do is either to maintain the status quo or to prolong the dying that will inevitably lead to death. Thus, the need for new definitions and criteria arises.

The standards for irreversible coma drawn up by an ad hoc committee at the Harvard Medical School in 1969 led to the concept of whole brain death: a person is dead when his or her entire brain, including the brain stem, ceases to function.[4] In this orientation, the brain is the locus of death because it is the organ that integrates all other organ systems and is the basis for the person's social presence in the world. The death of the brain removes the biological precondition for the person's existence precisely because of this irreversible disintegration of the physiology of the brain itself. The death of the whole brain (the brain stem, the cortex, and the neocortex) is equated with the death of the person because without this organ, the person has no means of being biologically, physiologically, and, therefore, socially integrated. For whole brain death, the criteria include unreceptivity and unresponsiveness, no spontaneous movements or breathing, no reflexes, with the confirmation of this situation by an electroencephalogram; these seek to give a means of knowing a total and irreversible lack of activity in the brain.

## Neocortical Death

One problem yet remains. Sometimes the brain stem of a person, typically someone in a permanent vegetative state, may remain operative even though the rest of the brain is irreversibly destroyed. Since the brain stem is responsible for our involuntary nervous system, this individual may be breathing spontaneously and his or her heart beating on its own. According to the whole brain death definition, this individual is not dead. Neocortical death addresses this situation by looking only to the neocortex of the human brain as the locus for a definition of death. Proponents of this definition select the neocortex because it appears to be the biological precondition for consciousness and self-awareness, distinctive personal characteristics, and other executive functions of personal life. In this definition, because disease or trauma irreversibly destroys the biological basis for self-awareness, this individual is no longer an integrated social whole and, therefore, no longer a person. The person is dead even though, paradoxically, involuntary aspects of physical life continue. By using this definition, we confront a situation with a cadaver that is still breathing under its own power, so to speak. The disposition of such a cadaver presents tremendous religious, philosophical, and psychosocial problems, such as dualism and other mind-body relation issues.

# LIMITS OF RESPONSIBILITY AND EXPANSION OF AUTHORITY

The defining of death requires awesome responsibilities. Some suggest that such attempts to redefine death are well beyond the responsibilities human beings have. Others argue that we have no choice, since not to decide is also to decide. Because there are limits to medicine, we must make a virtue of necessity and establish reasonable definitions and defensible criteria. In doing this, it may be prudent to keep in mind the sage advice of Paul Ramsey that while there may be limits to curing, there are never limits to caring.[5] Ramsey also warns us not to consider the definition of death along with needs that can be fulfilled by what a potentially dead person has to offer. For example, we ought not to consider the definition of death if by changing that definition we can harvest more organs for transplantation into patients who need them.

One common objection to redefining death (and using criteria that are not compatible with our certitude of death) is that it is "playing God," that is, appropriating to human beings what is the responsibility of God alone. The traditional understanding of God as author of life and death forms the basis of this objection. Hence, death is God's responsibility, and interfering with it is overstepping the limits of human responsibility. First, such a view confuses defining death with the authority to take life. The purpose of defining death and establishing criteria is to determine when it has occurred; the purpose is not to take a person's life. Second, this view uncritically, or perhaps naively, assumes that God is directly and immediately involved in each and every physical or biological event in the universe. While wanting to avoid the position that God created the world and then left it to its own devices, we must also reject the contrary position, which assumes that God directs each and every act occurring in the world. The former view overstates human responsibility; the latter devalues it.

A second problem with redefining death comes from the very practical issue of what to do with people in irreversible comas or permanent vegetative states. On the one hand, health care providers could maintain and care for those individuals in such conditions almost indefinitely. On the other hand, if we do maintain such individuals our health care facilities, including limited and expensive intensive care units, will become overburdened. Individuals who need an ICU as a transitional phase of their recovery may be at risk of not being admitted because of overcrowding in the unit. Thus, considerations of space and economics force the question of the status of these individuals upon us. Also, our own ethical concern for respect for persons and for life causes us to examine their situation. A person can be just as much violated by overtreatment as by undertreatment. We have a moral obligation to treat a cadaver with respect, but not to continue to provide it with expensive medical therapies. Thus, a reexamination of the definition of death can provide us with an orientation to some of these problems.

The issues raised by the definitions of death and corresponding obligations to provide treatment to persons generate other significant questions in health care decision making. For example, issues of medical futility, or disputes over what is medically beneficial, emerge when, if by declaring a patient dead, a health care provider indicates that his or her obligations to provide medical treatment to such a patient are no longer applicable. If families disagree with the reality of death, they will likewise disagree with the lack of obligations to provide treatments. Conversely, if a physician believes medical treatment is no longer beneficial to a patient because that patient is dead, then he or she may believe that he or she has reached the end of medicine based on its own reason for being.

Third, we need to consider the issue of suffering. Although suffering is an evil and is one of the major problems of human existence, we have nonetheless attempted to find meaning in it, again making a virtue of necessity. Some see suffering as contributing to the development of character, as strengthening one's personality. The discipline learned from suffering allows a person to make his or her way through the world and succeed. Others experience suffering in a religious context and see it as a means of transforming the self and the community. Such an experience of redemptive suffering can be an occasion for personal growth and the strengthening of the community. All of us know the inspiration that one can derive from witnessing such an experience of suffering.

Yet, when a person is comatose, when an individual cannot personalize the suffering or in some way appropriate the suffering to oneself and one's life project, may not such suffering simply be impersonal, unredemptive, meaningless? Although one may wish to make suffering a religious experience or an occasion for personal growth (indeed, one may even succeed in this), might there not come a time or a situation in which such efforts cease? The patient is in a coma or an irreversible vegetative state and cannot respond to the situation. The patient cannot interact with the family. One can make little or no sense of the situation; growth and development can no longer occur. Such destructive suffering may lead to the despair of all.

Finally, we must be cautious about when and how we entertain different definitions of death and their criteria. As mentioned above, Ramsey warns us to consider such a context because we might be prone to shape the definition in a way that favors one group over another. One subject within which this is preeminently a concern is organ procurement. Since the development of organ transplantation, organ procurement agencies have initiated efforts to increase the organ supply. One of those efforts includes institutionalizing donation after cardiac death through compliance standards (e.g., every hospital needs to have a policy on donation after cardiac death [DCD]). While organ donation historically occurred after cardiopulmonary death, organ transplantation standards evolved principally around whole brain death. Today, as agencies continue to increase the organ supply, they increasingly invoke the more traditional definition of death in DCD: cardiopulmonary death. This is why some use the phrase "back to the future" to describe DCD. Another set of questions in organ transplantation that relates to the definition of death involves anencephalic infants. If one uses the whole brain death definition, then one cannot harvest the newborn's organs without allowing it to die first (i.e., according to the definition). If one uses the neocortical brain death definition, however, then one could harvest the newborn's organs without waiting for the newborn's heart to stop or whole brain to die.

# CURRENT DIRECTIONS

Personal and technical considerations that give rise to attempts to redefine death continue to be with us. Such attempts are an effort to come to terms with the limits of medicine in seeking to cure an individual. They also are an effort to respect the rights of individuals and to maintain their dignity by prohibiting overtreatment or inappropriate treatment. In addition, the redefinition of death is an attempt to resolve the limbolike situations of many patients, in a variety of contexts, where technical interventions support their vital functions but whose status as alive or dead is questionable.

The continued press of events, ongoing debates of the appropriateness of various definitions of death, and the continuing problems presented by life-support systems led to a formal consideration of the definition of death by a presidential commission in 1981: The President's Commission for the Study of Ethical Problems in Medicine and Biomedical and Behavioral Research. This commission, recognizing that many states legislated differing definitions of death, proposed a uniform standard. The commission reached its conclusion about the definition of death and its implementation based on several considerations:[6]

1. Recent developments mandate such considerations.
2. This restatement ought to be a matter of statutory law.
3. Such laws ought to be, at present, enacted on the state level.
4. Such laws ought to be uniform.
5. The definition ought to address physiological standards rather than medical tests and criteria that can be rendered outdated by new knowledge and technical developments.
6. Death is a unitary phenomenon and can be determined by either traditional heart-lung criteria or brain criteria. This helps avoid perceptions of different degrees of death.
7. Definitions of death ought to be kept separate from provisions concerning organ donation and decisions to withhold or withdraw life support systems.

Given these considerations as well as the conclusion of various other studies, the commission recommended the following as a uniform definition of death: "An individual who has sustained either (1) irreversible cessation of circulatory and respiratory function, or (2) irreversible cessation of all function of the entire brain, including the brain stem, is dead. A determination of death must be made in accordance with accepted medical standards."[7]

The strength of this proposed definition is that it recognizes—to put it directly—that when one is dead, that particular death is the same reality regardless of which criteria a clinician uses in diagnosing it. Thus, (whole) brain death has the same validity as traditional cardiopulmonary death. Also, the definition does not lock anyone into the technology or knowledge of a particular time. The criteria for determining death are the responsibility of the medical profession and will change as knowledge and technology change.

Yet, this proposed definition has not resolved all problems. The commission has provided a framework for analysis, a location for determining criteria, and a validation of the concept of death, regardless of how one recognizes it. While not resolving all of the difficult and frequently tragic circumstances that surround death, its defining, or the applications of clinical criteria, the commission orients us to an understanding that can help us resolve many of our difficulties.

Neuroscience is one of the fastest growing fields in the biomedical sciences. Likewise, biomedical technology has matured, and greater dialogue about which diagnostic tools and techniques to use has cultivated a growing certitude over diagnosing death. Other pressures, however, may preclude appropriate use of the tools and techniques. Clinicians may be pressed for time and may not perform the diagnostic tests appropriately (e.g., apnea tests). In contrast, some clinicians may be worried about not being certain enough and may order tests that are not required; an electroencephalogram (EEG) is not required to determine death, it may merely affirm the evidence in other, less expensive tests. Yet, clinicians may order their use just to be sure. Recently, one study found variation in the guidelines for determining death by brain death criteria.[8] Furthermore, the growing interculturalism of contemporary American health care also creates a situation where individuals who differ in their views on death are faced with the prospect of having to reconcile divergent worldviews. For example, some cultures may outright reject whole brain death. How are clinicians to accommodate or respect those beliefs when, legally, they understand the patient to be dead? Thus, we must have greater sensitivity and vigilance in understanding what definitions of death we each have and how we apply our criteria for knowing while caring and respecting patients and their families.

Linda Emanuel, a physician, proposes a contemporary response to some of these issues, including some raised by Veatch. Her point is that although one may frequently consider life and death to be distinct states, with a relatively clear threshold between them, dying is, rather, a process that results not in a state *of death*, but a state *of not being*. Emanuel notes: "The traditional model of life and death as poles of a binary opposition is therefore in need of modification. The new model must have only one state; there is only life and its cessation. The challenge shifts from understanding death to understanding life and its loss. Attempts to define death must therefore be recast as attempts to define loss of life."[9]

For Emanuel, "the living person is the product of all the interacting systems of the body. Life is understood as the totality of biological and cognitive and spiritual life." The reality and experience of this model are critical in that "the activities of the whole system can cease while some components of the system continue, and any one component can cease to function while the whole continues, without in any way challenging the concept of life or person." This means that at various stages during the process of losing one's life there will be states of residual life left, perhaps the functioning of the heart, digestion, organic life, or cellular life. She continues, "Rather than categorizing all states as dead or alive it allows unhindered examination of the residual states *as* residual states. This opens up for inquiry what the appropriate behavior is toward particular states."[10]

This examination and inquiry occur in what Emanuel calls a bounded zone approach, which "identifies an *observable* state, complete with the physiological feature that may readily translate into criteria, and then asks what is the correct approach to it."[11] Determining loss of life is not a subjective or criteria-less judgment. Rather, the determination will seek to define upper and lower limits of forms of residual life and to determine the moral value appropriate to that stage of the loss of life.

Shifting to a kind of process model of death will make various demands on us. The model proposed by Emanuel, however, gives us a helpful way to begin such a transition by allowing us to "resolve the tension between conceptual understanding and real experience." This is a major problem with our current understanding: many of us have had the experience of reluctantly recognizing that though the body of a loved one may be functioning biologically, the loved one is absent and will not return. In addition, this understanding helps us to "define cessation of life and identify appropriate moral behavior toward specified states." Of critical importance is that this model not only recognizes that life is a value throughout the process of losing life, but it also affirms that different moral obligations are appropriate for the various stages.[12]

Finally, advances in biotechnology are creating significant moral questions. In particular, antiaging technology raises several questions in relation to death. As we attempt to expand the time we have as functioning adults, we may or may not alter the maximum life span of the human species (about 120 years of age). Alternatively, if we gain control over expanding the average life span, not just in a relative way against the maximum life span of 120 years (e.g., increasing average life span incrementally to 90, 100, 110, and so on up to 120 years), but in an ultimate way, say to 200 or even a 1,000 years or more, what are the implications for human relationships? For economic and environmental sustainability? Or for our relationships with God? These philosophical, theological, and gerontological questions are intimately connected with our senses of mortality, including a sense of our human finitude as well as our relationship to future generations (e.g., generativity).

## CONCLUSION

Discussions about the once seemingly simple or indisputable realities of life and death will continue. The President's Commission started us on the way by codifying the debate of the last three decades. As Emanuel shows us, however, developments in technology as well as moral reflection of the value of life in various stages are calling us to a new debate and possibly a reconceptualization of death and dying.

Outside of defining death and its criteria, we face significant moral questions with respect to illness and dying. Among these questions are whether and to what extent we are obligated to provide (or to accept) medical treatments. Under what circumstances can we justify foregoing or withdrawing medical treatment? It is in the next chapter that we will discuss these and other questions.

## DISCUSSION QUESTIONS

1. Why has defining death become so difficult?
2. What kinds of technical resources complicate defining death? How do they do this?
3. What are some of the social implications of redefining death?
4. Who should be responsible for redefining death? Who should be responsible for establishing the diagnostic criteria for death?
5. Does Emanuel's understanding of death as a process of losing life help resolve problems such as those caused by the irreversible loss of the neocortex or Alzheimer's disease?

## NOTES

1. Daniel Callahan, *The Troubled Dream of Life: In Search of a Peaceful Death* (Washington, DC: Georgetown University Press, 2000).

2. Average life span, however, varies significantly around the globe. In 2002, average life expectancy at birth ranged from seventy-eight years in women who were born in developed countries to less than forty-six years for men in Subsaharan Africa. See World Health Organization (WHO), "The World Health Report

2003: Shaping the Future," *WHO: The World Health Report 2003*, http://www.who.int/whr/2003/en/index.html, accessed January 9, 2008 (p. 4 of the PDF version).

3. Robert Veatch, *Death, Dying and the Biological Revolution* (New Haven, CT: Yale University Press, 1976), 21ff.

4. Ad Hoc Committee of the Harvard Medical School, "A Definition of Irreversible Coma," *Journal of the American Medical Association* 205 (August 1968): 337–40.

5. Paul Ramsey, *The Patient as Person* (New Haven, CT: Yale University Press, 1970).

6. President's Commission for the Study of Ethical Problems in Medicine and Biomedical and Behavioral Research, *Defining Death: Medical, Legal and Ethical Issues in the Determination of Death* (Washington, DC: US Government Printing Office, 1981).

7. Ibid., 1–2. These considerations and definitions ultimately informed the Uniform Determination of Death Act.

8. David M. Greer, Panayiotis N. Varelas, Shamael Haque, and Eelco F. M. Wijdicks, "Variability of Brain Death Determination Guidelines in Leading U.S. Neurologic Institutions," *Neurology* 70, no. 4 (January 22, 2008): 284–89.

9. Linda L. Emanuel, "Reexamining Death: The Asymptotic Model and a Bounded Zone Definition," *Hastings Center Report* 25, no. 4 (July–August 1995): 27.

10. Ibid., 30, 31 (italics in original).

11. Ibid., 31 (italics in original).

12. Ibid., 34.

# BIBLIOGRAPHY

Ad Hoc Committee of the Harvard Medical School, "A Definition of Irreversible Coma." *Journal of the American Medical Association* 205 (August 1968): 337–40.

Buckman, Robert. *How to Break Bad News: A Guide for Health Care Professionals*. Baltimore: Johns Hopkins University Press, 1992.

Callahan, Daniel. *The Troubled Dream of Life: In Search of a Peaceful Death*. Washington, DC: Georgetown University Press, 2000.

Emanuel, Linda L. "Reexamining Death: The Asymptotic Model and a Bounded Zone Definition." *Hastings Center Report* 25, no. 4 (July–August 1995): 27–35.

Greer, David M., Panayiotis N. Varelas, Shamael Haque, and Eelco F. M. Wijdicks. "Variability of Brain Death Determination Guidelines in Leading U.S. Neurologic Institutions." *Neurology* 70, no. 4 (January 22, 2008): 284–89.

Kübler-Ross, Elisabeth. *On Death and Dying*. New York: Macmillan, 1969.

President's Commission for the Study of Ethical Problems in Medicine and Biomedical and Behavioral Research. *Defining Death: Medical, Legal and Ethical Issues in the Determination of Death*. Washington, DC: US Government Printing Office, 1981.

Ramsey, Paul. *The Patient as Person*. New Haven, CT: Yale University Press, 1970.

Veatch, Robert. *Death, Dying and the Biological Revolution*. New Haven, CT: Yale University Press, 1976.

World Health Organization. "The World Health Report 2003: Shaping the Future." *WHO: The World Health Report 2003*. http://www.who.int/whr/2003/en/index.html. Accessed January 9, 2008.

Youngner, Stuart J., Robert M. Arnold, and Renie Schapiro, eds. *The Definition of Death: Contemporary Controversies*. Baltimore: Johns Hopkins University Press, 1999.

## Chapter 9

# FORGOING AND WITHDRAWING TREATMENT

## INTRODUCTION

Sometimes, in spite of the best intentions and the best medical care, health care providers cannot cure a disease. Alternatively, a cure might be possible, but the cost to the patient in terms of suffering and pain might be too much for the patient to bear. Or, the therapies that are available may not offer the patient an outcome that is acceptable. These situations occur daily in most hospitals. The patient may be a newborn, an adolescent, someone in the prime of life, or an older person who is frail or becoming senile.

The question is, must providers initiate treatment or continue it once initiated? Several factors complicate the answer to this question. The first factor is the technological imperative, which states that if we can do something then we are obligated to do so. This perspective would tend to mandate always treating as long and as intensely as possible. The second factor is the culture of modern medicine, which sees death as the enemy we must combat at all costs. If one ceases treatment, one loses to death; therefore, one continues to the end: *vive la résistance*! The third factor is the idea that death "has been moved out of nature into the realm of human responsibility."[1] Now that we can use technology or a therapy to make some difference in a patient's life, we assume that if we do not intervene in that way, then we are responsible for what happens. No distinction is made between what happens in the world of nature and human action. Providing cardiopulmonary resuscitation (CPR) is an example of this: there is a presumption that providers *must* administer CPR when someone's heart stops no matter what the burdens may be or how likely it is to succeed. But, if providers choose not to administer CPR, some may believe they are responsible for the death of the patient.

Despite these contemporary developments and perspectives, there is a tradition in bioethics that responds "No" to the question of whether we must initiate or continue treatment. That is, one may morally justify forgoing or withdrawing treatment. First, we will look at ethical issues in deciding whether treatment could be forgone or withdrawn. Second, we will examine the elements of the decision-making process even if the patient is incompetent.

## ETHICAL ISSUES IN FORGOING AND WITHDRAWING TREATMENT

Ethical issues in forgoing and withdrawing treatment fall into three thematic distinctions. First, the ordinary-extraordinary means distinction serves as a way to understand one's obligations to provide medical treatment. Second, the distinction between killing the patient and allowing the patient to die operates as a general framework for understanding whether it is permissible to forgo or withdraw treatment. Third, the tension between a sanctity of life perspective and a quality of life perspective functions as a corrective balance to figuring out whether forgoing or withdrawing treatment is morally wrong or right.

### Ordinary and Extraordinary Means of Treatment

These terms historically referred to a way of categorizing treatments or therapies in order to understand one's obligations to provide (e.g., as a physician) and to accept (e.g., as a patient) medical treatment.[2] On the one hand, *ordinary treatments are those that are morally obligatory*: they must be provided, and patients have a duty to preserve their lives by seeking them and accepting them. Ordinary therapies typically referred to medicines, treatments, or operations that offered a reasonable amount of benefit to a patient without excessive pain, expense, or other inconvenience. On the other hand, *extraordinary treatments are those that are not morally obligatory*: they are morally optional; they are supererogatory. Extraordinary therapies were those that, while offering only some or little benefit, were very costly, very painful, and exceptionally inconvenient.[3] The standard moral rule was that one was obligated to use only those treatments that were ordinary; otherwise, too high an ethical standard would be imposed on individuals.

There is much confusion here, however. One can interpret the ordinary-extraordinary distinction in a variety of ways. Take, for example, an *empirical* interpretation and a *moral* interpretation. An empirical interpretation would indicate that an ordinary treatment is readily available, relatively inexpensive, likely to work, and no longer experimental. A ventilator is an example of a modern, empirically understood ordinary treatment. Furthermore, empirically speaking, an extraordinary treatment is not readily available or rare, relatively expensive, not likely to work, and possibly experimental. In contrast, a moral interpretation would indicate that an ordinary treatment is an intervention wherein *the benefits are likely to outweigh the burdens*. Some refer to this as a *proportionate* treatment. Morally speaking, an extraordinary treatment is an intervention wherein *the benefits may not or do not outweigh the burdens*. These treatments are *disproportionate*. An example is a ventilator that is no longer helping the patient reach a meaningful level of recovery.

Notice that depending on the interpretation, a ventilator can be empirically ordinary or morally extraordinary. The judgment of whether the benefits outweigh the burdens should (a) always be made from the patient's perspective and (b) always be relative to a particular treatment. Technical interventions in medicine have complicated this traditional distinction, particularly with respect to its use in evaluating treatment modalities. The major problem here is that what is medically or empirically routine becomes confused with what is morally ordinary—they are not the same. For example, a Jehovah's Witness likely sees a blood transfusion as extraordinary because the religion prohibits it under penalty of eternal damnation. Yet, for most, it is both medically routine and typically morally ordinary.

## Killing the Patient and Allowing the Patient to Die

One can base decisions to forgo or withdraw medical treatment on a variety of principles or values. For example, a ventilator may no longer be beneficial or serve the patient's best interests; therefore, one may withdraw the ventilator. Recognizing one's obligations—either as a provider of health care or as a patient—informs these decisions and the moral judgments about them. Nevertheless, contemporary end-of-life decisions involving forgoing and withdrawing treatment demonstrate a tension between the rights of patients to refuse treatments and the obligations of health care professionals to provide them. A key ethical issue is that moral arguments rest on the importance of one's intent in morality and, consequently, a distinction between killing the patient and allowing the patient to die. Thus, when forgoing or withdrawing treatment is morally acceptable, the intent is *never* the death of the patient, but rather the cessation of harmful and/or nonbeneficial treatments or technology that is prolonging the natural dying process. This distinction is controversial, and many do not share the same perspective on the role of intention.

If one concludes that the treatment is extraordinary, then the treatment may be forgone or withdrawn. Generally speaking, the moral arguments for either forgoing or withdrawing treatment are identical. That is, the reasons for not initiating a ventilator frequently are the same as the arguments for withdrawing it. These arguments have to do with the patient's values, the expected benefits of the action, or the burdens of the treatment—that is, determining whether the treatment is morally ordinary or extraordinary.

While moral arguments may be parallel in forgoing and withdrawing treatment, there are significant psychosocial differences between them. These might be that in the patient, family, and medical team, a therapy has aroused certain expectations; momentum has developed and intensified during the treatment; and, all too common a party is unwilling to admit failure. Some even argue that seeing death in this context as a failure is problematic: death is not necessarily the enemy—suffering is a more insidious enemy. Thus, while most will frequently agree that a therapy is doing little, if any, good for the patient, disagreement will frequently arise about the appropriateness of withdrawing the therapy, primarily because it signifies the inability of anybody to do anything truly therapeutic for the patient.

## The Sanctity of Life and the Quality of Life

In addition to the distinctions between ordinary and extraordinary treatments and between killing and allowing the patient to die, another thematic distinction and set of ethical issues pertain to a perceived tension between the sanctity of life and the quality of life. To begin, the term *sanctity of life* refers to the inviolable value of human life. According to a sanctity of life ethos, one must protect human life at almost any cost; one must never, under *any* circumstances, deliberately and intentionally attack and end human life. An example of the sanctity of life ethos for some is the duty to preserve life in patients who are in a permanently unconscious state by providing medically assisted nutrition and hydration. Although the term derives from theological perspectives in bioethics, it and comparable concepts have experienced wide appeal outside of religious circles. Some may prefer a different term, however; for example, some may refer to a kind of human dignity. Sanctity of life positions would tend to rank human biological life as among the highest values, if not *the* highest value.

Next, the term *quality of life* can mean many different things, but it generally refers to a measure of the value of personal life, not purely biological life. According to a quality of life ethos, one may encounter circumstances in which the obligation to protect and preserve human physical life no longer exists. An example of a quality of life ethos is the idea that the duty to continue with chemotherapy in a patient with advanced cancer no longer exists if the chemotherapy causes more suffering than benefits for the patient and that the patient's entire life is subsumed by the struggle to continue physical life. The notions of sanctity of life and quality of life tend to inform moral arguments over forgoing and withdrawing medical treatments in opposing ways. Thus, someone who seeks to protect the sanctity of life of the patient will likely disagree with someone who recognizes the importance of the quality of the patient's life.

Notwithstanding this opposition, James J. Walter has argued that this tension is misleading: the values both terms—sanctity and quality of life—reflect are categorically different values;[4] Walter therefore seeks to reconcile these positions. To that end, he offers this understanding of quality of life:

> the word "quality" in the phrase quality of life does not and should not primarily refer to a property or attribute *of life*. Rather, the quality that is at issue is the quality *of the relationship* which exists between the medical condition of the patient, on the one hand, and the patient's ability to pursue life's goals and purposes (purposefulness) understood as the values that transcend physical life, on the other.[5]

Nevertheless, the debates between the sanctity of life proponents and the quality of life proponents have developed and merged into other debates. One such example is the debate between *the right to life* position (reflecting a sanctity of life ethos) and *the right to die* position (reflecting certain forms of a quality of life ethos). The right to life position argues that life is the most important value and if we do not protect and defend that value against assaults, then all else stands to be lost. When human life loses its value, then we also endanger other institutions and values. The value of life and the dignity of the person stand at the center of the moral and cultural universe, and if they are degraded or disregarded, we have lost our moral foundation.

However, many claim that a right to die—or, more precisely, a right to refuse treatment—is also important; they base such a claim on respecting the patient's quality of life. How people live or the conditions under which they live is often more important than whether they live. The defense in war of the values of democracy and liberty as well as human dignity itself is surely an example of occasions when some values are as important as or more important than life itself.

# THE CASE OF TERRI SCHIAVO

One of the most dramatic and drawn-out cases in recent years was the case of Terri Schiavo.[6] In this case, we were witness to the intensity of some of the aspects of the debates about end-of-life decision making. For about fifteen years, Mrs. Terri Schiavo remained in a permanent vegetative state (PVS), also called a state of post-coma unresponsiveness, until Michael Schiavo, her husband, requested that she be removed from medically assisted nutrition and hydration (ANH) and allowed to die. Although many details of the case remain elusive or misrepresented, Mrs. Schiavo suffered a heart attack in 1990 that caused her to enter a vegetative state shortly thereafter due to lack of oxygen to her brain. In 2000, Mr. Schiavo requested that her feeding tube (a way to provide ANH) be removed. When the Circuit Court judge in Florida agreed with Mr. Schiavo, Mrs. Schiavo's parents—the Schindlers—initiated a lengthy appeal process. Additionally, lawmakers and opinion leaders made several legislative initiatives aimed at protecting Mrs. Schiavo and other persons in her condition. Finally, Mrs. Schiavo's feeding tube was removed and she died on March 31, 2005, at forty-one years of age.

In the debates about Mrs. Schiavo's case, we can see the above distinctions demonstrated. For one, Catholic commentators argued whether medically assisted nutrition and hydration provided through a feeding tube for patients in a PVS was ordinary or extraordinary. Two, bioethicists and many others argued over whether removing the feeding tube was killing Mrs. Schiavo by starvation or was allowing her to die. Although patients in a PVS are not imminently dying, they are unable to participate actively and independently in the eating process. Another complication is that patients in PVS cannot experience starvation. Because these patients lack higher brain function, their bodies may register the neurological signals for starvation, but there is no consciousness to process those signals as the experience of starvation (or thirst). Many would claim that removing the feeding tube was euthanasia (see chapter 10); others would say that it is compassionate care and would allow Mrs. Schiavo to die peacefully. Finally, the debates more or less unfolded along the lines of those who embraced a sanctity of life position and those who held a quality of life position. For the former, we had an obligation to protect Mrs. Schiavo's life and to provide ANH no matter how long she lived. For the latter, we were prolonging Mrs. Schiavo's life, which no longer had any personal dimension to it. Because Mrs. Schiavo lost her higher functions, she could not pursue any of life's values. In this sense, Mrs. Schiavo did not have any quality of life. She simply remained in bed or was set up in a chair by caregivers. (Many, including Mrs. Schiavo's parents, claimed that Mrs. Schiavo could have benefited from brain injury rehabilitation and therapy. They alleged that she would respond to lights and other stimuli. Patients in a PVS, however, demonstrate certain behaviors that may be mistaken for purposeful behavior. For example, PVS patients have sleep-wake cycles, they react to noxious stimuli, which only requires an intact spinal cord, and their bodies are able to perform autonomic functions like respiration, circulation, and digestion. Mrs. Schiavo's autopsy revealed that her higher brain had deteriorated significantly; no therapy or rehab would have likely been helpful in her case.)

As bioethics emerged as a recognizable field, the Catholic tradition continued to provide reflections on many matters involving end-of-life decisions. The decision to forgo or withdraw ANH from patients has received attention alongside the debates in Mrs. Schiavo's case. In March 2004, Pope John Paul II delivered an allocution entitled, "Care for Patients in a 'Permanent' Vegetative State." In this speech, the Pope declared that patients in a vegetative state ought to receive nutrition and hydration:

> I should like particularly to underline how the administration of water and food, even when provided by artificial means, always represents a natural means of preserving life, not a medical act. Its use, furthermore, should be considered in principle ordinary and proportionate, and as such morally obligatory insofar as and until it is seen to have attained its proper finality, which in the present case consists in providing nourishment to the patient and alleviation of his suffering.[7]

This raised questions, however, pertaining to how Catholic health care services in the United States should understand Directive 58 in the *Ethical and Religious Directives for Catholic Health Care Services* (4th ed., 2001). Directive 58 states, "There should be a presumption in favor of providing nutrition and hydration to all patients, including patients who require medically assisted nutrition and hydration, as long as this is of sufficient benefit to outweigh the burdens involved to the patient."[8] Specifically, the allocution seemed to call into question the "presumption," which suggested that it was no longer a presumption but a requirement to provide nourishment and hydration to patients in a PVS.[9]

Thus, in response to the questions raised, the United States Conference of Catholic Bishops (USCCB) posed two questions in the form of an official submission, called a *dubium* ("doubts"), to the Sacred Congregation for the Doctrine of the Faith (CDF), the office of the Roman Curia responsible for moral matters. The CDF replied with its answers and a commentary to those answers (quoted here verbatim):

> *First question:* Is the administration of food and water (whether by natural or artificial means) to a patient in a "vegetative state" morally obligatory except when they cannot be assimilated by the patient's body or cannot be administered to the patient without causing significant physical discomfort?
>
> *Response:* Yes. The administration of food and water even by artificial means is, in principle, an ordinary and proportionate means of preserving life. It is therefore obligatory to the extent which, and for as long as, it is shown to accomplish its proper finality, which is the hydration and nourishment of the patient. In this way, suffering and death by starvation and dehydration are prevented.
>
> *Second question:* When nutrition and hydration are being supplied by artificial means to a patient in a "permanent vegetative state," may they be discontinued when competent physicians judge with moral certainty that the patient will never recover consciousness?

*Response:* No. A patient in a "permanent vegetative state" is a person with fundamental human dignity and must, therefore, receive ordinary and proportionate care which includes, in principle, the administration of water and food even by artificial means.[10]

In addition to reaffirming the pontiff's allocution, the CDF "Commentary" pointed out three conditions under which medically assisted nutrition and hydration could be removed from patients in a PVS:

1. *Physiological futility:* one is not obligated to provide medically assisted nutrition or hydration when the patient's body can no longer assimilate the substance(s).
2. *Excessive [Physical] Burdensomeness:* one is not obligated to provide medically assisted nutrition or hydration if such interventions cause, for example, significant physical discomfort.
3. *The Principle ad impossibilia nemo tenetur:* No one is obligated to do the impossible. Therefore, one is not obligated to provide medically assisted nutrition or hydration "in very remote places or in situations of extreme poverty," where the provision of "food and water may be physically impossible."[11]

Accordingly, the Catholic Health Association of the United States issued the following statement in response to the CDF answers and commentary:

The CDF document makes two important points. First, the provision of artificially administered nutrition and hydration to patients in a vegetative state is morally obligatory except when they cannot be assimilated by the patient's body (and, hence, don't achieve their purpose) or cause significant discomfort. Second, artificially administered nutrition and hydration cannot be discontinued for a patient in a persistent vegetative state even when physicians have determined with reasonable certainty that the patient will never recover consciousness. This is due to the fact that the person in a persistent vegetative state retains his or her fundamental human dignity and, therefore, must be provided ordinary and proportionate care which includes nutrition and hydration.[12]

Although the case of Mrs. Schiavo involves specific circumstances—the PVS condition and the question about ANH—her case also highlights key elements of forgoing or withdrawing medical treatments in general. As biomedical technology becomes more sophisticated, we will have to reexamine what is medically and morally ordinary or extraordinary, we will have to consider what constitutes killing or allowing the patient to die, and we will have to reflect on how to balance the perspectives of sanctity of life and quality of life.

# ELEMENTS IN THE
# DECISION-MAKING PROCESS

In his book *Contemporary Catholic Health Care Ethics*, David F. Kelly argues that beginning in the 1990s one could speak generally of an American consensus in end-of-life decision making, including decisions to forgo and withdraw treatments.[13] Thus, although there remain controversial aspects to this consensus as the Schiavo case demonstrates, one may choose to forgo or withdraw medical treatment, which one could morally justify with reference to what Kelly described as three pillars: (1) the ordinary-extraordinary distinction, (2) the killing–allowing to die distinction, and (3) the right to autonomy and the liberty to decide for oneself.[14] Thus, in health care decision making, especially in decisions to forgo or to withdraw treatment, one needs to consider carefully the elements of those decision-making processes. Therefore, we will now examine some of these elements. We covered aspects of patients making their own decisions in chapter 4 (e.g., under the concepts of informed consent and paternalism). Here, we will look at decision making on behalf of patients. Thus, we will look at two different surrogate decision-making situations: decision making for incompetent adult patients and for never-competent newborn patients.

## Decision Making for Incompetent Adult Patients

In health care, people often face situations in which patients are no longer able to make decisions for themselves. These are adult patients who were once able to make their own decisions but have since lost that capacity and are considered incompetent. Thus, the decision-making process requires others to participate. When another person makes decisions for the patient, that person is called a surrogate decision maker (or proxy decision maker). Sometimes patients may legally identify who they want as a surrogate decision maker; this person is known as the patient's health care agent and has the patient's durable power of attorney for health care. Other times, patients have not identified anyone. Health care providers must then enter into conversations with family members or friends to determine who should be the patient's surrogate and to begin the decision-making process. Occasionally, the state may assign a person to make decisions on behalf of an incompetent patient: i.e., a guardian or a conservator. Finally, some patients may not have any friends, family, or a conservator. Some commentators refer to this kind of patient as an unrepresented patient; in this situation, elaborate group-based decision-making mechanisms can be used to minimize conflicts of interest and to serve as advocates for these very vulnerable patients.[15] Whoever a surrogate decision maker is, there are several models for such decision making, and there are standards we must use in considering any evidence that a patient may have to have help in the decision-making process.

## Decision Making for Never-Competent Newborn Patients

The birth of a baby is one of the most profound and stirring human experiences we can have. Even though we know the biology of fertilization and development, the birth of a baby is still a profound mystery. It is also a significant life event for the mother and father. Parenthood is a new dimension of their relationship and helps evoke a deeper commitment to each other as well as a commitment to the new child. Sometimes all does not go as expected, however. The child that the parents desire is not the child they receive. There may be, for example, a premature birth, and the newborn may not be physically mature enough to survive outside the womb. Or the infant may have a physical impairment or be born with a disease. In this time of severe psychological trauma and grief, critical decisions must be made.

In this context, parents and health care providers are thrust into difficult situations requiring decisions, which may lead to the death of the newborn. Some commentators suggest that parents may not be emotionally stable enough to make decisions in the best interests of their newborn. Others contend that physicians should not impose their own medical morality onto the care of the newborn. Thus, a major issue in decision making for newborns is defining the roles and how much authority parents and doctors have. Furthermore, another difficulty is that newborns have never been competent nor have had decision-making capacity. In decision making for incompetent adult patients, one can reflect on the life that the patient lived and discern, to some extent, the values and preferences of that patient. For newborns, however, there is no set of life values to which surrogates can turn, and there is no advance directive; there has never been any expression of that individual's values or preferences. Decision making for never-competent patients is very different than decision making for once-competent patients.

## Medical Dimensions

Regardless of whether the patient was once competent or was never competent, one should consider the medical dimensions of the patient's situation in formulating a treatment decision. For the once-competent adult patient, several clinical factors function in decision making. First, one must know the patient's diagnoses. This includes more than what the patient's main complaint was or why the doctor admitted the patient to the hospital; this requires consideration of the various other conditions the patient may have and their combined effect. Second, one must know the patient's overall prognosis. In light of several different diagnoses as well as the process of consulting with physicians who are different specialists, the patient's overall prognosis may become clouded or miscommunicated. Third, one must also consider the resources and technology available to address those conditions. In fact, what is medically feasible informs one's overall prognosis. These factors require further reflection: in order to make the best decision, one needs to evaluate these factors in terms of the patient's values and preferences. Often, health care providers will appraise decisions differently than surrogates or patients because they may not know the patient's values or preferences. A physician's medical decision or recommendation is related to but distinct from a patient's personal health care decision.

For the never-competent newborn patient, two clinical factors play a role in decision making. The first is prenatal diagnosis in its various forms. While we covered some of this in chapter 7, it is important to note here that clinicians can diagnose many hundreds of genetic diseases as well as other anomalies *before birth*. What this means practically is that frequently the decision-making process begins well before birth occurs. The second factor is the neonatal intensive care unit (NICU); this is the place where health care professionals take premature infants as well as other newborns with various problems as soon as possible after birth. Developments in this area have occurred more rapidly than one could have imagined, and a variety of interventions and therapies are available that were not even imaginable thirty years ago. Decision making is becoming more complex as the technical and medical possibilities increase. Health care today has greater capacities to help newborns overcome their medical conditions and to push back the threshold of when a fetus is viable outside of the womb to an earlier time in the pregnancy. It is important to note, however, that despite all of the powers of modern medicine, there are still limits. Sometimes a decision to forgo or withdraw treatment in the NICU is the morally right decision.

## Identifying Appropriate Surrogates

One major element in the decision-making process is identifying appropriate surrogates. When patients lose the capacity to make their own decisions or when patients never had this capacity, health care providers must identify the appropriate surrogate. We should, however, make a distinction between a legally and a morally appropriate decision maker. A legally appropriate decision maker may be someone whom the patient explicitly (orally or in writing) identified in a legally legitimate way—for example, in an advance directive. Some states have statutes that define a list of persons who can legally serve as a surrogate decision maker when a patient has not identified his or her surrogate. Other states, however, do not have such a law; rather, the law in these states suggests that the best person to make decisions on behalf of a patient who has not identified a surrogate is the person who knows the patient's preferences or who knows the patient's values best. Thus, a spouse or an adult child is likely to fit that description; but in difficult family situations, the best person may be a friend or a nephew or niece. A legally appropriate decision maker is a person who should be the decision maker according to the letter of the law; a morally appropriate decision maker is a person who knows the patient best, who can communicate the patient's preferences and relevant values or who can express what the patient would have decided if the patient were still able to do so. Additionally, this person should act in good faith and be genuinely concerned for the patient's well-being. Ideally, the legally appropriate surrogate and the morally appropriate surrogate are the same person(s).

For once competent adult patients, one should appeal to a surrogate only when the patient has lost the capacity to make his or her own decisions (or when the patient forfeits his or her right to make decisions). This requires that a physician assess the patient's decisional capacity *for the particular decision at hand* and document the outcome of that assessment in the patient's hospital chart. If the doctor finds that the patient cannot make the decision, then he or she needs to identify a surrogate decision maker. As mentioned above, the patient may have already identified his or her surrogate in an advance directive or orally to a health care professional. In this case, this is the person to whom the physician should turn for decisions. In other circumstances, the health care team may need to seek out family members or to hold a meeting with people who know the patient in order to determine who the surrogate should be or who the spokesperson should be. In some cultures, it is not clear whether a *single* person will act as a surrogate. Instead, persons in these cultures may want a *group*-based surrogate decision-making process.[16] In any case, the health care team will need to identify a single spokesperson even if the decision was rendered by a family. In the end, the group or individual should be morally appropriate and ideally should be legally empowered to make decisions on behalf of the incompetent patient.

For never-competent newborn patients, bioethicists and others have proposed several decision makers. First, many argue that the parents should be the newborn's surrogates. Proponents of this position claim that parents are the ones who wanted the child; they are the ones who will experience the impact of raising the child; and they are the ones who have responsibility for the child. Historically, parents have been charged with making decisions for their children; and society assumes that, absent evidence to the contrary, parents decide in the best interests of the child. Second, many suggest that physicians should function as decision makers. Here, proponents argue that doctors have skill and experience in dealing with these cases; they have professional standards of care to uphold; and they are committed to preserving life. It is physicians' medical expertise that most often commends them as decision makers. Third, others claim that society, in the form of the court or law, should be the decision maker. Proponents of this position hope that these agents would be more objective and, therefore, give a fairer decision. The other purpose of having society involved is so that the decision making process will be in the open and that a certain amount of consistency will be obtained. Finally, some commentators argue that ethics committees should function as appropriate decision makers. Such committees could explicitly deal with the value dimensions of such cases. In this way, other decision makers could not cloak the decisions under the guise of medical or technical principles. Although an ethics committee would help surface the ethical aspects of a case, questions of its competence, authority, and scope are controversial.

## Bases for Making Decisions on Behalf of Others

Once one has identified the appropriate surrogate decision maker, that person still needs to make the decision(s). Therefore, it is essential to understand (a) what standards are applicable to surrogate decision making, especially standards pertaining to how surrogates *know* what the patient would want (i.e., the evidence of the patient's preferences); and (b) what models a surrogate can use in decision making on behalf of the patient.

In 1985, the New Jersey Supreme Court delivered its holding in the case of Claire Conroy; in the process, it established three specific standards for surrogate decision making.[17] One, surrogates may apply the *subjective standard* in which there exists relevant and trustworthy evidence of what the patient would want relative to a specific treatment decision. The subjectivity refers to the patient. An example of such evidence is an advance directive. Two, surrogates may employ the *limited-objective standard* in which there exists some relevant evidence but it is not entirely trustworthy. Therefore, surrogates must use some mixture of what they know to be the patient's preferences and of what they believe would be in the patient's best interests. Three, surrogates may use the *pure-objective standard* in which there exists no relevant evidence and/or it is entirely or virtually untrustworthy. Therefore, surrogates must appeal exclusively to some sort of objective criteria (e.g., a "best interests" or "reasonable person" set of criteria) in basing treatment decisions for patients. Thus, these three standards reflect a spectrum of ways to base surrogate decisions for patients, which range from the subjective to the pure-objective. This spectrum also reflects a range of available, trustworthy, and specific information regarding what the patient would want.

As we can see, decision making on behalf of others requires careful consideration and use of evidence of what the patient's preferences are or of what the patient's values are. Typically people are very concerned about ensuring the disposition of their property, money, possessions, and even their body. Historically, one's last will and testament, a legally sanctioned instrument that ensures that one's wishes will be carried out after death, resolve these and similar problems. The advance directive is a comparable instrument used in health care to express a patient's preferences even if the patient has lost that capacity.

In general, the concept of an advance directive proposes that while we are competent we indicate our wishes about how we wish to be treated if we become incompetent. The advance directive seeks to keep responsibility for decision making with the patient. In this way, control over issues such as whether the patient should be physically maintained, what is in the patient's best interest, and who the decision maker is remains with the patient as it is in other situations. Advance directives can contain both (1) an identification of an agent and/or (2) a set of instructions for medical treatments. The Karen Ann Quinlan, Nancy Cruzan, and Terri Schiavo cases alert us to how difficult and draining such decision making can be absent some kind of advance directive.

The major problem with health care instructions in an advance directive is that such instructions do not and cannot specify all possible circumstances and conditions of the patient. There is always an element of ambiguity about (a) when an advance directive is operable and (b) what the specific instructions mean in a given circumstance. Thus, one may genuinely be in doubt about the applicability of the directive. To respond to this, designating a particular individual as a surrogate decision maker may alleviate some of the uncertainty. To many health care providers, having a surrogate decision maker is preferable to vague and often unhelpful instructions.

If a hospital receives federal health care reimbursement money, federal regulations mandate that these hospitals provide patients with the opportunity to make an advance directive or give them the option of having information on advance directives. While this legislation adds another layer of bureaucracy to the hospital and to the admission process, discussing this with patients makes them aware of the option of the advance directive and can facilitate discussion of these issues with patients and their family.

In the end, states differ in the legal evidence standard they apply in determining whether a document is an advance directive or not. For some states, simply writing out your wishes on a piece of paper, signing it, and dating it is sufficient. In these states, the evidence standard is *the preponderance of evidence standard*. In other states, the requirements are much greater. In order for an advance directive to be legally recognized as such, the patient must sign it, date it, and have two witnesses sign it or have the document notarized. Here, the evidence standard is *clear and convincing*. The Court's holding in the Cruzan case established that it was not unconstitutional for states to have a clear and convincing evidence standard for advance directives. Nevertheless, even if a document is not *legally recognized*, one may still use it as evidence of the patient's preferences insofar as the content is trustworthy; it may still be *morally recognized* as significant to the decision(s) at hand.

There are two basic models of, or approaches to, surrogate decision making. On the one hand, a surrogate can provide a *substituted judgment* on behalf of the patient. In making a substituted judgment, a surrogate may echo the patient's own judgment (if known) or a surrogate may infer the patient's judgment from what he or she knows of the patient (and any available evidence). On the other hand, a surrogate can provide a *best interests judgment* for the patient. In making a best interests judgment, a surrogate appeals to what he or she believes the patient would judge to be in the patient's own best interests. Nevertheless, this ultimately requires the surrogate to turn to some objective criteria about what would constitute a patient's best interests. Thus, some surrogates may turn to the concept of a reasonable person: What would a reasonable person do in a similar circumstance?

# CONCLUSION

The ethical and psychosocial problems involved in deciding whether or not to forgo or withdraw treatment are complex. Moral arguments about forgoing or withdrawing treatment deal with three basic distinctions: between ordinary and extraordinary treatments, between killing the patient and allowing the patient to die, and between the sanctity of life perspective and the quality of life perspective.

Despite the complexity, the good news is that many more people are aware of these issues and have taken steps to ensure that others know their wishes. The bad news continues to be that often such information is not available when it is needed most. Also, there may be a gap between informing the physician of one's wishes and having them implemented, or there may be disputes among family members about what should be done, even though an advance directive may have been filled out and everyone is aware of the patient's wishes. Nonetheless, we must recognize that there comes a time when the treatment alternatives are exhausted, the burdens difficult or unbearable, and the benefits few. The sad but compelling conclusion is that we have done enough, that our resources are at their limits. The ethical task then is to stop the efforts to cure, and to intensify our care as we accompany the patient on his or her last journey.

## DISCUSSION QUESTIONS

1. Why has the advance directive become an issue?
2. Do you think the advance directive might open the door to the practice of mercy killing (i.e., euthanasia)?
3. Do you think the technology that provides nutrition and hydration to a person in a persistent vegetative state is ordinary or extraordinary therapy?
4. Do you think that the strategy of having a surrogate decision maker is better than the written document of an advance directive? Why or why not?
5. Do you think that the federal regulations requiring that information on advance directives be made available to anyone admitted to a hospital are a good idea? Try to think of reasons why people might be admitted to a hospital. Do you think these are good reasons to make out an advance directive?
6. Who should make decisions on behalf of an infant? On what basis?

# NOTES

1. Daniel Callahan, *The Troubled Dream of Life: In Search of a Peaceful Death* (Washington, DC: Georgetown University Press, 2000), 64.

2. See Pope Pius XII, "The Prolongation of Life," in *Artificial Nutrition and Hydration and the Permanently Unconscious Patient: The Catholic Debate*, ed. Ronald P. Hamel and James J. Walter (Washington, DC: Georgetown University Press, 2007), 91–97. See also Michael R. Panicola, "Catholic Teaching on Prolonging Life: Setting the Record Straight," in Hamel and Walter, *Artificial Nutrition*, 29–52; and Donald E. Henke, "A History of Ordinary and Extraordinary Means," in Hamel and Walter, *Artificial Nutrition*, 53–79.

3. Gerald Kelly, *Medical-Moral Problems* (St. Louis: Catholic Hospital Association, 1958), 129.

4. James J. Walter, "The Meaning and Validity of Quality of Life Judgments in Contemporary Roman Catholic Medical Ethics," in *Quality of Life: The New Medical Dilemma*, ed. James J. Walter and Thomas A. Shannon (Mahwah, NJ: Paulist Press, 1990), 78–88.

5. Ibid., 81–82.

6. See Thomas A. Shannon and James J. Walter, "Assisted Nutrition and Hydration and the Catholic Tradition," in Hamel and Walter, *Artificial Nutrition*, 223–35.

7. Pope John Paul II, "Care for Patients in a 'Permanent' Vegetative State," in Hamel and Walter, *Artificial Nutrition*, 205 (no. 4).

8. United States Conference of Catholic Bishops (USCCB), *Ethical and Religious Directives for Catholic Health Care Services*, 4th ed. (Washington, DC: USCCB, 2001), 31 (no. 58).

9. Shannon and Walter, "Assisted Nutrition and Hydration and the Catholic Tradition," 231.

10. Sacred Congregation for the Doctrine of the Faith (CDF), "Responses to Certain Questions of the United States Conference of Catholic Bishops Concerning Artificial Nutrition and Hydration," http://www.vatican.va/roman_curia/congregations

/cfaith/documents/rc_con_cfaith_doc_20070801_risposte-usa_en.html, accessed September 18, 2007.

11. CDF, "Commentary," http://www.vatican.va/roman_curia/congregations/cfaith/documents/rc_con_cfaith_doc_20070801_nota-commento_en.html, accessed September 18, 2007.

12. Catholic Health Association of the United States, "Comment Regarding Congregation for the Doctrine of Faith Clarification Concerning Nutrition and Hydration for Patients in a Persistent Vegetative State," News Releases, http://www.chausa.org/Pub/MainNav/Newsroom/NewsReleases/2007/r0709 14a.htm, accessed September 18, 2007.

13. See David F. Kelly, *Contemporary Catholic Health Care Ethics* (Washington, DC: Georgetown University Press, 2004), 127.

14. Ibid., 127–28.

15. Douglas B. White, J. Randall Curtis, Leslie E. Wolf, Thomas J. Prendergast, Darren B. Taichman, Gary Kuniyoshi, Frank Acerra, Bernard Lo, and John M. Luce, "Life Support for Patients without a Surrogate Decision Maker: Who Decides?" *Annals of Internal Medicine* 147 (2007): 34–40.

16. H. Russell Searight and Jennifer Gafford, "Cultural Diversity at the End of Life: Issues and Guidelines for Family Physicians," *American Family Physician* 71 (2005): 515–22.

17. "In the Matter of Claire Conroy: The Supreme Court, State of New Jersey (1985)," in *Source Book in Bioethics: A Documentary History*, ed. Albert R. Jonsen, Robert M. Veatch, and LeRoy Walters (Washington, DC: Georgetown University Press, 1998), 220–28.

# BIBLIOGRAPHY

Buchanan, Allen E., and Dan W. Brock. *Deciding for Others: The Ethics of Surrogate Decisionmaking*. New York: Cambridge University Press, 1989.

Callahan, Daniel. *Setting Limits: Medical Goals in an Aging Society*. Washington, DC: Georgetown University Press, 1995.

———. *The Troubled Dream of Life: In Search of a Peaceful Death*. Washington, DC: Georgetown University Press, 2000.

————. *The Tyranny of Survival and Other Pathologies of Civilized Life*. New York: Macmillan, 1973.

————. *What Kind of Life? The Limits of Medical Progress*. New York: Simon & Schuster, 1990.

Clark, Peter A. *To Treat or Not to Treat: The Ethical Methodology of Richard A. McCormick, S.J., as Applied to Treatment Decisions for Handicapped Newborns*. Omaha, NE: Creighton University Press, 2003.

Hamel, Ronald P., and James J. Walter, eds. *Artificial Nutrition and Hydration and the Permanently Unconscious Patient: The Catholic Debate*. Washington, DC: Georgetown University Press, 2007.

Jonsen, Albert R., Robert M. Veatch, and LeRoy Walters, eds. *Source Book in Bioethics: A Documentary History*. Washington, DC: Georgetown University Press, 1998.

Kelly, David F. *Contemporary Catholic Health Care Ethics*. Washington, DC: Georgetown University Press, 2004.

————. *Critical Care Ethics: Treatment Decisions in American Hospitals*. Kansas City, MO: Sheed & Ward, 1991.

————. *Medical Care at the End of Life: A Catholic Perspective*. Washington, DC: Georgetown University Press, 2006.

Kelly, Gerald. *Medical-Moral Problems*. St. Louis: Catholic Hospital Association, 1958.

Sacred Congregation for the Doctrine of the Faith. "Commentary." http://www.vatican.va/roman_curia/congregations/cfaith/documents/rc_con_cfaith_doc_20070801_nota-com mento_en.html. Accessed September 18, 2007.

————. "Responses to Certain Questions of the United States Conference of Catholic Bishops Concerning Artificial Nutrition and Hydration." http://www.vatican.va/roman _curia/congregations/cfaith/documents/rc_con_cfaith_doc_ 20070801_risposte-usa_en.html. Accessed September 18, 2007.

Searight, H. Russell, and Jennifer Gafford. "Cultural Diversity at the End of Life: Issues and Guidelines for Family Physicians." *American Family Physician* 71 (2005): 515–22.

United States Conference of Catholic Bishops. *Ethical and Religious Directives for Catholic Health Care Services*. 4th ed. Washington, DC: USCCB, 2001.

Walter, James J., and Thomas A. Shannon, eds. *Quality of Life: The New Medical Dilemma*. Mahwah, NJ: Paulist Press, 1990.

White, Douglas B., J. Randall Curtis, Leslie E. Wolf, Thomas J. Prendergast, Darren B. Taichman, Gary Kuniyoshi, Frank Acerra, Bernard Lo, and John M. Luce. "Life Support for Patients without a Surrogate Decision Maker: Who Decides?" *Annals of Internal Medicine* 147 (2007): 34–40.

## Chapter 10

# EUTHANASIA

## INTRODUCTION

Three major factors control our perceptions of dying. First, the diseases or problems associated with growing older are proving very difficult to cure. Various disabilities associated with senility, different forms of cancer, or Alzheimer's disease ultimately bring about death, but frequently only after a long, drawn-out process of suffering. Second, while individuals are in this debilitated state, technical interventions can prolong their lives *and* their dying. Most such interventions cannot cure; in fact, they were not designed to cure but rather to compensate temporarily for a particular body function. Once an individual is on a life-support system, however, many people are reluctant to remove the individual from it. Thus, there is a fear of being trapped on a machine. Third, there is what Daniel Callahan refers to as *technological brinkmanship*, "a powerful clinical drive to push technology as far as possible to save life while, at the same time, preserving a decent quality of life." In this context, brinkmanship is "the gambling effort to go *as close to that line as possible* before the cessation or abatement of treatment."[1] This, of course, rests on an assumption that we can control and fine-tune our technological interventions; in turn, this leads to an increasing reliance on technical interventions—even though, as noted above, such reliance is quite often futile.

These problems, perceptions, and experiences of being trapped on machines as well as genuine concern for those who experience prolonged dying have caused bioethicists to consider euthanasia anew. Some see euthanasia as an appropriate end to intolerable suffering or a hopeless situation. Others see it as a way of easing a transition that is already occurring. Still others see it as anticipating the inevitable. Euthanasia is also seen by some as a right or an entitlement: a person's last expression of autonomy and human dignity. Homicide is still another way of understanding euthanasia. From this perspective, it is an unjustified usurpation of power over oneself or another; it is going beyond the bounds of stewardship over our bodies.

Public events have also generated greater awareness of euthanasia. In 1984, Governor Lamm of Colorado suggested that older citizens may have a duty to die so that they will not deplete scarce resources for others. Elizabeth Bouvia, a twenty-six-year-old cerebral palsy patient, asked to be allowed to starve herself to death. Roswell Gilbert became the first person convicted of homicide for an act of direct euthanasia in 1985. Mrs. Gilbert was suffering from Alzheimer's disease and osteoporosis that left her disoriented and in considerable pain. After she told her husband she wanted to die, he shot her.

In the past two decades, there has also been a developing national and international debate on euthanasia. In the Netherlands and Belgium, the practice of euthanasia is legally and socially tolerated as long as certain guidelines are met.[2] In the United States, this debate has been led primarily by two individuals: Derek Humphry, founder of the Hemlock Society and author of *Final Exit* (a how-to manual for both euthanasia and assisted suicide), and Jack Kevorkian, MD, an advocate of euthanasia and an active participant in physician-assisted suicide. Finally, in an eight-to-three 1996 ruling, the United States Court of Appeals for the Ninth Circuit in San Francisco struck down a Washington State law that made assisted suicide a felony. The court said: "A competent, terminally ill adult, having lived nearly the full measure of his life, has a strong liberty interest in choosing a dignified and humane death rather than being reduced at the end of his existence to a childlike state of helplessness, diapered, sedated, incompetent."[3] More recently, three U.S. Supreme Court cases have shaped our reflections over euthanasia in general and physician-assisted suicide in particular: *Vacco v. Quill*, *Washington v. Glucksberg*, and *Gonzalez v. Oregon*. Since these pertain to physician-assisted suicide, we will discuss them in detail in the next chapter.

In the current U.S. debate, we see a typical American response to this issue: a rush to implement a seemingly merciful policy. The general pattern is the following: After little public discussion of the issue, there is some form of implementation of the practice, which is then followed by ethical, social, political, and legal problems. The fact that the practice is already instituted complicates the resolution of these problems. This has been the pattern for all major technical developments from atomic energy to artificial reproduction. Thus, even though there have been state referenda on physician-assisted suicide, we need to think this issue through much more carefully before we rush to implement euthanasia as social policy. We bene-fited individually and socially by the prolonged—though painful—debate over the removal of life-prolonging technologies in the Quinlan, Cruzan, and Schiavo cases. The protraction of the debate gave us time to think and to test various responses. Today, a similar pause for reflection would prove very helpful, particularly given the finality of the euthanasia option.

# CONCEPTIONS OF EUTHANASIA

The word *euthanasia* comes from Greek words meaning "good death." In this chapter, we understand *euthanasia* to be the voluntary and intentional ending of a person's life. Prior to the actual consideration of the ethics of euthanasia, we note three crit-ical distinctions many have made in the debate. First, there is a dis-tinction between voluntary and involuntary euthanasia. *Voluntary* euthanasia is performed either by or at the request of the recipient of the act. *Involuntary* euthanasia is performed without the consent of the individual, either because the patient is incompetent, because the patient's wishes are not known, or because it is a policy to end the life of a person with certain traits (e.g., Nazi euthanasia policies). Most discussions of euthanasia reject any consideration of involuntary euthanasia, particularly in this last sense.

Second, there is a distinction between active and passive euthanasia. *Active* euthanasia occurs when someone performs an action that results in the death of the patient. Thus, one understands active euthanasia positively as the *commission* of a death-inducing action. *Passive* euthanasia occurs when someone does not perform an action, which results in the death of the patient. Thus, one understands passive euthanasia negatively as the *omission* of a life-preserving action. An example of active euthanasia is a doctor's injecting a lethal dose of barbiturates into a patient to bring about the death of the patient. An example of passive euthanasia is a doctor's intent to kill a patient by refusing to administer antibiotics to a patient suffering from a treatable form of pneumonia.

Third, there is a distinction between direct and indirect euthanasia. Here, as we saw in the last chapter, intention plays a key role in establishing whether the action is *direct* or *indirect*. Also, the Principle of Double Effect is applicable, which enables one to determine the nature of the agent's intent and whether the action is morally permissible or not. In *direct* euthanasia an agent *intends the death of the patient* as the sole end. In *indirect* euthanasia an agent does not intend the death of the patient either as the end sought or as a means to a further end. Many prefer not to use the term *indirect euthanasia*, however, because this may confuse forgoing or withdrawing treatment with the intentional killing of a patient.

Historically, many conflate the last two distinctions: an active euthanasia was direct, a passive euthanasia was indirect. However, this is misleading because (a) there are two sets of criteria that differentiate these two distinctions (i.e., observation in the former, and the Principle of Double Effect in the latter) and (b) one distinction is descriptive of the action (i.e., commission versus omission), the other distinction is evaluative of the action (i.e., direct euthanasia is not morally permissible whereas an indirect euthanasia might be). Therefore, we suggest that these distinctions remain separate and avoided. Additional reasons for avoiding these terms include the following. First, using the generic term euthanasia to speak of both direct killing and withdrawing therapy is confusing methodologically and psychologically. Second, many ethicists debate whether there is in fact a moral difference between active and passive euthanasia. Limiting the term euthanasia to the intentional killing of an individual at least circumvents that debate. Third, we think it is better to identify the moral legitimacy of forgoing or withdrawing a therapy as a separate issue. In this instance, one is focusing on benefit to the patient, which precludes considerations of killing the patient. Thus, we will use the term euthanasia to mean an act of voluntary and intentional ending of a patient's life.

Many bioethicists frequently discuss the ethics of voluntary euthanasia in connection with the ethics of physician-assisted suicide. In fact, many see physician-assisted suicide as a form of voluntary euthanasia. There are key differences, however, and we will treat them separately. First, suicide is a self-induced interruption of the life process and typically occurs in a nonmedical context; that is, many individuals who commit suicide are not suffering from a life-threatening disease. Second, while voluntary euthanasia and physician-assisted suicide may share motivations (e.g., mercy, compassion, and respect of autonomy), the means by which one carries them out differ significantly. In voluntary euthanasia, a physician or another person *commits* the act. In physician-assisted suicide, a physician *cooperates but does not commit* the act. Instead, the physician helps *the patient commit* the act. Third, many debate the distinction between voluntary euthanasia and palliative care. This does not occur in the context of physician-assisted suicide. Therefore, there are important issues to untangle in considering voluntary euthanasia in the continuum of care in modern hospitals. There is less of a need to disentangle issues between physician-assisted suicide and other forms of medical care.

Indeed, one study compared the clinical practices of terminal sedation (a palliative care protocol that induces a coma to relieve pain) and euthanasia in the Netherlands.[4] These researchers found that both practices frequently involve patients who suffer from cancer. On the one hand, clinicians tended to use terminal sedation to address severe physical and psychological suffering in dying patients; on the other hand, clinicians tended to engage in euthanasia to protect patients' dignity during their last phase of life. In addition, clinicians employing terminal sedation tended to order benzodiazepines and morphine; clinicians participating in euthanasia tended to order barbiturates. Furthermore, the time interval between the administration of the drug and the patients' deaths ranged from one to twenty-four hours up to three to seven days for terminally sedated patients and tended to be less than one hour for euthanized patients.

# ETHICAL ISSUES IN VOLUNTARY EUTHANASIA

## *The Anti-Euthanasia Perspective*

The standard libertarian argument for euthanasia is that since this act harms no one and since the motive is relief of pain, or mercy, one cannot justify interfering with one's liberty in choosing death via euthanasia. Whether such an act harms no one is a disputable question. It may well be that, though relatives or friends sympathize with the act, they suffer genuine harms because of the loss of a loved one, the way it was done, and the lack of opportunity to bring some closure to the terminal condition of the patient. There also may be a social stigma with which relatives of the deceased have to contend. Moreover, though the act may be autonomous, may it not also be one that reflects isolation or separation? That is, the act of euthanasia may represent that the patient has little confidence in our willingness to accompany him or her on the final journey. Thus, may it not be a sign of alienation or abandonment from the community?

America seems to be a death-denying society. We have the strong suspicion that if we just spend a little more money on medicine, do a little more research, eat just a little less fat, and do low-impact step aerobics, within a few decades we will have death beaten. We seek to have total control over our lives and over disease and death, the ultimate evils. We view efforts not supporting such control as moral failures—or worse as un-American. As Daniel Callahan notes in his book *What Kind of Life?*, if ultimate control is the appropriate goal of modern medicine, then to relinquish that goal—to not intervene and allow a disease to take its course—is a moral and medical failure.[5] But because we in fact cannot cure this particular disease, we now claim euthanasia as our consolation prize. Since we cannot control our lives by curing all diseases and continuing to live, we claim control by demanding the right to end our life.

Many people, having seen that modern medicine frequently does a better job of preserving individual organs or organ systems than the life of the person in whom the organs function, simply do not want to submit themselves to that system when they are terminally ill. The fact and tragedy of modern high-tech medicine is that while it can frequently replace or compensate for most body parts or systems, ultimately such medical interventions cannot cure us. This is not a moral judgment against medicine; it is simply a fact. But it is a fact that many people will neither recognize nor accept. Therefore, they turn to euthanasia as the solution to this problem.

The major theological reason that people oppose euthanasia morally is that since God is the Creator and alone has full dominion over life and death, such a taking of life is an overstepping of human responsibility. Human beings are stewards of their lives and, as such, have limited control over what they may do. This opposition to euthanasia is closely related to the rejection of abortion based on the sanctity of life arguments we discussed earlier. Because life is inherently precious and valuable, no one under any circumstances may end it.

Many people oppose voluntary euthanasia because of fear of sliding down the slippery slope. If one allows others to kill dying patients or persons in irreversible comas—even if voluntary and for whatever good motive—what is to stop us from expanding the categories to include the involuntary killing of newborns, the mentally ill, the retarded, the unproductive, the socially undesirable? Once we lower the barriers to killing, then no one is safe.

If voluntary euthanasia becomes acceptable, this may have a detrimental effect on the relation between patients and physicians and on the perceptions of health care facilities. If seriously ill persons know that physicians or hospitals could administer euthanasia, individuals might be reluctant to seek treatment and even to enter such facilities.

## The Pro-Euthanasia Perspective

Proponents put forward several arguments supporting euthanasia. First, if a person is dying and nothing can be done, why should a person not be able to choose death now rather than later? The person is dying; the act of euthanasia anticipates what will inevitably happen. The key issue is control over one's life and death. The Principle of Autonomy grounds this argument; here, we understand this principle as the right to determine one's own destiny. Many see attempts to deny autonomy at this last and most critical time of one's life as a denial of one's dignity and an unjustified paternalistic intervention into one's life. If self-determination means anything, then it should mean the right to determine one's fate and the circumstances that surround it.

Second, if the only means of controlling patients' pain is to keep them unconscious or if patients are in an irreversible state of unconsciousness, then why not end their misery? These are individuals for whom nothing can be done except to maintain the status quo. Intervening directly to end their lives will end their misery. This continues to be the primary and most compelling argument for euthanasia. The fear of dying out of control because of uncontrollable pain is a powerful one. We cannot relieve this fear by assurances that we will control pain because frequently this means that physicians must sedate patients and keep them unconscious until death occurs. Thus, the person loses all autonomy and, therefore, his or her dignity. Although physicians control the pain, to be sure, the person is no longer there.

Third, such situations of helplessness and hopelessness take a serious toll on the family of patients. The inability of a family to do anything for their relative may cause pain and suffering almost as great as that experienced by the patient. Also, the dramatically increasing costs of medical care may totally deplete the resources of a family within days or weeks. Thus, voluntary euthanasia is justified because of the helpless condition of the patient and the greater good of the other family members.

# THE INTERNATIONAL EUTHANASIA DEBATE

## *The Netherlands*

As early as 1987, reports appeared describing the practice of euthanasia in the Netherlands. The discussion and practice of

euthanasia are complex because Article 293 of the Dutch Constitution prohibits taking someone's life, even with his or her
explicit permission. A violation of this carries with it a sentence of
twelve years of imprisonment. Since 1972, no one has been convicted or imprisoned for violating this article in performing
euthanasia. In 1993, after about two decades of debate, "the Dutch
Parliament approved by a 91 to 45 vote a law that sanctioned
euthanasia under strict conditions."[6] Technically, this vote did not
repeal Article 293 but stated that such acts would not be prose-
cuted. The 2002 Termination of Life on Request and Assisted
Suicide Act essentially cataloged and presented Dutch case law on
euthanasia and physician-assisted suicide, which had developed
over about twenty-five years.[7] The conditions under which one can
perform euthanasia are: the patient must freely request it; the
patient must be informed and have the option of alternatives;
the decision must be a clear one and not a result of depression; the
patient must be experiencing unacceptable suffering; the physician
administering euthanasia must consult with another colleague; and
the act of euthanasia must be reported to the coroner.

This practice has attracted a great deal of attention and controversy. One element is the basic debate over whether euthanasia
is murder, even though done voluntarily. Another element is the
exact number of instances of euthanasia. In 1995, Dutch physicians received approximately 9,700 explicit requests for euthanasia or physician-assisted suicide, of which 37 percent were
honored.[8] An earlier report indicated that there were about one
thousand cases of euthanasia without a request by the patient.[9]

## Belgium

In May 2002, the Belgian House of Representatives passed
the Act Concerning Euthanasia, which became effective in
September of that year. In contrast to the Dutch law, the Belgian
act only explicitly addresses euthanasia, not physician-assisted
suicide. Adams and Nys write, however,

In our opinion the most likely explanation for the
exclusion of assisted suicide is concerned with the ide-

ological and political context within which the legislative process in Belgium was played out. From the very beginning of the parliamentary process, a hostile atmosphere prevailed between the government and opposition parties. Proponents and opponents of the bill did not hesitate from portraying each other as extremists (conservative or liberal) in the interests of political image formation. In this context, from the very beginning of the debate, the term "assisted suicide" for a great many members of Parliament came to mean literally simply killing someone at their request with no additional conditions....The fact that the distinction between the two Acts [i.e., between the Dutch and Belgian statutes] lies only in the way the physician goes about his work, was at a certain moment no longer relevant for many of those involved.[10]

According to one study in 2000, there were 2,501 cases in Flanders, Belgium, involving active termination of life; among these, 640 cases involved euthanasia and 65 involved assisted suicide.[11]

## Australia

On May 25, 1995, by a vote of fifteen to ten, the "Northern Territory Legislative Assembly became the first parliament in the world to legalize voluntary euthanasia."[12] To make the legislation binding, the government needed to proclaim it to enable euthanasia to be performed. In 1997, however, the Australian Federal Parliament overturned this legislation. An amendment made to the Northern Territory (Self-Government) Act 1978 of the Commonwealth made the Rights of the Terminally Ill Act of 1995 ineffective.[13]

## Switzerland

In contrast to the Netherlands, Belgium, and Australia, Switzerland has taken a unique approach to these practices.[14] In Switzerland, assisted suicide is legally permissible, and non-physicians can perform it: it is not exclusively *physician*-assisted suicide. In contrast, euthanasia is currently illegal; though the country is currently debating decriminalization of it.

# CONCLUSION

Because euthanasia is an intentional ending of a person's life, its practice raises serious moral difficulties. The contexts of these difficulties—the hopelessness of a patient's condition and the pain and suffering of the patient—are also important moral considerations. Thus, the ethical debate on voluntary euthanasia is between *motive* (mercy) and *rule* (do not murder) as well as between the value and dignity of life and the indignities to which a person is submitted during a terminal illness.

Euthanasia seems to be the perfect "American" response to several problems, whether for good or for ill. It is physiologically efficient in that the administration of an agent of euthanasia is fast-acting and there is no need to wait around for the disease to do its work. It is cost efficient—that is, inexpensive—in that one dose of the agent costs about the same as ten seconds of time in a nursing home. Euthanasia may also be the ultimate autonomous act in which the individual shapes not only his or her life but also his or her death. It represents a triumph of privacy over the family or community; it is the final marking-off of a zone of separateness from the intervention of all others. Euthanasia finally and ultimately puts us in control by giving us the last word on our lives. Combining, as it does, these many all-American values, how could one be rationally against it?

Let us make several observations as to why, despite its present popularity and cost effectiveness, euthanasia may have less to commend it than one might initially think.

Note that we are not arguing that disease is good, that pain and suffering are blessings, or that death is a joyful event, for they most certainly are not. What we are arguing is that disease and death are parts of life, and since we will not do away with them, we might better begin by rethinking some of our attitudes.

Particularly, we need to think about long-term quality care for our elderly.[15] This is one element in our society that we have tended to ignore. We seem more willing to spend billions of dollars on developing an implantable artificial heart than to spend that same amount of money on visiting-nurse programs or other assistance programs such as meal programs to ensure that seniors can live at home with dignity. We need to think about what we mean when we say our medical system is the best. Best with respect to what: high-tech interventions benefiting a relative few? Or rehabilitation interventions, quality primary care, and various prevention initiatives?

We also need to resist the cultural imperative that mandates intervention at all times and at all costs. Possibly the greatest service we can do for some elderly patients is to stop intervening and help them be comfortable in their last days. We might do well to implement the saying of the Buddha: "Don't just do something, stand there."

If families and patients knew they would have help, assistance, and companionship in the last months or days of an illness, we suspect the move for euthanasia would likely lose much of its impetus. For we rightly fear being prisoners of technology, we rightly fear interventions that prolong our dying, we rightly fear abandonment, and we rightly fear having no money to provide for our final days. A step toward allaying those fears would be a health care system that provides care and support as we live our final days.

Finally, the argument for euthanasia based on autonomy hinges on a narrow understanding of freedom. In fact, there are a few other ways to understand freedom. Proponents of euthanasia principally see freedom as a capacity to choose among several options: it is a *freedom of choice*. Alternatively, we might consider freedom to be a capacity to be who we really are or want to be: it is a *freedom of self-actualization*. If we believe that human persons are fundamentally relational, then a choice for euthanasia is the ultimate incarceration. Choosing to sever any possible community, to abandon oneself from community, could be the ultimate forfeiture of freedom, not an expression of it. Thus, euthanasia would close off any possible self-actualization, in community, as one journeys toward his or her transformation in death.

A practical problem in the euthanasia debate is that frequently when a person has considered the ethical issues in euthanasia and has opted for it, it is at precisely that moment that the person has neither the means nor the ability; that is, the person may not have the drug necessary to end his or her life or may lack the ability to swallow the drug, even if it were available. This dimension of the euthanasia debate leads us to the next phase of it—physician-assisted suicide—which we will consider in the following chapter.

## DISCUSSION QUESTIONS

1. Do you think the distinction between euthanasia and suicide is relevant?
2. Do you think that euthanasia is an autonomous and a private act, or are there social consequences to it as well?
3. Do you think legalizing euthanasia would complicate the physician-patient relationship?
4. Do you think that the legalization of euthanasia would open the door to other socially sanctioned forms of killing?
5. Do you agree with the practice of giving increasing levels of pain relievers, even though they may hasten the death of the patient?

## NOTES

1. Daniel Callahan, *The Troubled Dream of Life: In Search of a Peaceful Death* (Washington, DC: Georgetown University Press, 2000), 40–41 (italics in original).

2. See Paul Schotsmans and Tom Meulenbergs, eds., *Euthanasia and Palliative Care in the Low Countries* (Leuven: Peeters Publishers, 2005).

3. Tamar Lewin, "Ruling Sharpens Debate on 'Right to Die,'" *New York Times*, March 8, 1996, A14.

4. Judith A. C. Rietjens, Johannes J. M. van Delden, Agnes van der Heide, Astrid M. Vrakking, Bregje D. Onwuteaka-Philipsen, Paul J. van der Maas, and Gerrit van der Wal, "Terminal Sedation and Euthanasia: A Comparison of Clinical Practices," *Archives of Internal Medicine* 166 (April 10, 2006): 749–53.

5. Daniel Callahan, *What Kind of Life? The Limits of Medical Progress* (Washington, DC: Georgetown University Press, 1995).

6. Marlise Simons, "Dutch Parliament Approves Law Permitting Euthanasia," *New York Times*, February 10, 1995, A10.

7. Maurice Adams and Herman Nys, "Euthanasia in the Low Countries: Comparative Reflections on the Belgian and Dutch Euthanasia Act," in Schotsmans and Meulenbergs, *Euthanasia and Palliative Care*, 5–33.

8. Ilinka Haverkate, Bregje D. Onwuteaka-Philipsen, Agnes van der Heide, Piet J. Kostense, Gerrit van der Wal, and Paul J. van der Maas, "Refused and Granted Requests for Euthanasia and Assisted Suicide in the Netherlands: Interview Study with Structured Questionnaire," *British Medical Journal* 321 (October 7, 2000): 865–66.

9. Henk Jochemsen, "Euthanasia in Holland: An Ethical Critique of the New Law," *Journal of Medical Ethics* 20, no. 4 (December 1994): 213.

10. Adams and Nys, "Euthanasia in the Low Countries," 9.

11. L. Deliens, F. Mortier, J. Bilsen, M. Cosyns, R. Stichele, J. Vanoverloop, and K. Ingels, "End-of-Life Decisions in Medical Practice in Flanders, Belgium: A Nationwide Survey," *The Lancet* 356, no. 9244 (2000): 1806–11.

12. Peter Singer, "The Legislation of Voluntary Euthanasia in the Northern Territory," *Bioethics* 9, no. 5 (1995): 419.

13. See Legislative Assembly of the Northern Territory, "Select Committee on Euthanasia: Schedule 1—Amendment of the Northern Territory (Self-Government) Act 1978," http://www.nt.gov.au/lant/parliament/committees/rotti/euthlaw.shtml, accessed February 19, 2008.

14. See Samia A. Hurst and Alex Mauron, "Assisted Suicide and Euthanasia in Switzerland: Allowing a Role for Non-

Physicians," *British Medical Journal* 326 (February 1, 2003): 271–73.

15. For example, see Lisa Sowle Cahill, *Theological Bioethics: Participation, Justice, Change* (Washington, DC: Georgetown University Press, 2005), esp. 70–130.

# BIBLIOGRAPHY

Cahill, Lisa Sowle. *Theological Bioethics: Participation, Justice, Change.* Washington, DC: Georgetown University Press, 2005.

Callahan, Daniel. *The Troubled Dream of Life: In Search of a Peaceful Death.* Washington, DC: Georgetown University Press, 2000.

———. *What Kind of Life? The Limits of Medical Progress.* Washington, DC: Georgetown University Press, 1995.

Deliens, L., F. Mortier, J. Bilsen, M. Cosyns, R. Stichele, J. Vanoverloop, and K. Ingels. "End-of-Life Decisions in Medical Practice in Flanders, Belgium: A Nationwide Survey." *The Lancet* 356, no. 9244 (2000): 1806–11.

Haverkate, Ilinka, Bregje D. Onwuteaka-Philipsen, Agnes van der Heide, Piet J. Kostense, Gerrit van der Wal, and Paul J. van der Maas. "Refused and Granted Requests for Euthanasia and Assisted Suicide in the Netherlands: Interview Study with Structured Questionnaire." *British Medical Journal* 321 (October 7, 2000): 865–66.

Hurst, Samia A., and Alex Mauron. "Assisted Suicide and Euthanasia in Switzerland: Allowing a Role for Non-Physicians." *British Medical Journal* 326 (February 1, 2003): 271–73.

Jochemsen, Henk. "Euthanasia in Holland: An Ethical Critique of the New Law." *Journal of Medical Ethics* 20, no. 4 (December 1994): 212–17.

Keown, John, ed. *Euthanasia Examined: Ethical, Clinical, and Legal Perspectives.* New York: Cambridge University Press, 1995.

Lewin, Tamar. "Ruling Sharpens Debate on 'Right to Die.'" *New York Times.* March 8, 1996, A14.

Rietjens, Judith A. C., Johannes J. M. van Delden, Agnes van der Heide, Astrid M. Vrakking, Bregje D. Onwuteaka-Philipsen, Paul J. van der Maas, and Gerrit van der Wal. "Terminal

Sedation and Euthanasia: A Comparison of Clinical Practices." *Archives of Internal Medicine 166* (April 10, 2006): 749–53.

Scherer, Jennifer M. *Euthanasia and the Right to Die: A Comparative View.* Lanham, MD: Rowman & Littlefield Publishers, 1999.

Schotsmans, Paul, and Tom Meulenbergs, eds. *Euthanasia and Palliative Care in the Low Countries.* Leuven: Peeters Publishers, 2005.

Simons, Marlise. "Dutch Parliament Approves Law Permitting Euthanasia." *New York Times.* February 10, 1995, A10.

Singer, Peter. "The Legislation of Voluntary Euthanasia in the Northern Territory." *Bioethics* 9, no. 5 (1995): 419–24.

## Chapter 11

# PHYSICIAN-ASSISTED SUICIDE

## INTRODUCTION

A variation of the right to die discussion is the intense national debate over physician-assisted suicide. This debate recognizes what many proponents of euthanasia have argued for many years: there is a large number of individuals who want to end their lives but are unable to secure either necessary means or desirable means. For example, most of the drugs needed to end one's life are available only with a prescription. Because of legal risks, many physicians are reluctant to write such a prescription.

In the last few years, a major national debate has emerged over the issue of whether or not a physician might assist patients in ending their lives by providing appropriate and adequate medical means to do so. This is not voluntary euthanasia because neither the physician nor anyone else administers the drug or other agent to the patient. Rather, the physician lends assistance in that he or she provides access to the appropriate chemical agent for patients, but then these patients administer the agent to themselves. If this assistance were legal, the physician would be able to prescribe the appropriate dosage to achieve the end that patients desire.

In 1991 citizens in the state of Washington voted on Referendum 119, and in 1992 citizens in California voted on Referendum 161. These referenda sought to sanction legally both euthanasia and physician-assisted suicide, or physician-assisted dying. Voters defeated both of these referenda by very narrow margins—about 54 percent to 46 percent in both instances. In 1994, however, the citizens of Oregon were asked to vote on Measure 16, which asked "Shall law allow terminally ill adult Oregon patients voluntary informed choice to obtain physician's prescription for drugs to end life?"[1] Here, the measure passed, which ultimately led to the Oregon Death with Dignity Act (DDA).[2] The critical difference between the Oregon statute and those of Washington and California was its restriction to physician-assisted suicide only.

Eli Stutsman, the legal counsel for Oregon Right to Die, suggests this act appeals to three major groups: patients, health care professionals, and the public in general. First, the DDA is intended to advance the interests of patient autonomy by making the right to die through assisted suicide "a fundamental civil right." Second, the DDA would ensure that health care professionals can provide the form of care that best promotes the patient's welfare with guarantees of legal immunity. Finally, the DDA offers to the public a model of "reasonable regulation" of physician assistance in suicide with safeguards that the public will understand as being "sensible without being onerous."[3]

Oregonian voters approved this measure on November 8, 1994, by a very narrow margin, and thus Oregon at the time became "the only place in the world where doctors may legally help patients end their lives."[4] That was not the end of the story, however. The day before the measure was to become law, its enactment was "blocked by a court challenge." In August 1995, a federal judge ruled the measure unconstitutional because "with state-sanctioned and physician-assisted death at issue, some 'good results' cannot outweigh other lives lost due to unconstitutional errors and abuses."[5]

In March 1996, the situation in the nine western states in the jurisdiction of the United States Court of Appeals for the Ninth Circuit, including Oregon, changed radically. In an eight to three opinion, this court struck down a Washington State statute that made assisting in a suicide a felony. While this ruling held only for the states in the Ninth Circuit, a very critical precedent was set. The grounds for the ruling were privacy and autonomy. Judge Stephen Reinhardt, writing for the majority, said: "Like the decision of whether or not to have an abortion, the decision how and when to die is one of 'the most intimate and personal choices a person may make in a lifetime,' a choice 'central to personal dignity and autonomy.'"[6] The ruling also argued that not only doctors should be protected from prosecution "but others like pharmacists and family members 'whose services are essential to help the terminally ill patient obtain and take' medication to hasten death" should be protected as well.[7] Thus, the door was opened for a round of appeals and argumentation. This position was reinforced by a unanimous ruling of the three-judge Second Circuit Court of Appeals in New York in April 1996. This court ruled "that doctors in New York State could legally help terminally ill patients commit suicide in certain circumstances."[8] As the ruling was appealed, a critical bicoastal debate began.

Moreover, the state of Michigan passed a law explicitly prohibiting physician-assisted suicide. This was in response to the activities of Jack Kevorkian, MD, many of whose activities include physician-assisted suicide. This law has passed out of existence, however, because of the time limits imposed in the original passage of this law. Furthermore, Kevorkian was brought to trial for acts committed while this law was in effect but was found not guilty based on the jury's decision that his intent was to relieve pain, not to cause death. Nevertheless, another murder charge was made against Kevorkian in 1999; in this case, he was convicted and sentenced to prison.

In November 2008, Washington voters passed a new ballot measure allowing physician-assisted suicide. This proposition, Initiative 1000, passed with a wider margin than in Oregon: 59 percent to 41 percent. According to one article, the law would impose safeguards and procedures comparable to the Oregon law.[9]

Finally, as we mentioned in the last chapter, three U.S. Supreme Court cases have become landmark cases in the legal and ethical debates over physician-assisted suicide. In 1997, the U.S. Supreme Court adjudicated on two related cases.[10] First, the main question before the Court in *Vacco v. Quill* was whether New York's prohibition on assisting suicide violated the Equal Protection Clause of the Fourteenth Amendment. The Court held that it did not. Second, the main question before the Court in *Washington v. Glucksberg* was whether the "liberty" (i.e., the right to refuse wanted life-saving medical treatment) specifically protected by the Due Process Clause includes a right to commit suicide, which includes a right to assistance in suicide. The court held that the "right" to assistance in suicide is not a fundamental liberty interest protected by the Due Process Clause. In the 2006 case of *Gonzalez v. Oregon*, the main question before the Court was whether the Controlled Substances Act allows the U.S. attorney general to prohibit doctors from prescribing regulated drugs for use in physician-assisted suicide, notwithstanding a state law prohibiting it.[11] Previously, the court of appeals held that the interpretive rule exercised by the attorney general to restrict use of certain drugs was invalid; the Supreme Court held that the court of appeals was correct: its decision was affirmed. In effect, these cases demonstrate that (a) it is not unconstitutional for states to ban assisted suicide while at the same time protecting patients' rights to refuse life-sustaining treatment; (b) one cannot claim that physician-assisted suicide is a fundamental liberty interest protected in the same way as the right to refuse treatment; and (c) the executive branch at the federal level cannot use the Controlled Substances Act to restrict physician-assisted suicide at the state level (which basically protects the practice of physician-assisted suicide in Oregon and Washington).

## VOLUNTARY EUTHANASIA VERSUS PHYSICIAN-ASSISTED SUICIDE

Timothy Quill, MD, became one of the leading spokespersons for physician-assisted suicide. In 1991, Quill published a very moving and compelling case study entitled "Death and Dignity: A Case of Individualized Decision Making" in the *New England Journal of Medicine*.[12] In it, he recounted the case of "Diane," a long-term patient who, having successively come to terms with several other difficulties in her life, was diagnosed with cancer. She elected not to have therapy because of her judgment that the low probability of success did not justify the burdens of the therapy. She wished to die under her own control, however. This led to several discussions with Quill through which he came to understand her position. He prescribed appropriate medication for her to end her life when she wanted. After having made her farewells to her family, Diane asked to be left alone. She then took the drugs and died as she wished within an hour.

The publication of this article set off a major debate not only because of what was done but also because Quill signed his name to it. Furthermore, the case was extremely compelling, and many could identify with Diane, Quill, and all the tragedy and sorrow of the case. Nonetheless, the practice of physician-assisted suicide raises critical issues that simply cannot be resolved by appeals to compassion, no matter how tragic the case.

As we described in the last chapter, there are several reasons why one should distinguish voluntary euthanasia from physician-assisted suicide. One, in voluntary euthanasia someone other than the patient (or requester) commits the act; in physician-assisted suicide the patient commits the suicide with the cooperation of the physician. Two, in addition to differing agents, the contexts of voluntary euthanasia and physician-assisted suicide also tend to differ. Physician-assisted suicide can be a private matter, at home and in solitude; that is, it can occur in a nonmedical context away from the public. In contrast, voluntary euthanasia is a public event; at a minimum, it occurs between two people: the patient and the physician or person committing the act. Furthermore, voluntary euthanasia tends to occur in a medical context. Three, in voluntary euthanasia, the death of the patient is not only anticipated, it is generally imminent; in physician-assisted suicide, the death of the patient may be anticipated, but it is likely not imminent. This reinforces the first reason: physician-assisted suicide requires that patients have the ability to self-administer the lethal agent *before they lose that ability*. Furthermore, there is less of a tendency to confuse physician-assisted suicide with palliative care than there is with voluntary euthanasia.

# ETHICAL ISSUES IN PHYSICIAN-ASSISTED SUICIDE

## *The Pro–Physician-Assisted Suicide Perspective*

In many ways, the case for physician-assisted suicide is an extension of many of the battles in bioethics over the last decades to secure various rights: autonomy, informed consent, and the right to refuse treatment. Thus, the primary argument for physician-assisted suicide is that this is a matter of patients' choices, a matter of their values, and expressions of their desire to control how they die. One can describe the decision for physician-assisted suicide as an autonomous, free choice of the patient, and one, therefore, that we should respect. To refuse such a choice is to tell someone we know what is best for him or her. This is paternalism at its worst because we impose an alien set of values on a competent patient. Thus, to prohibit physician-assisted suicide is to violate the cornerstone of American bioethics: autonomy.

Second, one can justify physician-assisted suicide as a way of relieving pain and suffering. As Quill says, "One of our most troubling challenges as physicians and caregivers is to respond to these patients for whom comprehensively applied comfort care is unable to adequately relieve their suffering, so that death seems the only sensible escape."[13] Many patients afflicted with various diseases do not have easy or peaceful deaths. Frequently these deaths are drawn out, filled with pain and suffering.

Third, physician-assisted suicide should be an option for persons who are not on life-support out of fairness; here, the moral argument rests on justice as equal opportunity to choose death. In this way, one can remove those who are on life-support systems, such as a ventilator or hemodialysis, from these machines and let them die rather rapidly and painlessly. This seems unfair to those who are not being similarly supported and are left to suffer through their last days. As Quill notes, "Those who are dependent on life-sustaining treatments are the only patients who receive the medical right to choose death."[14] Some respond to this situation by secretly planning their own death and act on their own to take their lives. However, "the notion that such patients have to face this agonizing decision alone, often in secrecy, violates basic principles of humane care."[15]

The key ethical issues, then, for physician-assisted suicide are the motive of mercy (i.e., to relieve patients of pain and suffering), respect for self-determination, and the role of physicians in not abandoning the ones for whom they care. These are surrounded by a desire to expand the concept of humane medical care by including in it the option for assisting the patient in committing suicide.

## The Anti–Physician-Assisted Suicide Perspective

Not all are in favor of this expansion of medical care to include physician-assisted suicide. First, many recognize that there is a problem in that we still consider death the enemy and we resist it as long and as intensely as possible. The solution to this problem would seem to be recognizing that death is a part of life and that one need not resist it as long as possible. While this will not solve all problems raised by those who support physician-assisted suicide, it will go a long way toward decreasing the pressure for that solution. If we respect people's decisions about the removal of therapies, this will diminish the fear and reality that one's death is more dependent on technological failure than on the disease itself.

Second, in contrast to cooperating in the death of a patient, physicians, like other people, often have an aversion to death and seek to avoid it. This avoidance behavior could cause physicians to abandon patients while they are dying. "The problem of medical abandonment will not be solved by legalizing physician-assisted suicide. The problem may be worsened by such legalization because it would instruct patients and physicians that when death looms, a quick exit is the approved treatment."[16] In other words, attempts to apply such a quick fix to suffering may be a more subtle form of medical abandonment.

Third, the New York State Task Force on Life and the Law made an interesting distinction. It argued that "the imposition of life-sustaining medical treatment against a patient's will requires a direct invasion of bodily integrity and, in some cases, the use of physical restraints, both of which are flatly inconsistent with society's basic conception of personal dignity." The right against bodily intrusion is not "a general right to control the timing and manner of death [that in turn] forms the basis of the constitutional right to refuse life-sustaining treatment."[17] This is an important distinction because frequently one understands the right to refuse treatment as derived from the right to privacy, which is then extended to cover individual decisions in cases of physician-assisted suicide. The argument is misplaced, however, because the right to be free from bodily intrusion is not a privacy right but rather one of personal dignity manifested through bodily integrity. Therefore, the right to refuse treatment cannot be used to justify physician-assisted suicide.

Finally, there is the morality of suicide itself. The moral question is whether humans have this degree of responsibility over their lives. Many argue that such an act exceeds human responsibility and is a violation of human dignity. Thus, even though one is sympathetic to the situation of the patient, many judge the use of suicide to relieve pain to be immoral.

## Procedural Issues

All recognize that physician-assisted suicide is not something that one should enter into easily or without some safeguards. The issues are critical, and the outcome is clear and lethal. The following safeguards are from the Oregon DDA (§3.01):[18]

1. Determination of whether the patient (1) has a terminal disease; (2) is capable of making this decision [for physician-assisted suicide]; and (3) has made the request voluntarily and free of any coercion.
2. Provision of information to the patient including the patient's medical diagnoses, prognosis, potential risks associated with the medications under consideration, probable result of taking the medications, and feasible alternatives.
3. Referral of the patient to another consulting physician for confirmation of medical information, the patient's capacity to make decisions, and that the patient made the decision voluntarily.
4. Referral for psychological counseling if appropriate.
5. Request that the patient notify his or her next-of-kin.
6. Provision of information to the patient regarding the opportunity the patient has to rescind his or her decision at any time.

7. Verification, immediately prior to writing the prescription, that the patient is making an informed
   decision.
8. Fulfillment of documentation requirements in the
   patient's medical record.
9. Assurance that all steps were carried out in accordance with the Act prior to writing the lethal prescription.

These criteria seem to be reasonable, responsible, and adequate.
They also are comparable to the guidelines Quill proposed.[19] The
patient is protected, the physician is safeguarded, autonomy is
upheld, and the patient's wishes will be respected. All is seemingly well.

Yet, some issues may emerge. First, while suffering is a critical
element in any disease and particularly terminal ones, it is not the
same as pain and is not the immediate responsibility of the physician. Pain is a consequence of a particular biological situation; suffering occurs from an interpretation of one's situation. Obviously
the two are related, but it is unclear how the primary role of the
physician should relate to suffering versus pain. Clearly a physician
will be concerned about the suffering of a patient, but he or she
may not have particular expertise or responsibility in that area.

Second, who is the judge of when suffering, to use Quill's
terminology, is "severe, unrelenting, and intolerable"? Some may
judge that the mere diagnosis of a terminal illness constitutes
such a level of suffering. Others may think it is unfair that there
may be a type of "suffering quota" one has to endure before one
can gain assistance. Data suggest that the principal reason why
patients seek physician-assisted suicide is fear of losing autonomy, control, or dignity; it is not a fear or experience of pain.[20]

Third, what qualifications should the consulting physician
have, and can he or she have a prior relation to the patient? Also,
what if the consulting physician disagrees with either the patient
or the attending physician? The guidelines are unclear here.

Finally, while documentation is appropriate, what is its purpose? Quill suggests that the documentation will give assurance
to the participants that "they will be free from criminal prosecu-

tion for their role in assisting the patient to die."[21] Should not the motivation rather be to ensure that the rights of the patient are protected? Furthermore, who receives the documentation? If the hospital personnel receive it, what are they to do with it? Conflict of interest issues loom large here, too. Should the government receive and review these data? While this would be certain to cause apoplexy among the antigovernment forces, at least a government agency might have fewer conflicts of interest.

## CONCLUSION

The practices of euthanasia and physician-assisted suicide have been occurring in the Netherlands over the last twenty-five years under moderately controlled circumstances. Over the last decade, two interesting developments have occurred. First, the practice of aiding in suicide has been extended to psychiatric patients: the context has expanded from suffering caused by bodily dysfunction to a range that includes suffering caused by mental anguish.[22] Two factors play a part in this extension: (1) suffering is caused not only by somatic diseases, and (2) patients with mental illnesses are not always incompetent. A 1994 decision by the Dutch Supreme Court was important in this connection. A fifty-year-old woman who suffered severe depression because of the failure of her marriage and the death of her two sons—one from suicide and one from a terminal illness—wished to end her life. A psychiatrist assisted her in this request. Two lower courts acquitted him, but the psychiatrist was found guilty—but not punished—by the Supreme Court. "According to the Supreme Court, the psychiatrist had acted sufficiently carefully in all respects except the last one: the experts he had consulted had not themselves examined the patient. Therefore he was convicted." No one, however, challenged his aiding the patient in dying. The critical issue here is the extension of criteria from somatic disease to mental illness. The next question is: "What if a person's suffering is not caused by a disease, not even by a mental illness?"[23]

A second issue is the growing discomfort with many doctors who perform euthanasia: the context and professionalism of medicine are shifting to a preference for physician-assisted suicide over euthanasia. From the perspective of some physicians, it is better if patients do the deed themselves. The continuing question in this regard will be what to do with individuals who are not physically able to perform the act by themselves. Additionally, many in the disability rights movement worry about these debates precisely because they may be threatened and are vulnerable to the judgment—in a slippery slope argument—that they may be targets for euthanasia. Or, they may see that physician-assisted suicide offers a seductive exit to life's problems. How can we protect them when the culture around us is building momentum toward these options?

Finally, the perceptions of medicine as a profession continue to shift and to change. How will we think of physicians as physician-assisted suicide becomes more pervasive in society? Will the practice of physician-assisted suicide further erode patients' trust in doctors and health care institutions? Will physician-assisted suicide infuse new—and some would say inappropriate— goals (i.e., assistance in causing death) with more traditional goals (e.g., healing, curing, and preventing disease) in the practice of medicine?

## DISCUSSION QUESTIONS

1. Do you see any dangers in physician-assisted suicide?
2. What benefits are there in this practice?
3. Is it important to distinguish between pain and suffering in thinking about physician-assisted suicide?
4. Should physician-assisted suicide be limited to somatic illnesses, or should mental illnesses be included as well?
5. Do you think procedural safeguards such as those suggested by Oregon's Death with Dignity Act will protect patients against abuses?

# NOTES

1. Quoted in Courtney S. Campbell, "The Oregon Trail to Death: Measure 16," *Commonweal* 121, no. 14 (August 19, 1994): 9.

2. See "The Oregon Death with Dignity Act," in *Contemporary Issues in Bioethics*, 7th ed., ed. Tom L. Beauchamp, LeRoy Walters, Jeffrey P. Kahn, and Anna C. Mastroianni (Belmont, CA: Thomson Wadsworth, 2008), 404–6.

3. Campbell, "Oregon Trail to Death," 9.

4. Timothy Egan, "Suicide Law Placing Oregon on Several Uncharted Paths," *New York Times*, November 25, 1994, A1.

5. "Judge Strikes Down Oregon's Suicide Law," *New York Times*, August 4, 1995, A15.

6. Tamar Lewin, "Ruling Sharpens Debate on 'Right to Die,'" *New York Times*, March 8, 1996, A14.

7. Ibid.

8. Frank Bruni, "Federal Ruling Allows Doctors to Prescribe Drugs to End Life," *New York Times*, April 3, 1996, A1.

9. Jane Gross, "Landscape Evolves for Assisted Suicide," *New York Times* (www.nytimes.com), published November 10, 2008; accessed January 20, 2009.

10. See Beauchamp et al., *Contemporary Issues in Bioethics*, 407–12.

11. Ibid., 413–18.

12. Timothy Quill, "Death and Dignity: A Case of Individualized Decision Making," *New England Journal of Medicine* 324 (March 7, 1991): 691–94. The article is also available in Quill's book *Death and Dignity: Making Choices and Taking Charge* (New York: W. W. Norton, 1993).

13. Quill, *Death and Dignity*, 98.

14. Ibid., 109.

15. Ibid., 107.

16. Robert A. Burt, "Death Made Too Easy," *New York Times*, November 16, 1994, A19.

17. The New York State Task Force on Life and the Law. Quoted in Yale Kamisar, "Assisted Suicide and Euthanasia: The Cases Are in the Pipeline," *Trial* 30, no. 12 (December 1994): 30, 32, 34–35.

18. See "Oregon Death with Dignity Act" in Beauchamp et al., *Contemporary Issues in Bioethics*, 404.

19. Quill, *Death and Dignity*, 162–63.

20. See Oregon Department of Human Services, "Eighth Annual Report on Oregon's Death with Dignity Act," http://www.oregon.gov/DHS/ph/pas/docs/year8.pdf, March 9, 2006, accessed February 19, 2008.

21. Quill, *Death and Dignity*, 164.

22. Sjef Gevers, "Physician Assisted Suicide: New Developments in the Netherlands," *Bioethics* 9 (1995): 310.

23. Ibid., 311, 312.

## BIBLIOGRAPHY

Beauchamp, Tom L., LeRoy Walters, Jeffrey P. Kahn, and Anna C. Mastroianni. *Contemporary Issues in Bioethics*. 7th ed. Belmont, CA: Thomson Wadsworth, 2008.

Bruni, Frank. "Federal Ruling Allows Doctors to Prescribe Drugs to End Life." *New York Times*. April 3, 1996, A1.

Burt, Robert A. "Death Made Too Easy." *New York Times*. November 16, 1994, A19.

Campbell, Courtney S. "The Oregon Trail to Death: Measure 16." *Commonweal* 121, no. 14 (August 19, 1994): 9–11.

DuBose, Edwin R. *Physician Assisted Suicide: Religious and Public Policy Perspectives*. Chicago: Park Ridge Center, 1999.

Egan, Timothy. "Suicide Law Placing Oregon on Several Uncharted Paths." *New York Times*. November 25, 1994, A1.

Foley, Kathleen, and Herbert Hendin, eds. *The Case against Assisted Suicide: For the Right to End-of-Life Care*. Baltimore: Johns Hopkins University Press, 2002.

Gevers, Sjef. "Physician Assisted Suicide: New Developments in the Netherlands." *Bioethics* 9, no. 3 (July 1995): 309–12.

Gorsuch, Neil M. *The Future of Assisted Suicide and Euthanasia*. Princeton, NJ: Princeton University Press, 2006.

"Judge Strikes Down Oregon's Suicide Law." *New York Times*. August 4, 1995, A15.

Kamisar, Yale. "Assisted Suicide and Euthanasia: The Cases Are in the Pipeline." *Trial* 30, no. 12 (December 1994): 30, 32, 34–35.

Lewin, Tamar. "Ruling Sharpens Debate on 'Right to Die.'" *New York Times.* March 8, 1996, A14.

McLean, Sheila. *The Case for Physician Assisted Suicide.* London: Pandora, 1997.

Mitchell, John B. *Understanding Assisted Suicide: Nine Issues to Consider.* Ann Arbor: University of Michigan Press, 2007.

Oregon Department of Human Services. "Eighth Annual Report on Oregon's Death with Dignity Act." http://www.oregon.gov/DHS/ph/pas/docs/year8.pdf. Published March 9, 2006. Accessed February 19, 2008.

Quill, Timothy. "Death and Dignity: A Case of Individualized Decision Making." *New England Journal of Medicine* 324 (March 7, 1991): 691–94.

————. *Death and Dignity: Making Choices and Taking Charge.* New York: W. W. Norton, 1993.

Yount, Lisa. *Physician-Assisted Suicide and Euthanasia.* New York: Facts On File, 2000.

*PART IV*

---

# ISSUES IN BIOTECHNOLOGY

## Chapter 12

# GENETIC ENGINEERING: NONHUMAN ORGANISMS

## INTRODUCTION

To get a practical idea of how far we have come in the science of genetics and in applications through genetic technologies, one could read or reread *Brave New World* by Aldous Huxley, which he wrote in 1932. At that time, James Watson, Francis Crick, and Rosalind Franklin had not yet described the now instantly recognizable double-helix structure of the DNA molecule (1953), scientists had not thought of the technology of recombinant DNA (1970s), commercial interests had not patented new life-forms (1980s), clinical researchers had yet to design and perform the first gene therapy (1990), and the public collaborative initiative, the Human Genome Project, and the private company, Celera Genomics, had not completed the sequence of nucleotides of the human genome (2001–2003).[1]

Yet, Huxley assumed or used these and other technologies in his book. On the one hand, one can regard—and perhaps dismiss—the book as a particularly lucky, though inspired, guess about future technological developments. On the other hand, the book clearly reveals how far and how rapidly one can go when individuals in power obtain the critical insight. Absent the aspects of the mass production of fetuses, the capacity to get ninety individuals out of a single egg, some manufacturing details, and the sociopolitical system favorable to such a process, we can do almost everything Huxley described.

Along with these new and tremendous powers has come a new attitude toward science. Traditionally, scientists studied natural phenomena to understand them, to be able to formulate the laws that stood behind nature. Thus, the major purpose of science was *to describe* nature. Scientists achieved their primary purpose when they were able to formulate basic laws that described how nature operated.

Two major events changed that orientation, though such a change was not their primary intent.[2] The first event was the expansion of applied research, primarily in physics, that led to the building and detonation of the atomic bomb. In this research, the intent was not so much to discover and describe the laws of nature as to discover, describe, and then *use* the laws of nature to achieve a particular goal. This marks a shift from basic to applied research. The second event was the discovery and description of the structure of the DNA molecule by Watson, Crick, and Franklin in 1953. This discovery opened the door to significant developments in genetics, which culminated in a capacity to recombine genetic material from one organism into another to make a new entity. These discoveries gave human beings the capacity to *change* nature.

We have now—under the general heading of genetic engineering—a large number of capacities that enable us to intervene at a basic and fundamental level into nature—including human life—and change it according to our designs and wishes. This capacity to change nature and redesign it raises several ethical problems. In this chapter, we will describe several types of interventions in the plant and animal world and the ethical problems they raise, both specifically and generally.

## Notes on Terms

First, it is important to note that the word *gene* can mean many different things, which has implications for how we interpret and understand biotechnology in general and genetic engineering in particular. The era of modern genetics arose around the turn of the twentieth century marked by the rediscovery of Mendelian genetics. This caused many debates including those involving theories of inheritance and "genetic material." Ernst Mayr, a naturalist and philosopher of biology, suggested that the main problem in this early era was the ambiguity between phenotype and genotype and an insufficient understanding of the concept of the gene.

In describing how to define the word *gene*, Petter Portin, a philosopher, suggests that an operational definition of a gene includes four phenomena: genetic transmission, genetic recombination, gene mutation, and gene function.[3] Genetic transmission means the ability to transmit genetic information from one generation to the next. Genetic recombination is the capacity for genetic information (e.g., whole genes or parts of chromosomes) to recombine in different configurations and combinations in offspring. Genetic mutation is the phenomenon where genetic information can spontaneously change. For example, single nucleotide polymorphisms (SNPs) are well-known forms of genetic mutations that sometimes cause genetic disease. Finally, gene function is the ability of cells and genetic information to express genes as proteins or to control the expression of genes. These capacities are interdependent; for example, one cannot have genetic transmission without gene function. Therefore, a gene can be a biochemical structure (i.e., a nucleotide sequence), a unit of inheritance, and a set of information.

Given the last understanding of the word *gene*, one can see that genetic engineering is the intentional modification of genetic information in an organism for human purposes. There are a number of ways to modify an organism's genetic information. Two examples are traditional cross-pollination of plant species or animal husbandry and breeding techniques. In addition, if one had enough patience, one could change the environment of an organism and let natural selection effect the desired change(s). For the purposes of this chapter, however, we are principally discussing genetic modifications where scientists employ recombinant DNA (rDNA) technology.

## GENETIC ENGINEERING OF NONHUMAN ORGANISMS

The rise of recombinant DNA technology in molecular biology and genetics in the 1970s was a culmination of research and technology development beginning in the 1950s. By 1970, all the techniques necessary for controlled genetic engineering with bacteria were available. The major scientific and technological breakthrough that enabled the first genetic engineering and gene transfer experiments of the early 1970s involved restriction enzymes, which allowed researchers to cut DNA at specific locations and splice in new segments of DNA. The first genetic engineering experiments involved prokaryotic organisms (bacteria) and bacteriophages (viruses). Between 1970 and 1971, two independent research groups used restriction enzymes to splice DNA while using viruses as vectors to carry the new genetic information into cells. Peter Lobban and Paul Berg of Stanford University independently developed similar processes.[4]

The initial impetus for these projects was to use bacteria as factories to produce mammalian proteins. As the work of Lobban and Berg became known in 1972 and 1973, several researchers set out to collaborate on a genetic engineering project to explore their findings. In the fall of 1972, Herbert Boyer, Robert Helling, Stanley Cohen, and Annie Chang worked together to splice DNA from one species into another. This research group chose to use bacteria plasmids instead of viruses as vectors because the restriction enzymes they were using cut the viral genetic code in multiple places, making precise control of DNA splicing virtually impossible. In 1973, this group had successfully transferred toad DNA into the bacterium *E. Coli*. The research team was also able to replicate the bacterium and confirm that the toad DNA was transcribed into RNA.[5]

After these initial genetic engineering experiments, which include the first gene transfers across species, genetic engineering entered the commercial arena between 1976 and 1979, thus ushering in the biotechnology industry. Since the first successful gene transfer experiments, the technology continues to grow rapidly and is evolving constantly. The rise of recombinant DNA (rDNA) technology also marks the entry into a new era. Since life forms on Earth share the same basic genetic material (DNA or RNA), we can, in principle, apply rDNA technology to modify the genetic information of those life forms. Thus, plants, animals, fungi, bacteria, and viruses are all open to genetic modification for human purposes.

## Agricultural Biotechnology: Plants

There are four basic categories of plant-based genetic modifications in agricultural biotechnology (agbiotech). They are medicine-added, nutrition-added, protection-added, and production-added plants.

1. *Medicine-added plants*: Here, one genetically engineers plants in such a way that infuses medicinal value. The basic paradigm for this has been the development of edible vaccines in plants, like bananas or potatoes.[6] Proponents argue that medicine-added plants will facilitate delivery of medicine and vaccines to individuals in whose communities it would otherwise be difficult to do so (e.g., in rural areas and/or developing countries). This could be because the community lacks clean needles, trained professionals, or other infrastructures necessary to deliver these health care products safely.

2. *Nutrition-added plants*: Like medicine-added plants, nutrition-added plants contain an added value that promotes good health in human beings. A primary example of this type of plant is golden rice.[7] Developers of golden rice sought to alleviate health problems due to malnutrition, especially vitamin A deficiency (e.g., blindness), by genetically engineering rice to produce beta-carotene, the precursor to vitamin A. Taken together, we generally recognize the food that medicine-added plants and nutrition-added plants produce as *functional foods*. Commentators refer to the enriched nature of these plants as *biofortification*.

3. *Protection-added plants*: Protection-added plants use genes for proteins that confer greater protection against pesticides, herbicides, or the pests themselves. Thus, developers desire for these plants to be more hardy and resilient if farmers apply the appropriate pesticides or herbicides: only the pests or

weeds feel the effect of the poisons in these chemicals, not the agricultural plant itself. In turn, the hope is also to reduce the overall amount of chemical pesticides and herbicides used. The development of *Bt* corn and *Bt* cotton are examples of protection-added plants. Scientists spliced genes from the bacterium *Bacillus thuringiensis* that produces a toxic chemical to insect pests. Thus, the plants themselves produce these toxins to ward off pesky pests on their own. Controversy ensued, however, when some data began to surface that showed these plants affected populations of Monarch butterflies.[8]

4. *Production-added plants*: Rather than protection, production-added plants use genes for proteins that increase farmers' yields or that allow the plants to grow in areas where they would otherwise be unable to grow. For example, scientists have spliced into plants genes that confer resistance to high-salt content soil, allowing the plants to grow in desert conditions. Similarly, Calgene developed a now-famous tomato, the Flavr Savr, which was resistant to rotting. Likewise, DNA Plant Technology Corp. developed a tomato with a gene from an arctic flounder in order to confer resistance to frost. Thus, tomato crops could be protected from unexpected frosts and/or farmers could expand the seasonal harvests into colder months.[9]

## Agricultural Biotechnology: Animals

Like plants, we can genetically engineer animals to serve human needs. In principle, the same four categories apply for animals. There has been less success, however, in developing and commercializing agbiotech in animals. This lack of success has to do with social perspectives on genetic modification in general as well as biological (e.g., reproductive) and logistical limitations. Nevertheless, scientists continue to pursue this aspect of agbiotech, and there are interesting developments on several fronts.

1. *Medicine-added animals*: Medicine-added animals contain genes that produce proteins that make the animals clinically useful for human beings. For example, in xenotransplantation, scientists splice into a pig certain human genes so that the surfaces of the cells of the pig's organs contain human proteins. In this way, the human recipient's immune system will be more likely to recognize the pig's organ as "human" rather than "porcine." In another example, scientists genetically engineer dairy cows to produce therapeutic proteins in their milk. This increases the manufacturing capacity for these proteins.[10]

2. *Nutrition-added animals*: Here, scientists use genetic engineering to produce nutrition-added animals. This means that the animals could possess leaner meat or more nutritious meat.[11]

3. *Protection-added animals*: Some developers use genetic engineering to confer disease resistance to farm animals. Thus, farmers are less dependent on veterinary interventions to save or to protect their livestock.

4. *Production-added animals*: In production-added animals, scientists splice genes for proteins that promote a particular characteristic or add a new characteristic in which human beings are interested. For example, one may engineer dairy cattle to produce greater amounts of milk without injecting specific hormones. Likewise, one may engineer beef cattle to be beefier, thus increasing the yield of meat. In addition, scientists have genetically engineered a goat to produce spider silk in its milk. Spider silk, the stuff out of which a spider makes its web, has a tensile strength-to-weight ratio that is very desirable for building materials and other human uses. It is practically impossible for one to rely on spiders to produce the amounts of spider silk necessary. Thus, like

producing therapeutic proteins, developers use animals as biological factories, or bioreactors, to produce the desired substances. In recent developments, scientists are combining recombinant DNA technology with cell-based biotechnologies (i.e., nuclear transfer) to increase quality production in livestock (see chapter 14).[12]

A related use of biotechnology includes the development of recombinant bovine growth hormone (rBGH) farmers use in cattle. In this case, scientists genetically modify bacteria to produce the hormone that farmers apply to their livestock. So, the cattle are not genetically modified directly, but one uses genetic engineering to increase production of milk.[13]

## Health Care and Biotechnology

In addition to using plants and animals to produce and, in some cases, deliver medicines or vaccines, one can apply genetic engineering in a variety of ways for human health care outside of agriculture. While clinicians can utilize biotechnology on human beings themselves, we will address those interventions in the next chapter. There are two ways, however, one can use biotechnology in this context that we will discuss here: (1) the use of animals as models for human diseases and (2) the use of microbes as factories that manufacture human therapeutic proteins.

1. *Animal Models for Research*: Generally, scientists perform research in animals before they do research in human beings. This is to protect humans and minimize the potential harms that the research might cause them. Scientists also use this research to weed out potential products that will likely fail when used in human beings. In order to test products and perform clinically relevant research on animals, however, scientists need to show how the biology of an animal relates to the biology of a human being. To do this, scientists seek animal models for human dis-

eases. There are a variety of ways one can accomplish this. For example, scientists genetically engineer transgenic mice with human genes; they splice a human gene (or genes) into the mouse genome. These genes result in the mice contracting human or humanlike diseases such as cancer and Alzheimer's disease. Another example is the knockout mouse. In these mice, particular genes are shut off, or knocked out, in order to understand the effects of that gene's function. Since scientists can measure the relatedness of mice genes to human genes, and because humans and mice are similar in genetically important ways, these mice prove to be valuable research tools.

2. *Microbes as Bioreactors*: Scientists and others in the biotechnology industry use microbes in a variety of ways. One use of microorganisms is the bioreactor. One can genetically modify bacteria and grow them in big vats in order to produce massive quantities of a therapeutic protein or other substance humans use in health care. Examples of this include the use of the bacterium *E. Coli* to produce human insulin for diabetes patients. In 1982, the recombinant human insulin produced through *E. Coli* by Genentech was the first biotechnology product that received FDA approval.[14]

## Industrial and Environmental Biotechnology

Industrial or environmental uses of biotechnology include a wide range of goods, including food, energy, chemicals, pollution prevention, and fabric. In fact, the Biotechnology Industry Organization (BIO) claims that biotechnology is fostering a cleaner, more sustainable industrial revolution.[15] Biotechnology enables the convergence and merging of previously separate industrial sectors: farmers of corn, for example, can now participate in the development of energy (e.g., ethanol) and of chemicals (e.g., by-products of the production of ethanol, which could include nylon).

1. *Protecting the Environment with Oil-Eating Bacteria*: One way to protect the environment through biotechnology is the application of oil-eating bacteria.[16] Here, scientists have genetically modified a common bacterium to thrive off of spilled oil. Using the bacteria in this way accelerates the clean-up process after an accidental oil spill.

2. *Promoting Public Health with Arthropods*: Another health-related use of biotechnology is the development of genetically modified arthropods (e.g., insects) or their bacterial symbionts. For example, scientists genetically engineer mosquitoes to be sterile and release the modified insects to mate with wild mosquitoes, thus controlling the population of malaria- or West Nile virus–carrying bugs. Alternatively, scientists can engineer the bacteria that live inside particular insects to control the spread of diseases.[17]

3. *Producing Biofuels from Biomass*: One area of industrial biotechnology that has received a lot of attention recently is the production of energy sources (called *biofuels*). This reduces dependence on foreign oil and increases national security. To produce biofuels, scientists engineer bacteria to process leftover plant material and wood (e.g., from agriculture, grass clippings, or forestry), which is called biomass, into ethanol, biodiesel, or other chemicals.[18]

4. *Ensuring National Security and Germ Warfare*: One unfortunate use of biotechnology in nonhuman organisms includes the development of germ warfare or biological weapons.[19] While officially the United States can only use biotechnology to develop defenses against biological weapons, the distinction between a defense and an offense in germ warfare may be difficult to determine. In this context, scientists can develop special vaccines or other defenses against weapons and/or they can develop "super-

bugs" that one can release against the soldiers (or entire population) of the enemy.

# ETHICAL ISSUES IN GENETIC ENGINEERING OF NONHUMAN ORGANISMS

## Benefits to Human Beings

The genetic engineering of nonhuman organisms provides several potential benefits to human beings. First, scientists can improve health care for human beings by using plants, animals, or microbes to manufacture therapeutic proteins or other products. Second, scientists can promote good nutrition for human beings by adding nutritional value (e.g., provitamins, vitamins, or other beneficial substances) to edible plants. We can also accomplish this by enabling farming and food production in impoverished areas such as deserts in developing nations. Third, scientists gain valuable knowledge about the world and human beings, which has a value in itself. In addition, one can apply that knowledge to develop new technologies or other solutions to human needs. Finally, scientists can use biotechnology to increase national security. For example, one can accomplish this by decreasing dependence on foreign oil or energy sources as well as by increasing defenses against biological weapons.

## Risks of Harm to Human Beings

However, the genetic engineering of nonhuman organisms also poses several potential risks to human beings. One, the genetic modifications may expose humans to significant health risks caused by allergies. Novel substances in the genetically modified organism (GMO) or existing substances in the GMO can induce a serious immune response. Here, one question is what constitutes a "new" substance. On the one hand, genetic engineering could result in a brand-new, never-occurred-before-in-nature protein, which might cause an immune reaction. If the GMO or food product does contain a new substance, then developers need to submit it to the Food and Drug Administration (FDA), which will analyze it, label it, and regulate it (i.e., review its safety and, if approved, license it for the market in the United States). On the other hand, genetic engineering could result in a gene (and its corresponding product or function) that is new *for the particular species*. For example, scientists who introduced the arctic flounder gene into a tomato plant introduced a new gene for the tomato plant. The gene was not new itself—it occurs naturally in the fish—but it is new for the tomato. The gene is not altered or changed in any significant way; it is just relocated from the fish to the plant. Here, the newness is the result of genetic engineering between species. To respond to this question of newness, which would subject the product to FDA oversight, the FDA developed a safety assessment program within a regulatory framework to ensure the safety of foods and animal feeds.[20] For example, when one uses soybeans as food for domesticated animals, one must supplement the soybeans with the amino acid methionine. Thus, "[t]he 2S albumin gene from the Brazil-nut has been introduced into soybeans" to increase their nutritional quality.[21] Serum from these transgenic soybeans caused allergenic reactions in human beings allergic to Brazil nuts. Appropriate labeling and regulatory policies are necessary to address this issue.

Two, genetic engineering could result in diseases caused by new viruses or bacteria as well as increased resistance to antibiotics. For example, one safety issue arises from the use of rBGH to increase milk production. The problem has two impacts: one on cows and the other on human beings. For the cows, some veterinarians note that the use of this hormone puts stress on the cows, which weakens their immune system and leads to infections of the udders. The consequences of this include an increased use of antibiotics to counter these infections.[22] For humans, the impact would be on consumers. Here, the increased levels of these antibiotics and their residues in the food chain could harm people who drink milk produced with rBGH.

Three, genetic engineering could expose researchers to dangerous material or pathogens. Here, the scientists themselves are at risk while doing research or studying a genetically modified plant, animal, or microbe.

## Rights and Welfare of Other Organisms

Another issue involves the rights and welfare of animals, plants, and other organisms. To begin, the Union of Concerned Scientists identified a set of concerns in its 1993 report, *Perils Amidst the Promise*. The report identifies four issues. First, because of the vast array of new genes from which one can draw, this technology "can add more genes with harmful potential than traditional breeding." Second, "the organisms containing these new gene combinations may be less predictable in their traits and behaviors than those produced by traditional breeding." Third, because the genes being transferred are advantageous to plants, these plants could "overcome obvious limits on population growth." Finally, "we simply have no experience with the use and behavior of organisms with the novel genetic makeups of transgenics."[23]

Next, transgenic crops and livestock could create new viruses and diseases. In a process similar to the one in nature, Richard F. Allison, a plant virologist, and Ann E. Greene, a graduate student at the time, showed that "pieces of a virus that have been inserted through genetic engineering [to increase viral resistance] can combine with a newly introduced virus to make a new virus." Their concern is that "inserting such viral resistance into plants could lead to new, and perhaps more virulent, plant viruses."[24] Similarly, if one engineers an animal to be resistant to a particular pathogen, the pathogen could mutate to a new form to which the animal is not resistant. Such engineering can change the microenvironment of the pathogen, which "in turn could result in these pathogens becoming dangerous to humans or to other animals."[25]

Furthermore, one of the early issues evoked by the development of transgenic animals was the traditional one of animal rights and welfare. For several years now, there has been a growing animal rights movement that focuses on the use of animals in research, especially in what some consider frivolous research, such as the use of animals by the cosmetics industry. Another concern of the movement is the treatment of animals during research procedures, for example, intentionally blinding animals, destroying animals' brain centers, and infecting animals with diseases of interest to humans. Proponents of the animal rights movement also criticized the use of animals as practice models for surgical techniques. In addition, they denounced the housing of animals, which they claimed as inadequate. As a result of this outcry, researchers have made numerous changes in the housing of animals, established committees at research centers to evaluate the use of animals, and discontinued certain forms of research.

## Species Integrity

A new set of issues involved in genetically engineering non-human organisms includes the question of species integrity. More specifically, the use of rDNA across different species raises the question of whether scientists should protect the natural boundaries between species. Under natural circumstances, genes would not "jump" species because such organisms are what biologists call *reproductively isolated*: they do not reproduce with each other and therefore do not share genes. Though there are some examples of naturally shared genes, such as transposons in plants and insects, we know little about the effects of these jumper genes. Notwithstanding this possibility, scientists enter uncharted territory when they develop or test transgenic crops and livestock using genes from different species. Concerns here relate to the welfare of the genetically modified organism (and species) itself as well as to the potential impact on the environment (whether wilderness or farmland).

## Threats to Biodiversity and the Environment

One major concern with GMOs is the threat they pose to biodiversity and the environment. Naturalist Edward O. Wilson recognizes that diversity in ecosystems represents a significant value—both for the environment itself as well as for human beings.[26] The concern is that the more widespread GMOs are, the less diverse the environment becomes. Thus, the more susceptible to catastrophic damage the organisms are. For example, if entire crops are of a single, homogenous plant, that whole crop may be devastated by one infection. Entire yields and harvests may be lost. Thus, biodiversity supplies nature and ecosystems with the ability to adapt to different stresses—naturally occurring or induced by humans.

Other threats to the environment include the potential of GMOs to take over their natural counterparts, driving them to extinction, and disrupting the delicate balance in the environment. There may be other, long-term consequences that we simply do not know yet.

One risk assessment strategy and approach to biotechnology is the adoption of the precautionary principle.[27] Basically, this principle states that when in doubt or when the data are not sufficient we should not proceed with developing or using certain technologies. Opinion leaders and policymakers, however, tend to use the principle in a much more conservative way; one can use it as a mechanism to rule out the new technology altogether.

Beginning in 2000, members of the international community adopted a precautionary approach to biotechnology in order to protect biodiversity and the environment.[28] Known as the Cartagena Protocol on Biosafety, signatories agreed to implement certain regulations on living modified organisms. In early 2008, the United States had not signed, accepted, or ratified the protocol.[29] Some opponents might argue that the regulations are too restrictive for or interfere with commercial development and industry; others claim that they are necessary for sustainable development and the future of a healthy global environment. Surely, the debate will continue.

## Distribution and Uses of Commercial Biotechnology

Finally, there are justice issues involving the distribution and uses of commercial biotechnology. Some opponents claim that these biotechnologies drive small farmers out of business unfairly because they create a market in which they cannot compete. Other opponents argue that seed companies create dependence on purchasing new seeds each year, which is an expensive enterprise for small farms or farms in a developing country. Others note, however, that the seeds are manufactured in such a way as to limit the spread of genetically modified organisms. Thus, scientists have created seeds that produce sterile plants; farmers cannot reseed the plants because of the need to control the GMOs.

Another issue involves commutative justice between a company that is seeking valuable genetic information—a process called bioprospecting—and the community or region in which that search is occurring. For example, say a U.S. seed company uses information obtained from an indigenous community in South America to find, develop, and use a gene from a tropical plant native to the community's home in order to add nutritional value to a crop in the United States. What does the U.S. company owe the indigenous people? Or the country in which it finds the gene? Is the gene from the tropical plant a natural resource, which may be subject to international trade agreements? Here, ethicists call the issue of stealing this genetic information *biopiracy.*[30]

## PATENTING OF LIVING THINGS

The development and patenting of a bacterium by General Electric that disposes of oil slicks by eating the oil was the opening salvo in a debate over the development, use, ownership, and licensing of transgenic organisms. In 1980, the U.S. Supreme Court resolved the question of whether a single-celled living thing could legally be patented in the case *Diamond v. Chakrabarty.* The Court addressed whether the "invention was a product of nature or an invention made by human intervention."[31] Nevertheless, when the question about multicellular organisms, including animals, arose, the editors of the *New York Times* argued that if one can own a cow, then why cannot one patent the cow, too? They further stated that if it is acceptable to engineer an organism genetically, then patentability should be acceptable also.[32] The fact that the major premises of both arguments raised substantive questions seemed to be irrelevant to the editors, presumably in light of current practice of owning animals and manipulating them genetically.

The move from bacteria to animals came with an application to patent a polyploid Pacific oyster. While the United States Patent and Trademark Office (USPTO) rejected the claim, the patent board noted that the oyster did fall within the Court's decision in *Diamond v. Chakrabarty*. Then, the commissioner of the USPTO released a notice that the office would consider "nonnaturally occurring nonhuman multicellular living organisms, including animals, to be patentable subject matter within the scope of 35 U.S.C. Para. 101." In addition, the notice stated that "the grant of a property right in a human was prohibited by the U.S. Constitution and that, therefore, any claim which included humans within its scope would not be considered patentable subject matter under 35 U.S.C. Para. 101." In 1988, Harvard University received the first patent for a nonhuman mammal, its cancer-susceptible mouse, and the debate intensified.[33]

The debate over the patenting of living things raised three particular issues. The first issue is the sanctity of or reverence for life. Since the paradigm for patents is mechanical invention, will patenting lead us to think of organisms as machines? The key issue is that "living things are distinguished by their having a certain kind of history rather than by their having a certain kind of composition."[34] Making transgenic organisms would force us to look at their composition rather than their origin. If we separate the concept of being alive and being born, the concept of the sanctity of life could be weakened for we would return to the Cartesian position of seeing bodies as autonomously functioning machines.

The second issue related to patenting animals is that the use of human DNA with other animals raises the question of "the moral category in which transgenic animals belong." Robert Wachbroit raises the very interesting question of the use of such techniques on what he calls *higher animals*—for example, monkeys or chimpanzees: "How ought we to regard such a 'halfway' creature? As an augmented ape or as a diminished human?"[35] While National Institutes of Health rules expressly prohibit practices such as the transfer of human embryos to animals for gestation and the creation of human-animal chimeras, or cross-species fertilization,[36] fears remain, and the rules cover only research subsidized by the federal government. (We will discuss this chimera and hybrid technology in chapter 14.)

The third issue related to patenting animals looks to a specific consequence: Can such patented methods and materials be used without cost? For example, Ohio University developed a

patent "for microinjection, the process many scientists use to add
new genes to mice."[37] DNX, a Princeton-based biotech company,
has the rights to the patent. Currently DNX does not ask for a fee
for using the technique unless a commercial product is involved.
GenPharm International, a California biotech company, received
a license from various universities to market knockout mice. The
company charged between $80 and $100 per mouse. "The company also prohibited labs from breeding the mice, which effectively forced researchers to pay GenPharm for every mouse they
used." Such a pricing practice would obviously be prohibitive for
many labs. The GenPharm decision that resolved the issue was to
"allow researchers to breed as many mice as they want for an
annual fee of $1,000 and the initial purchase of a breeding pair.
One time breeding, to see if the pups have birth defects, for example, will be free."[38]

In March 1995, the European Parliament rejected a directive
that would have "set common standards of patent protection for
biotechnological inventions." This brought to closure a six-year
debate. Animal rights activists and environmentalists are pleased
with this decision because they reject "the basic premise of the
directive, that life is patentable." Geneticists, however, are concerned because "the existing practice of patent offices may give
commercial companies too much control over genetic data, thereby
restricting research." Plus, some parliamentarians "opposed the
directive because it would not have explicitly banned human
germline gene therapy, which introduces permanent, inheritable
traits into genes." Thus, officials will resolve patenting issues on the
basis of precedents that are being established on a case-by-case
basis. The fear is that this approach could "result in a patchwork of
different regulations in different European countries."[39]

## REGULATORY CHALLENGES FOR
## GENETIC ENGINEERING

There are four basic reasons why regulating genetically engineered plants, animals, and microorganisms is challenging. First,
and perhaps most importantly, there are significant value differ-

ences across regulatory communities. Different people in different countries assess risks differently. Thus, there is a significant difference between how the European community views and assesses GMOs versus how the U.S. community does.[40] This is one reason why biotechnology has been more successful in the United States than elsewhere in the world. Second, the containment and nature of genetic information pose serious challenges to regulating its exchange.[41] Genetic information has passed from generation to generation, and in some cases from species into new species, since life began on Earth. How can humans regulate such phenomena? Third, there is overlap in the scopes of responsibility of different regulatory agencies. For example, in the United States, GMOs may come under one or more of the following government agencies: the FDA, the Environmental Protection Agency (EPA), the U.S. Department of Agriculture (USDA), the Centers for Disease Control and Prevention (CDC), and the National Institutes of Health (NIH). Finally, the sheer volume and uncertainty in risk assessment and regulations of GMOs create significant logistical challenges.

## CONCLUSION

Genetic interventions in the plant, animal, and microbe worlds are proving to be interesting and controversial. On the one hand, these interventions are the testing ground for the study of possible consequences of such interventions without necessarily involving human subjects (see chapter 16). On the other hand, these tests are proving that similar kinds of interventions could be replicated in human beings.

In addition, these genetic interventions are raising broader environmental questions as well as questions about the moral and biological value of the integrity of particular species. While many interventions offer the promise of new foods, increased production, and immunity to various pathogens, the environmental impact of these new organisms is not clear. Moreover, various human-animal interactions—through xenotransplantation, for example—have yet to be subjected to critical testing.

Finally, the scientific and commercial communities in biotechnology are just beginning to address adequately the arguments and objections of the animal rights and environmental protection movements. Clearly, the members of the biotechnology community have a lot to gain from such research. The public may have much to gain from it, too. However, nonhuman organisms will bear much of the burden for such gains. An example of this is recent efforts to demonstrate whether a particular gene—called *eyeless*—is indeed the gene responsible for the development of the eye. To test this, scientists inserted the gene on developing wings, legs, and antennae of the fruit fly. "The ectopic eyes appeared morphologically normal and consisted of groups of fully differentiated ommatidia with a complete set of photoreceptor cells."[42] Whether this caused physical harm to the fruit fly was unclear. Aesthetically, however, the experiment did not appear to enhance the appearance of the fruit fly.

Genetic interventions are indeed exciting, but much work remains to close the gap between the promise offered and its fulfillment. Navigating the uncertain as well as the known ethical problems will require a delicate balance of courage, caution, and wisdom.

## DISCUSSION QUESTIONS

1. Do you think the power to intervene in nature and change it is any more dangerous than our previous abilities to alter nature?
2. What is an appropriate length of time to monitor or test for long-term consequences of genetic interventions?
3. Do you think patenting of life-forms is a violation of the sanctity of life?
4. Do animals have any rights that are violated when they are used as subjects of experiments?
5. Do you think genetically engineered foods are a cause for worry?

## NOTES

1. J. D. Watson and F. H. C. Crick, "Molecular Structure of Nucleic Acids: A Structure for Deoxyribose Nucleic Acid," *Nature* 171 (April 25, 1953): 737–38; see Susan Wright, "Recombinant DNA Technology and Its Social Transformation, 1972–1982," *Osiris* 2 (1986): 303–60; see John J. Doll, "The Patenting of DNA," *Science* 280, no. 5364 (May 1, 1998): 689–90; W. F. Anderson, "Human Gene Therapy," *Science* 256, no. 5058 (May 8, 1992): 808–13; see Francis S. Collins, Michael Morgan, and Aristides Patrinos, "The Human Genome Project: Lessons from Large-Scale Biology," *Science* 300, no. 5617 (April 11, 2003): 286–90; and J. Craig Venter et al., "The Sequence of the Human Genome," *Science* 291, no. 5507 (February 16, 2001): 1304–51.

2. See Wright, "Recombinant DNA Technology."

3. Petter Portin, "Historical Development of the Concept of the Gene," *Journal of Medicine and Philosophy* 27, no. 3 (2002): 257.

4. Wright, "Recombinant DNA Technology," 305, 309, 310–12.

5. Ibid., 312–15.

6. For example, see Tsafrir S. Mor, Miguel A. Gómez-Lim, and Kenneth E. Palmer, "Perspective: Edible Vaccines—A Concept Coming of Age," *Trends in Microbiology* 6, no. 11 (November 11, 1998): 449–53; and William H. R. Langridge, "Edible Vaccines," *Scientific American* 283, no. 3 (September 2000): 66–71.

7. See Paola Lucca, Susanna Poletti, and Christof Sautter, "Genetic Engineering Approaches to Enrich Rice with Iron and Vitamin A," *Physiologia Plantarum* 126 (2006): 291–303; J. A. Paine et al., "Improving the Nutritional Value of Golden Rice through Increased Pro-Vitamin A Content," *Nature Biotechnology* 23, no. 4 (April 2005): 482–87; and X. Ye et al., "Engineering the Provitamin A (Beta-Carotene) Biosynthetic Pathway into (Carotenoid-Free) Rice Endosperm," *Science* 287, no. 5451 (January 14, 2000): 303–5.

8. See David A. Andow, Gábor L. Lövei, and Salvatore Arpaia, "Ecological Risk Assessment for *Bt* Crops," *Nature Biotechnology* 24, no. 7 (July 2006): 749–50; Richard H. French-Constant and Nicholas R. Waterfield, "Ground Control for Insect

Pests," *Nature Biotechnology* 24, no. 6 (June 2006): 660–61; Sarah L. Bates, Jian-Zhou Zhao, Richard T. Roush, and Anthony M. Shelton, "Insect Resistance Management in GM Crops: Past, Present, and Future," *Nature Biotechnology* 23, no. 1 (January 2005): 57–62; and Jian-Zhou Zhao et al., "Transgenic Plants Expressing Two *Bacillus thuringiensis* Toxins Delay Insect Resistance Evolution," *Nature Biotechnology* 21, no. 12 (December 2003): 1493–97; Mark K. Sears et al., "Impact of *Bt* Corn Pollen on Monarch Butterfly Populations: A Risk Assessment," *Proceedings of the National Academy of Sciences* 98, no. 21 (October 9, 2001): 11937–42.

9. See M. Kasuga et al., "Improving Plant Drought, Salt, and Freezing Tolerance by Gene Transfer of Single Stress-Inducible Transcription Factor," *Nature Biotechnology* 17, no. 3 (March 1999): 287–91; Belinda Martineau, *First Fruit: The Creation of the Flavr Savr Tomato and the Birth of Biotech Food* (New York: McGraw-Hill, 2001); see also Glenn Thorlby, Nicolas Fourrier, and Gareth Warren, "The *SENSITIVE TO FREEZING2* Gene, Required for Freezing Tolerance in *Arabidopsis thaliana*, Encodes a β-Glucosidase," *The Plant Cell* 16 (August 2004): 2192–203.

10. Working Party on Xenotransplantation, Committee of Ministers of the Council of Europe, *Report on the State of the Art in the Field of Xenotransplantation* (Strasbourg: Council of Europe, 2003), 28–29; see Karl A. Thiel, "Biomanufacturing, from Bust to Boom...to Bubble?" *Nature Biotechnology* 22, no. 11 (November 2004): 1365–72.

11. M. N. Sillence, "Technologies for the Control of Fat and Lean Deposition in Livestock," *The Veterinary Journal* 167 (2004): 242–57.

12. For an interesting discussion, see Alan Dove, "Milking the Genome for Profit," *Nature Biotechnology* 18, no. 10 (October 2000): 1045–48.

13. See Frederick H. Buttel, "The Recombinant BGH Controversy in the United States: Toward a New Consumption Politics of Food?" *Agriculture and Human Values* 17 (2000): 5–20; see also Barnaby J. Feder, "Monsanto Has Its Wonder Hormone. Can It Sell It?" *New York Times*, March 22, 1995, F8.

14. See Cory L. Nykiforuk et al., "Transgenic Expression and Recovery of Biologically Active Recombinant Human Insulin from *Arabidopsis thaliana* Seeds," *Plant Biotechnology Journal* 4, no. 1 (January 2006): 77–85; see Biotechnology Institute, "History of Biotechnology—Timeline," http://www.biotechinstitute.org/what_is/timeline.html, accessed March 12, 2008.

15. Biotechnology Industry Organization (BIO), "Industrial and Environmental Biotechnology: Publications," http://bio.org/ind/pubs/, accessed March 12, 2008.

16. Víctor de Lorenzo, "Blueprint of an Oil-Eating Bacterium," *Nature Biotechnology* 24, no. 8 (August 2006): 952–53.

17. Charles B. Beard, Ravi V. Durvasula, and Frank F. Richards, "Bacterial Symbiosis in Arthropods and the Control of Disease Transmission," *Emerging Infectious Diseases* 4, no. 4 (October–December 1998): 581–91; see Guoliang Fu et al., "Female-Specific Insect Lethality Engineered Using Alternative Splicing," *Nature Biotechnology* 25, no. 3 (March 2007): 353–57; Andrea Crisanti et al., "An Anopheles Transgenic Sexing Strain for Vector Control," *Nature Biotechnology* 23, no. 11 (November 2005): 1414–17; and Bart G. J. Knols et al., "GM Sterile Mosquitoes—A Cautionary Note," *Nature Biotechnology* 24, no. 9 (September 2006): 1067–68.

18. David Pimentel and Tad W. Patzek, "Ethanol Production Using Corn, Switchgrass, and Wood; Biodiesel Production Using Soybean and Sunflower," *Natural Resources Research* 14, no. 1 (March 2005): 65–76; Richard G. Lugar and R. James Woolsey, "The New Petroleum," *Foreign Affairs* 78, no. 1 (January/February 1999): 88–102.

19. See Judith Miller, Stephen Engelberg, and William Broad, *Germs: Biological Weapons and America's Secret War* (New York: Simon & Schuster, 2001).

20. David A. Kessler, Michael R. Taylor, James H. Maryanski, Eric L. Flamm, and Linda S. Kahl, "The Safety of Foods Developed by Biotechnology," *Science* 256, no. 5065 (June 26, 1992): 1747–49 and 1832.

21. Julie Nordlee, Steve Taylor, Jeffery Townsend, Laurie Thomas, and Robert Bush, "Identification of a Brazil-Nut Allergen

in Transgenic Soybeans," *New England Journal of Medicine* 334, no. 11 (March 14, 1996): 688.

22. Keith Schneider, "U.S. Approves Use of Drug to Raise Milk Production," *New York Times*, November 6, 1993, A9.

23. Jane Rissler and Margaret Nellon, *Perils Amidst the Promise: Ecological Risks of Transgenic Crops in a Global Market* (Cambridge, MA: Union of Concerned Scientists, 1993), 12.

24. Keith Schneider, "Study Finds Risk in Making Plants Viral Resistant," *New York Times*, March 11, 1994, A16.

25. B. E. Rollin, "The Frankenstein Thing: The Moral Impact of Agricultural Animals on Society and Future Science," in *Genetic Engineering of Animals: An Agricultural Perspective*, ed. J. W. Evans and A. Hollaener (New York: Plenum Press, 1988), 292.

26. Edward O. Wilson, *The Future of Life* (New York: Vintage Books, 2003), 105.

27. Kenneth R. Foster, Paolo Vecchia, and Michael H. Repacholi, "Science and the Precautionary Principle," *Science* 288, no. 5468 (May 12, 2000): 979–81.

28. Convention on Biological Diversity, "Background," *The Cartagena Protocol on Biosafety*, http://www.cbd.int/biosafety/background.shtml, accessed March 12, 2008.

29. Convention on Biological Diversity, "Ratifications," *The Cartagena Protocol on Biosafety*, http://www.cbd.int/biosafety/signing list.shtml, accessed March 12, 2008.

30. See Ikechi Mgbeoji, *Global Biopiracy: Patents, Plants and Indigenous Knowledge* (Ithaca, NY: Cornell University Press, 2006).

31. Jeffrey Auerbach, "Transgenic Animals and Patenting," *ATCC Quarterly Newsletter* 9 (1989): 10.

32. "Yes, Patent Life," *New York Times*, April 21, 1987, A30.

33. Auerbach, "Transgenic Animals and Patenting," 10.

34. Robert Wachbroit, "Eight Worries about Patenting Animals," *Report from the Institute for Philosophy and Public Policy* 8, no. 3 (Summer 1988): 6.

35. Ibid., 8.

36. Eliot Marshall, "Rules on Embryo Research Due Out," *Science* 265, no. 5175 (August 19, 1994): 1024.

37. David L. Wheeler, "Biologists Discuss Ways to 'Share' Genetically Engineered Mice," *Chronicle of Higher Education*, April 7, 1993, A14.

38. Christopher Anderson, "Researchers Win Decision on Knockout Mouse Pricing," *Science* 260, no. 5104 (April 2, 1993): 23.

39. Claire O'Brien, "European Parliament Axes Patent Policy," *Science* 267, no. 5203 (March 10, 1995): 1417–18.

40. Cf., for example, Susan Hornig Priest, "US Public Opinion Divided over Biotechnology?" *Nature Biotechnology* 18, no. 9 (September 2000): 939–42; George Gaskell, "Agricultural Biotechnology and Public Attitudes in the European Union," *AgBioForum* 3, nos. 2 and 3 (2000): 87–96; and J. L. Lusk and A. Rozan, "Consumer Acceptance of Biotechnology and the Role of Second Generation Technologies in the USA and Europe," *Trends in Biotechnology* 23, no. 8 (August 2005): 386–87.

41. For example, see Henry Daniell, "Molecular Strategies for Gene Containment in Transgenic Crops," *Nature Biotechnology* 20, no. 6 (June 2002): 581–86.

42. George Hadler, Patrick Callaerts, and Walter J. Gehring, "Induction of Ectopic Eyes by Targeted Expression of the *Eyeless* Gene in *Drosophila*," *Science* 267, no. 5205 (March 24, 1995): 1788.

## BIBLIOGRAPHY

Anderson, Christopher. "Researchers Win Decision on Knockout Mouse Pricing." *Science* 260, no. 5104 (April 2, 1993): 23–24.

Anderson, W. F. "Human Gene Therapy." *Science* 256, no. 5058 (May 8, 1992): 808–13.

Andow, David A., Gábor L. Lövei, and Salvatore Arpaia. "Ecological Risk Assessment for *Bt* Crops." *Nature Biotechnology* 24, no. 7 (July 2006): 749–50.

Auerbach, Jeffery. "Transgenic Animals and Patenting." *ATCC Quarterly Newsletter* 9 (1989): 10.

Bates, Sarah L., Jian-Zhou Zhao, Richard T. Roush, and Anthony M. Shelton. "Insect Resistance Management in GM Crops:

Past, Present, and Future." *Nature Biotechnology* 23, no. 1 (January 2005): 57–62.

Beard, Charles B., Ravi V. Durvasula, and Frank F. Richards. "Bacterial Symbiosis in Arthropods and the Control of Disease Transmission." *Emerging Infectious Diseases* 4, no. 4 (October–December 1998): 581–91.

Biotechnology Industry Organization. "Industrial and Environmental Biotechnology: Publications." http://bio.org/ind/pubs/. Accessed March 12, 2008.

Biotechnology Institute. "History of Biotechnology—Timeline." http://www.biotechinstitute.org/what_is/timeline.html. Accessed March 12, 2008.

Buttel, Frederick H. "The Recombinant BGH Controversy in the United States: Toward a New Consumption Politics of Food?" *Agriculture and Human Values* 17 (2000): 5–20.

Collins, Francis S., Michael Morgan, and Aristides Patrinos. "The Human Genome Project: Lessons from Large-Scale Biology." *Science* 300, no. 5617 (April 11, 2003): 286–90.

Convention on Biological Diversity. *The Cartagena Protocol on Biosafety.* http://www.cbd.int/biosafety/. Accessed March 12, 2008.

Crisanti, Andrea, et al. "An Anopheles Transgenic Sexing Strain for Vector Control." *Nature Biotechnology* 23, no. 11 (November 2005): 1414–17.

Daniell, Henry. "Molecular Strategies for Gene Containment in Transgenic Crops." *Nature Biotechnology* 20, no. 6 (June 2002): 581–86.

Doll, John J. "The Patenting of DNA." *Science* 280, no. 5364 (May 1, 1998): 689–90.

Dove, Alan. "Milking the Genome for Profit." *Nature Biotechnology* 18, no. 10 (October 2000): 1045–48.

Evans, J. W., and A. Hollaener, eds. *Genetic Engineering of Animals: An Agricultural Perspective.* New York: Plenum Press, 1988.

Feder, Barnaby J. "Monsanto Has Its Wonder Hormone. Can It Sell It?" *New York Times.* March 22, 1995, F8.

Foster, Kenneth R., Paolo Vecchia, and Michael H. Repacholi. "Science and the Precautionary Principle." *Science* 288, no. 5468 (May 12, 2000): 979–81.

French-Constant, Richard H., and Nicholas R. Waterfield. "Ground Control for Insect Pests." *Nature Biotechnology* 24, no. 6 (June 2006): 660–61.

Fu, Guoliang, et al. "Female-Specific Insect Lethality Engineered Using Alternative Splicing." *Nature Biotechnology* 25, no. 3 (March 2007): 353–57.

Gaskell, George. "Agricultural Biotechnology and Public Attitudes in the European Union." *AgBioForum* 3, nos. 2 and 3 (2000): 87–96.

Hadler, George, Patrick Callaerts, and Walter J. Gehring. "Induction of Ectopic Eyes by Targeted Expression of the *Eyeless* Gene in *Drosophila*." *Science* 267, no. 5205 (March 24, 1995): 1788–92.

Hanson, Mark J., ed. *Claiming Power over Life: Religion and Biotechnology Policy*. Washington, DC: Georgetown University Press, 2001.

Hornig Priest, Susan. "US Public Opinion Divided over Biotechnology?" *Nature Biotechnology* 18, no. 9 (September 2000): 939–42.

Kasuga, M., et al. "Improving Plant Drought, Salt, and Freezing Tolerance by Gene Transfer of Single Stress-Inducible Transcription Factor." *Nature Biotechnology* 17, no. 3 (March 1999): 287–91.

Kessler, David A., Michael R. Taylor, James H. Maryanski, Eric L. Flamm, and Linda S. Kahl. "The Safety of Foods Developed by Biotechnology." *Science* 256, no. 5065 (June 26, 1992): 1747–49 and 1832.

Knols, Bart G. J., et al. "GM Sterile Mosquitoes—A Cautionary Note." *Nature Biotechnology* 24, no. 9 (September 2006): 1067–68.

Langridge, William H. R. "Edible Vaccines." *Scientific American* 283, no. 3 (September 2000): 66–71.

Lorenzo, Víctor de. "Blueprint of an Oil-Eating Bacterium." *Nature Biotechnology* 24, no. 8 (August 2006): 952–53.

Lucca, Paola, Susanna Poletti, and Christof Sautter. "Genetic Engineering Approaches to Enrich Rice with Iron and Vitamin A." *Physiologia Plantarum* 126 (2006): 291–303.

Lugar, Richard G., and R. James Woolsey. "The New Petroleum." *Foreign Affairs* 78, no. 1 (January/February 1999): 88–102.

Lusk, J. L., and A. Rozan. "Consumer Acceptance of Biotechnology and the Role of Second Generation Technologies in the USA and Europe." *Trends in Biotechnology* 23, no. 8 (August 2005): 386–87.

Marshall, Eliot. "Rules on Embryo Research Due Out." *Science* 265, no. 5175 (August 19, 1994): 1024–26.

Martineau, Belinda. *First Fruit: The Creation of the Flavr Savr Tomato and the Birth of Biotech Food*. New York: McGraw-Hill, 2001.

Mgbeoji, Ikechi. *Global Biopiracy: Patents, Plants and Indigenous Knowledge*. Ithaca, NY: Cornell University Press, 2006.

Miller, Judith, Stephen Engelberg, and William Broad. *Germs: Biological Weapons and America's Secret War*. New York: Simon & Schuster, 2001.

Mor, Tsafrir S., Miguel A. Gómez-Lim, and Kenneth E. Palmer. "Perspective: Edible Vaccines—A Concept Coming of Age." *Trends in Microbiology* 6, no. 11 (November 11, 1998): 449–53.

Nordlee, Julie, Steve Taylor, Jeffery Townsend, Laurie Thomas, and Robert Bush. "Identification of a Brazil-Nut Allergen in Transgenic Soybeans." *New England Journal of Medicine* 334, no. 11 (March 14, 1996): 688–92.

Nykiforuk, Cory L., et al. "Transgenic Expression and Recovery of Biologically Active Recombinant Human Insulin from *Arabidopsis thaliana* Seeds." *Plant Biotechnology Journal* 4, no. 1 (January 2006): 77–85.

O'Brien, Claire. "European Parliament Axes Patent Policy." *Science* 267, no. 5203 (March 10, 1995): 1417–18.

Paine, J. A., et al. "Improving the Nutritional Value of Golden Rice through Increased Pro-Vitamin A Content." *Nature Biotechnology* 23, no. 4 (April 2005): 482–87.

Pimentel, David, and Tad W. Patzek. "Ethanol Production Using Corn, Switchgrass, and Wood; Biodiesel Production Using Soybean and Sunflower." *Natural Resources Research* 14, no. 1 (March 2005): 65–76.

Portin, Petter. "Historical Development of the Concept of the Gene." *Journal of Medicine and Philosophy* 27, no. 3 (2002): 257–86.

Rissler, Jane, and Margaret Nellon. *Perils Amidst the Promise: Ecological Risks of Transgenic Crops in a Global Market.* Cambridge, MA: Union of Concerned Scientists, 1993.

Schneider, Keith. "Study Finds Risk in Making Plants Viral Resistant." *New York Times.* March 11, 1994, A16.

———. "U.S. Approves Use of Drug to Raise Milk Production." *New York Times.* November 6, 1993, A9.

Sears, Mark K., et al. "Impact of *Bt* Corn Pollen on Monarch Butterfly Populations: A Risk Assessment." *Proceedings of the National Academy of Sciences* 98, no. 21 (October 9, 2001): 11937–42.

Sillence, M. N. "Technologies for the Control of Fat and Lean Deposition in Livestock." *The Veterinary Journal* 167 (2004): 242–57.

Thiel, Karl A. "Biomanufacturing, from Bust to Boom…to Bubble?" *Nature Biotechnology* 22, no. 11 (November 2004): 1365–72.

Thorlby, Glenn, Nicolas Fourrier, and Gareth Warren. "The *SENSITIVE TO FREEZING2* Gene, Required for Freezing Tolerance in *Arabidopsis thaliana,* Encodes a β-Glucosidase." *The Plant Cell* 16 (August 2004): 2192–203.

Venter, J. Craig, et al. "The Sequence of the Human Genome." *Science* 291, no. 5507 (February 16, 2001): 1304–51.

Wachbroit, Robert. "Eight Worries about Patenting Animals." *Report from the Institute for Philosophy and Public Policy* 8, no. 3 (Summer 1988): 6–8.

Watson, J. D., and F. H. C. Crick. "Molecular Structure of Nucleic Acids: A Structure for Deoxyribose Nucleic Acid." *Nature* 171 (April 25, 1953): 737–38.

Wheeler, David L. "Biologists Discuss Ways to 'Share' Genetically Engineered Mice." *Chronicle of Higher Education.* April 7, 1993, A14.

Working Party on Xenotransplantation, Committee of Ministers of the Council of Europe. *Report on the State of the Art in the*

*Field of Xenotransplantation*. Strasbourg: Council of Europe, 2003.

Wright, Susan. "Recombinant DNA Technology and Its Social Transformation, 1972–1982." *Osiris* 2 (1986): 303–60.

Ye, X., et al. "Engineering the Provitamin A (Beta-Carotene) Biosynthetic Pathway into (Carotenoid-Free) Rice Endosperm." *Science* 287, no. 5451 (January 14, 2000): 303–5.

"Yes, Patent Life." *New York Times*. April 21, 1987, A30.

Zhao, Jian-Zhou, et al. "Transgenic Plants Expressing Two *Bacillus thuringiensis* Toxins Delay Insect Resistance Evolution." *Nature Biotechnology* 21, no. 12 (December 2003): 1493–97.

## Chapter 13

# GENETIC ENGINEERING: HUMAN BEINGS

## INTRODUCTION

By applying the same genetic engineering technology used in plants, animals, and microorganisms, we can change genetic information in human beings. This application is usually in the context of genetic medicine where researchers and clinicians aim to cure or to prevent certain diseases or predispositions to diseases. While there has been clinical research involving gene therapy in human beings, there has not been unequivocal success.[1] The state of the art includes evidence that the basic principle works: changing the genetic information in humans can cure, reverse, or prevent certain diseases. Significant safety and efficiency concerns remain, however. Although genetic medicine can include genetic counseling, which we discussed in chapter 7, we will focus on the application of recombinant DNA and other biotechnologies to change genetic information in human beings.

### Notes on Terms

Using the term *gene therapy* exclusively to refer to genetic engineering in humans can be misleading. First, gene therapy is not the only form of genetic engineering in humans. As we will see, parents may one day be able to change the genes in their gametes and confer certain traits onto their children but not be affected by the genetic changes themselves (i.e., germ-line genetic modification). In such cases, there is no existing patient that

231

receives the therapy. Moreover, we recognize that nuclear transfer cloning is also a way to modify genetic information in humans. We treat this technology separately in the next chapter. Second, the word *therapy* implies a particular end, goal, or good in medicine. One can use the technology to pursue ends other than curing. For example, is it "therapeutic" to prevent a disease from ever manifesting? One can also apply the technology to enhance certain traits. Is genetic enhancement really a form of therapy? Therefore, the scientific and bioethical communities prefer to use the term *gene transfer* to refer to this broad set of genetic engineering technologies. In particular, the term *human gene transfer* refers to modifying genetic information in human beings—either in particular individuals, across populations, or in the next generation.

## KNOWING THE HUMAN GENOME

The genome is the totality of the genetic information of the organism. Efforts to sequence and map the human genome formally began in 1988. Beginning in 1990, the U.S. Department of Energy and the National Institutes of Health established a budget of $3 billion, which included 3 to 5 percent to study the *e*thical, *l*egal, and *s*ocial *i*ssues of genetics (known as ELSI, the largest public bioethics project in history). In 2000, scientists published a rough draft of nearly 90 percent of the human genome's sequence of nucleotides—the building-blocks of DNA and a genome. By 2003 (two years earlier than expected), both the public collaborative initiative known as the Human Genome Project (HGP) and the private company Celera Genomics, led by Craig Venter, completed the nucleotide sequence of the human genome. While this is a major milestone in the history of human civilization, likened to landing on the moon and the (re-)discovery of the New World, it was only the beginning.[2]

We have gained a significant amount of knowledge about the human genome, but we have much more to learn. Thus, there has been a shift in the scientific community to understanding the functions, interactions, and other aspects of the genome that we previously could not have known. For example, early estimates of the number of genes human beings had reached over one hundred thousand; now, the estimated number of genes is between twenty thousand and twenty-five thousand.[3] How can the complexity (and beauty) of human life be accounted for by only twenty-five thousand genes? What about the genetic material between genes? Previously, many referred to this material as "junk DNA." By studying the functions of genes—a subfield called functional genomics—scientists are uncovering hidden messages, control mechanisms, and other functions of this unexpressed DNA. That is, just because a DNA sequence is not translated into a protein does not mean it is unimportant to the life and health of an organism.

Besides direct intervention to change the genetic material in human beings, knowledge of the human genome is quickly opening other opportunities in society. Even in the medical arena, this knowledge is accelerating the development of personalized medicine. For example, in the field of pharmacogenomics, clinicians can use genetic information, or patient genotypes, to determine and prescribe the right drug, at the right dose, for the right patient. This will likely have a major effect on clinical judgment and will potentially reduce the uncertainty that comes with practicing the art of medicine. Other uses include applications in the criminal justice system. We are now familiar with forensic science through popular TV shows such as *CSI*. DNA evidence has become a major element in prosecuting or acquitting suspects. Similarly, law enforcement officials use entire DNA databases to store criminal DNA and other forms of biological evidence in protecting citizens. Notwithstanding these amazing and intriguing applications, we will focus on health-related applications of human gene transfer.

# HUMAN GENE TRANSFER

## *Strategies of Gene Transfer*

There are three basic strategies in human gene transfer: inhibition, insertion, and revision. First, *inhibition* refers to the process of stopping a gene from expressing. Sometimes, scientists call this gene silencing. There are a variety of ways one can accomplish this, but the basic principle is to prevent a gene from working. For example, if one wants to suppress the function of a cancer-causing gene, then clinicians will aim to inhibit that gene from working. Second, *insertion*, the most popular strategy, refers to the procedure of placing a gene (or, more precisely, a shortened version of the gene) into human cells. Sometimes, scientists can splice the gene into the cell's genomic DNA; other times they simply put the gene in the cell and have the cell's transcription and translation machinery take over. In general, scientists cannot control where the gene inserts in a cell's genomic DNA; the insertion strategy is usually a somewhat random one. Plus, insertion does not remove the preexisting gene; it simply adds genetic material. Finally, *revision* involves leveraging a cell's own capacity for correcting—that is, revising—DNA; here, scientists use small nucleotide-based molecules that trigger the cell's editing process. Scientists have especially designed these molecules to contain the intended genetic change. So, when the cell "revises" its DNA, it makes the changes the scientist wants. Usually, this only occurs one nucleotide at a time. Diseases that involve many mutations pose a logistical problem for this strategy. The advantages, however, include that (at least in principle) the process is targeted and specific: the genetic change does not occur randomly as it might in the insertion strategy.[4]

## Tactical Aspects of Gene Transfer

There are several important concrete aspects of human gene transfer (HGT) protocols that influence one's evaluation of it; we will discuss only four. One, in order to get the genetic material *into* a patient's cells, clinicians must utilize a vector. A vector can be an engineered virus that no longer causes disease, typically a retrovirus or adenovirus, or some other courier for the genetic information. Some scientists have used microscopic cellular sacks (e.g., liposomes or nanoparticles), bacterial plasmids, artificial chromosomes, and even direct DNA microinjection. Two, HGT protocols differ in the location where researchers perform the gene transfer. In the early gene therapy trials, researchers removed the patient's cells, treated them with the vector out of the body (*ex vivo*), and then placed the cells back in the patient's body. Other times, researchers injected the modified vectors directly into the patient's bloodstream (*in vivo*), or they applied the vector directly to the diseased tissue (*in situ*). Three, HGT protocols may be different in terms of how long the genetic change will last. In some HGT protocols, the change is temporary and may require repeated exposure to the vector and transferred gene. Other times, the change is permanent. Four, HGT protocols differ in the target cells. Sometimes, the target cells are specific tissues affected by the genetic disorder. In the widely publicized gene therapy trials to date, these were immune cells found in patients' bone marrow. Traditionally, commentators referred to these target cells as somatic cells or body cells. Other target cells may include gametes or the precursors to gametes. Commentators referred to these as germ-line cells. One should note that a temporary gene transfer in a germ-line cell does not mean that the offspring will inherit the genetic modification.[5]

## *Two Moral Questions*

Taken together, the strategies and the different aspects of HGT protocols give us a good sense of what human gene transfer involves and how each protocol may differ from another. One may still ask, however, What does an ethicist make of all this? Fortunately, there has been a lot of debate over genetic modifications in human beings; this has given us a rich literature on which we can reflect.

In considering human gene transfer in genetic medicine, there are two basic moral questions one needs to address: (1) *Who receives the genetic intervention?* and (2) *What is the nature of the intervention?*[6] The first question pertains to whether the genetic intervention applies only to the recipient of the change (e.g., a patient) or if it can be transmitted to others. Traditionally, this related to the target cell: *somatic cells* or *germ-line cells*. Now, however, commentators use the language of heritability: Is the genetic change *heritable* or *nonheritable*? Will it be passed on from generation to generation, or will it remain "in" one person?

The second question asks about the effects of the intervention. Traditionally, this distinction referred to a difference between *therapy* and *enhancement*. Many have critiqued this distinction as either nonexistent or too difficult (if not impossible) to determine. We suggest that it may be better to think in terms of the goals of medicine: Does the intervention fit *within the goals of medicine* or is it *outside the goals of medicine*? This distinction has functioned as a moral boundary: generally, ethicists viewed therapeutic procedures positively (with extreme, but mixed, caution about germ-line gene therapy), whereas they viewed enhancement procedures more negatively (or at least as more morally problematic).[7] Of course, there is still controversy over what the goals of medicine are. But this allows one to evaluate HGT by appealing to its context—genetic medicine—rather than viewing it in an unknown ether of genetic modification. Thus, the second question becomes this: Does the HGT serve the good of the patient? It also forces us to probe what that good is. One should also note that simply because a genetic modification is outside the goals of medicine does not necessarily mean it is immoral or unethical. It requires further reflection, however, in order for one to justify it.

As a result of these two moral questions, one can envision four basic categories of human gene transfer: (1) nonheritable gene therapy, (2) heritable gene therapy, (3) nonheritable gene enhancement, and (4) heritable gene enhancement.

## ETHICAL ISSUES OF HUMAN GENE TRANSFER

Many of the concerns we addressed in the chapters on reproductive technology and early diagnosis are applicable here, too. For example, assisted reproductive technology (ART) can allow clinicians to perform genetic changes on embryos before they transfer them to the mother's womb. In fact, those who reject ART may reject genetic modification principally because it would require the use of ART even if they do not reject genetic modification in and of itself. In addition, the knowledge of a genetic diagnosis may lead to an alteration of a child's genetic makeup. We will address the issues that derive from the challenges HGT poses.

## Benefiting the Recipient(s)

A key issue in HGT is what constitutes a benefit for the recipient of the intervention. To begin, one could consider any effect of HGT comparable to a conventional medical intervention: the central issue in therapy is the intent to restore the patient to a state of health or well-being. What serves the patient's (or recipient's) best interests? What cures the recipient's condition? If an HGT protocol corrects a disease-causing gene resulting in a healthy phenotype, then one could say that the HGT benefited the recipient—it resulted in the medical good of the recipient. This would be similar to taking a drug or having surgery. Currently, most therapeutic HGT trials involve cancer.[8] Here, researchers apply HGT to cancer patients to destroy tumor cells either directly, causing the self-destruct cycle in those cells, or indirectly, by changing immune cells to attack the tumors or by shutting off the mechanism that feeds tumor cells (stopping blood vessels from growing into the tumors).[9] Likewise, HGT also serves the medical good of the recipient by preventing a disease or unhealthy phenotype from ever arising. So, for example, a gene therapy that corrects the genetic mutation causing Huntington's disease before the onset of the disease would be prevention. Some also believe that one day we might be able to develop and use a vaccine for HIV by leveraging a genetic mutation that results in human immunity from the virus that causes AIDS.[10]

Interestingly, though, Kevin FitzGerald states that many wonder whether this kind of prevention is actually a form of enhancement.[11] Indeed, the patient or recipient may not ever experience illness; how can an HGT treatment be therapeutic if there is no disease? What distinguishes genetic modification that prevents disease from a genetic modification that enhances one's immune system?

Needless to say, many will claim that there are clear-cut genetic enhancements. Thus, if the intent is enhancement, one is attempting to augment through active intervention specific characteristics or to give individuals a capacity they might not have had before. For example, there may one day be enhancements for muscle mass, for vision, for memory, and for a host of other benefits for an individual. Some already consider certain forms of cosmetic surgery (different from reconstructive surgery) as enhancements: face lifts, breast augmentation, and calf implants. These procedures enhance the aesthetic quality of the client within a given culture. Likewise, the use of certain drugs (e.g., selective serotonin reuptake inhibitors, SSRIs) may increase memory and attention in persons, who may use them even in the absence of a neurological disorder such as attention deficit and hyperactivity disorder (ADHD).[12]

A major question behind this discussion of therapy, prevention, and enhancement is the relationship between what is *statistically normal* and what is *morally normative*. If the average height of white men is 5 feet 10 inches, does that mean that all white men (or *all* men *and* women) *should be* at least 5 feet 10 inches tall? We say "at least" because many would want to be taller than average. In fact, there are sociological data that show social and economic advantages to being taller: men who are over a certain height tend to get better jobs and incomes as well as to be more socially and professionally influential.[13] In other words, just because a certain trait is *normal* does not necessarily mean that it determines what the *norm* should be. Height is a classic example of this problem because it is sometimes difficult to demarcate between dwarfism, short stature, and "appropriate" stature.

There are two types of judgments here: there is a *descriptive* judgment of what is statistically normal; and there is an *evaluative* and *normative* judgment of what is morally normative. In addressing the ethical issues of HGT, we should always be aware of what kind of judgments we are making. What is also critical here is the desire to *go beyond* the standard to *enhance* a particular characteristic or to design a new or different characteristic. At present, we do not have, in our judgment, a good set of criteria for evaluating such interventions or their social outcomes.

## Who Receives and Who Decides

In all current HGT research, the recipients of an HGT intervention are patients. If these patients consent to participate in the research, they both make that decision for themselves and receive the experimental intervention. Thus, the subjects of these research protocols are the sole recipients of the genetic modification.

In many other trials, however, children are the recipients. In these cases, their parents decide and consent to the procedures. As this technology matures, parents will have more and more options available to them to intervene early in the lives of their children (or even before they conceive children). This will go beyond the options available through preimplantation genetic diagnosis. Parents who seek HGT may change the genetic information of their offspring in a few different ways; some may be heritable, others may not be. On the one hand, if a preimplantation embryo is genetically modified through HGT to prevent a genetic disorder (e.g., cystic fibrosis) that modification will be inherited in that embryo's offspring (should she or he reproduce). On the other hand, if a fetus or child is genetically modified in a way that excludes modifying the germ cells, then those modifications will not be passed down to the next generation. In either case, the parents are making decisions while the children are receiving the change. In cases involving heritable modifications, the parents would be making the decision for every subsequent generation in their lineage. C. S. Lewis describes this problem in his book *The Abolition of Man*,

> In order to understand fully what Man's power over Nature, and therefore the power of some men over other men, really means, we must picture the race extended in time from the date of its emergence to that of its extinction. Each generation exercises power over its successors: and each, in so far as it modifies the environment bequeathed to it and rebels against tradition, resists and limits the power of its predecessors. This modifies the picture which is sometimes painted of a progressive emancipation from tradition and a progressive control of natural processes resulting in a continual increase of human power. In reality, of course, if any one age really attains, by eugenics and scientific education, the power to make its descendants what it pleases, all men who live after it are the patients of that power.

They are weaker, not stronger: for though we may have put wonderful machines in their hands we have pre-ordained how they are to use them.[14]

## Risks and Harms of Gene Transfer

Human gene transfer trials have been plagued with minimal success and overwhelming tragedy.[15] There are four problems for the recipient associated with HGT. First, there are massive immune reactions against the vector.[16] Although scientists remove the pathogenic aspects of the viral vectors, recipients may still experience a massive immune reaction against them. This phenomenon is similar to a life-threatening allergy or a rejection of a transplanted organ. After Jesse Gelsinger died in a famous failed gene therapy trial, scientists determined that his death was caused by such a massive reaction against the adenovirus that researchers used.[17] Second, the insertion strategy currently relies on random insertion into genomic DNA, which may trigger other negative consequences as mentioned above. In the gene therapy studies in France, the therapeutic genes were inserted into tumor-suppressing genes, which resulted in the participants contracting a form of leukemia.[18] While the gene therapy fixed the immune deficiency these participants had, it also caused cancer. Third, there are functional problems, which relate inefficiency with a concern for the risks. Not every HGT protocol will work, and there may be significant risks in administering the vectors or procuring the target cells (i.e., from the patient's body). Because the HGT protocol may simply not work and in view of the added risks of the procedure, the proportion of benefits to burdens may not be worth it. Fourth, there are risks involved in moving from preclinical experiments in animals to clinical trials in humans to widespread practice in health care. Major medical innovations require this process, and some researchers and some human subjects must at some point be courageous enough to try it. There's one caveat to this process, however. What about interventions that are inherited by the next generation? The researchers' generation may not experience the risks, but the risks and possible burdens could be shouldered by the next generation and the offspring of those who were willing to participate (possibly at no or minimal risk to themselves) in the research. Thus, the process of informed consent becomes a major factor in the moral acceptability of these interventions; only if the recipient is able and willing to accept the risks and potential harms should one administer HGT. Indeed, HGT poses significant challenges to our understanding of informed consent, especially when we cannot obtain the consent of the potential recipients as we saw in the previous section (Who Receives and Who Decides).

## Fairness of Enhancements

There are two aspects to the issue of fairness of enhancements. On the one hand, many commentators are concerned over whether there will be *fair access* to enhancement HGT. Like the concerns over access to health care in general, opponents worry that only those who are wealthy enough to afford these technologies will have access to them. On the other hand, many commentators are also concerned that the enhancements themselves present *unfair advantages*. Since enhancements will likely result in significant competitive advantages for the recipients, this unequal access to enhancement technology may further exacerbate the disparity between the haves and the have-nots. We see a similar debate of this in professional sports. Performance enhancing substances are not allowed; arguably everyone in the given sport has equal access to these substances, but critics worry that it changes the nature of the game. Thus, extending the argument into genetic modification, critics would worry that enhancing human beings would change or alter society in fundamental and unfair ways. It shifts the distribution of resources in favor of those who have the enhancements.[19]

## Fairness in Research and Development

The issue of whether there will be fairness in research and development of HGT interventions relates to the justice questions of high-tech medicine in general.[20] Will the allocation of research money for HGT be fair when compared to other social goods that may need more money (e.g., education, national security, or alternative energy sources)? How should Congress decide to appropriate money to the National Institutes of Health for research, to Medicare for health care, to the Department of Energy for research, or to the Department of Education for subsidies (for example)?

Related to the question of allocation of research money is fairness in the patent system. Originally developed in England in 1642, intellectual property laws and patent protection are very important inventions to protect one's return on investment. This promotes innovation in society; it is meant to function in fair market exchanges by giving the owner of the patent exclusive rights to market his or her invention. In the words of Abraham Lincoln, the patent system "added the fuel of *interest* to the *fire* of genius."[21] Thus, the inventor can recover his or her financial investment in developing new technology. Here, one is concerned with setting a fair price for a new technology. Although this is not unique to HGT, what is of specific concern here is the potential for competition. Many worry that given the nature of HGT and similar biotech products, inventors will not be able to produce generics. Thus, true competition that drives the price down among competing products may never occur; the only possibility for choices lies in the hope for more innovation.[22]

## THE HERITABLE GENE TRANSFER DEBATE

We have adapted the summary of the arguments presented by Nelson A. Wivel and LeRoy Walters on gene therapy for the debate over heritable forms of gene transfer.[23]

### Arguments for Heritable Genetic Modification

1. Health care professionals have an obligation to use the *best available* treatment methods to achieve the goals of medicine—that is, to benefit the patient (or recipient). Heritable genetic modification is more efficient and cost-effective than nonheritable forms of HGT: heritable HGT is the best treatment.

2. Public health officials have an obligation to employ methods to control and/or prevent genetically transmitted diseases and predispositions for other diseases.
3. Parents have an obligation to seek the best interests of children or any possible children.
4. Parents possess autonomy to access available technology for purposes of having a healthy child or benefiting their children in any way they see fit.
5. Society should enjoy maximal freedom of scientific inquiry, which reflects the significant value of the knowledge gained itself as well as the technology derived from that inquiry.

## Arguments against Heritable Genetic Modification

1. Heritable genetic modification is expensive, experimental, and limited; its current applicability is uncertain.
2. There are other technologies or techniques available to treat, prevent, or manage the symptoms of diseases addressed by heritable genetic modification.
3. There are unavoidable, uncertain, and/or possibly irreversible mistakes of heritable genetic modification for future generations.
4. There are inevitable pressures and ambiguous distinctions to use heritable forms of genetic modification for enhancement (where enhancement negatively affects fairness in society).
5. Heritable genetic modification is outside the domain of human responsibility. The theological corollary of this argument is that this kind of genetic engineering is "playing God."
6. The freedom of future generations should be respected by not imposing the will of current generations on any contingent generation or people.

# CONCLUSION

Developments in plant and animal genetics cannot be seen in isolation from human genetics because many of the techniques discovered and applied in the former will also find application in the latter. Techniques, for example, to develop transgenic animals can be used to develop transgenic humans. Thus, one needs to keep in mind potential human applications when thinking about plant and animal genetics, too.

In addition, we need to consider very carefully the power that the capacity to alter our genetic structure gives us. Obviously, human beings have evolved and continue to evolve. But this process is very slow and responsive to a wide variety of conditions. What is new is our capacity to intervene and effect an instant change. We have a growing capacity to make a dramatic impact on the human gene pool somewhat independent of the little-known and poorly understood system of evolutionary checks and balances in biological evolution. This is not an anti-intervention argument. Rather, it is a call for careful intervention based on a concern for future outcomes.

We also need to think carefully about the possibility of the new genetics turning into the new eugenics. What a particular culture sees as desirable may not be beneficial for the individual recipient, for society, or for human beings as a group. Furthermore, such preferences may reflect a variety of racist or sexist attitudes that would not be to anyone's benefit. The rush to have "designer genes," while perhaps well intentioned, might also release the worst features of a consumer or capitalist society.

Finally, such words of caution ought to be considered as exactly that: words of caution. The new genetics is giving us a marvelous power that has the capacity to prevent or alleviate much human misery. Yet that power can have a dark side, and we would do well to recall past experiments with eugenics.

We are genuinely at a new moment of human history with few precedents to guide us. Wisdom and caution must be creatively joined with scientific discovery and clinical application.

# DISCUSSION QUESTIONS

1. How do you think that having a map of the entire human genome impacts our understanding of human nature?
2. Who do you think will receive most of the benefits of genetic interventions?
3. Do you think using HGT to prevent genetic predispositions and diseases is a medical goal or an enhancement goal?
4. Should we consider someone who receives a genetic enhancement a client or a patient?
5. Do you approve of the therapeutic use of gene transfer? Why or why not?
6. Do you see any problems with heritable genetic interventions?
7. Is there any difference between sending a child to a high-quality school to enhance his or her intellectual capabilities and trying to do this through genetic interventions?

# NOTES

1. Nicholas J. Kockler, "Courage for a Brave New World: Medical Genetics, Evolution, and a Roman Catholic Approach to Human Gene Transfer" (Ph.D. diss., Duquesne University, 2006), 24–81.

2. U.S. Department of Energy, Office of Science, "The Human Genome Project Information," http://www.ornl.gov/sci/techresources/Human_Genome/home.shtml, accessed March 14, 2008; Tyra G. Wolfsberg et al., "Guide to the Draft Human Genome," *Nature* 409 (February 15, 2001): 824–26; see Francis S. Collins, Michael Morgan, and Aristides Patrinos, "The Human Genome Project: Lessons from Large-Scale Biology," *Science* 300, no. 5617 (April 11, 2003): 286–90; and J. Craig Venter et al., "The Sequence of the Human Genome," *Science* 291, no. 5507 (February 16, 2001): 1304–51. See also James Shreeve, *The*

*Genome War: How Craig Venter Tried to Capture the Code of Life and Save the World* (New York: Alfred A. Knopf, 2004).

3. International Human Genome Sequencing Consortium, "Finishing the Euchromatic Sequence of the Human Genome," *Nature* 431 (October 21, 2004): 931–45.

4. Kockler, "Courage for a Brave New World," 47–49.

5 Ibid., 50–53.

6. See LeRoy Walters and Julie Gage Palmer, *The Ethics of Human Gene Therapy* (New York: Oxford University Press, 1997), xvii–xviii.

7. Eric T. Juengst, "What Does Enhancement Mean?" in *Enhancing Human Traits: Ethical and Social Implications*, ed. Erik Parens and Adrienne Asch (Washington, DC: Georgetown University Press, 1998), 29–47, esp. 29–31; Juengst argues that commentators use the term *enhancement* to describe a particular effect of an intervention as well as to proscribe such effects. One use is descriptive, the other use is normative.

8. Recombinant DNA Advisory Committee (RAC), "Human Gene Transfer Protocols," Documents, updated November 19, 2007, http://www4.od.nih.gov/oba/rac/PROTO COL.pdf, accessed March 19, 2008.

9. Kockler, "Courage for a Brave New World," 38 and 54.

10. Kevin T. FitzGerald, "The Need for a Dynamic and Integrative Vision of the Human for the Ethics of Genetics," in *Genetics, Theology, and Ethics: An Interdisciplinary Conversation*, ed. Lisa Sowle Cahill (New York: Herder and Herder, 2005), 80–83.

11. Ibid., 81.

12. See President's Council on Bioethics, *Beyond Therapy: Biotechnology and the Pursuit of Happiness* (Washington, DC: U.S. Government Printing Office, 2003), 71–92.

13. For a discussion of this, see, e.g., David Blane, George Davey Smith, and Carole Hart, "Some Social and Physical Correlates of Intergenerational Social Mobility: Evidence from the West of Scotland Collaborative Study," *Sociology* 33, no. 1 (February 1999): 169–83.

14. C. S. Lewis, *The Abolition of Man* (New York: Harper, 1974), 56–57.

15. See Kockler, "Courage for a Brave New World," 24–33.

16. Ibid., 58.

17. Sheryl Gay Stolberg, "The Biotech Death of Jesse Gelsinger," *New York Times Magazine*, November 28, 1999, 136–40, 149–50; and Huntly Collins, "U Penn Scientists Discover Reason for Death of Gene-Therapy Teen," *The Philadelphia Inquirer*, January 26, 2001, A01.

18. Kockler, "Courage for a Brave New World," 30.

19. Allen Buchanan, Dan W. Brock, Norman Daniels, and Daniel Wikler, *From Chance to Choice: Genetics and Justice* (New York: Cambridge University Press, 2000), 318, 320.

20. See Karen Lebacqz, "Fair Shares: Is the Genome Project Just?" in *Genetics: Issues of Social Justice*, ed. Ted Peters (Cleveland: Pilgrim Press, 1998), 82–107; and Thomas A. Shannon, "Embryonic Stem Cell Therapy," in *The New Genetic Medicine: Theological and Ethical Reflections*, ed. Thomas A. Shannon and James J. Walter (Lanham, MD: Rowman & Littlefield, 2003), 149.

21. Abraham Lincoln, "Second Lecture on Discoveries and Inventions, February 11, 1859," in *The Collected Works of Abraham Lincoln*, vol. 3, ed. Roy P. Basler (New Brunswick, NJ: Rutgers University Press, 1953), 363.

22. See Alan Dove, "Betting on Biogenerics," *Nature Biotechnology* 19 (February 2001): 117–20.

23. Nelson A. Wivel and LeRoy Walters, "Germ-Line Gene Modification and Disease Prevention: Some Medical and Ethical Perspectives," *Science* 262, no. 5133 (October 22, 1993): 536.

## BIBLIOGRAPHY

Basler, Roy P., ed. *The Collected Works of Abraham Lincoln*. Vol. 3. New Brunswick, NJ: Rutgers University Press, 1953.

Blane, David, George Davey Smith, and Carole Hart. "Some Social and Physical Correlates of Intergenerational Social Mobility: Evidence from the West of Scotland Collaborative Study." *Sociology* 33, no. 1 (February 1999): 169–83.

Buchanan, Allen, Dan W. Brock, Norman Daniels, and Daniel Wikler. *From Chance to Choice: Genetics and Justice*. New York: Cambridge University Press, 2000.

Cahill, Lisa Sowle, ed. *Genetics, Theology, and Ethics: An Interdisciplinary Conversation*. New York: Herder and Herder, 2005.

Collins, Francis S., Michael Morgan, and Aristides Patrinos. "The Human Genome Project: Lessons from Large-Scale Biology." *Science* 300, no. 5617 (April 11, 2003): 286–90.

Collins, Huntly. "U Penn Scientists Discover Reason for Death of Gene-Therapy Teen." *The Philadelphia Inquirer*. January 26, 2001, A01.

Dove, Alan. "Betting on Biogenerics." *Nature Biotechnology* 19 (February 2001): 117–20.

Gay Stolberg, Sheryl. "The Biotech Death of Jesse Gelsinger." *New York Times Magazine*. November 28, 1999.

International Human Genome Sequencing Consortium. "Finishing the Euchromatic Sequence of the Human Genome." *Nature* 431 (October 21, 2004): 931–45.

Kockler, Nicholas J. "Courage for a Brave New World: Medical Genetics, Evolution, and a Roman Catholic Approach to Human Gene Transfer." Ph.D. diss., Duquesne University, 2006.

Lewis, C. S. *The Abolition of Man*. New York: Harper, 1974.

Parens, Erik, and Adrienne Asch, eds. *Enhancing Human Traits: Ethical and Social Implications*. Washington, DC: Georgetown University Press, 1998.

Peters, Ted, ed. *Genetics: Issues of Social Justice*. Cleveland: Pilgrim Press, 1998.

President's Council on Bioethics. *Beyond Therapy: Biotechnology and the Pursuit of Happiness*. Washington, DC: U.S. Government Printing Office, 2003.

Recombinant DNA Advisory Committee. "Human Gene Transfer Protocols." Documents. Updated November 19, 2007. http://www4.od.nih.gov/oba/rac/PROTOCOL.pdf. Accessed March 19, 2008.

Shannon, Thomas A., and James J. Walter. *The New Genetic Medicine: Theological and Ethical Reflections*. Lanham, MD: Rowman & Littlefield, 2003.

Shreeve, James. *The Genome War: How Craig Venter Tried to Capture the Code of Life and Save the World*. New York: Alfred A. Knopf, 2004.

U.S. Department of Energy, Office of Science. "The Human Genome Project Information." http://www.ornl.gov/sci/techresources/Human_Genome/home.shtml. Accessed March 14, 2008.

Venter, J. Craig, et al. "The Sequence of the Human Genome." *Science* 291, no. 5507 (February 16, 2001): 1304–51.

Walters, LeRoy, and Julie Gage Palmer. *The Ethics of Human Gene Therapy*. New York: Oxford University Press, 1997.

Wivel, Nelson A., and LeRoy Walters. "Germ-Line Gene Modification and Disease Prevention: Some Medical and Ethical Perspectives." *Science* 262, no. 5133 (October 22, 1993): 533–38.

Wolfsberg, Tyra G., et al. "Guide to the Draft Human Genome." *Nature* 409 (February 15, 2001): 824–26.

*Chapter 14*

# CELL-BASED BIOTECHNOLOGIES

## INTRODUCTION

Thus far, we have considered the recombinant DNA (rDNA) technology of genetic engineering in humans, animals, plants, and microorganisms. Scientists also employ other methods, however, to control biological information in living things. Here, they generally rely on cells and their processes more than on DNA molecules per se. Furthermore, whereas clinical researchers primarily employ human gene transfer (HGT) in genetic medicine, biomedical scientists employ cell-based biotechnologies in the fields of tissue engineering and regenerative medicine. There have been recent developments wherein scientists use the tactics of gene transfer to achieve desired goals in regenerative medicine (i.e., inducing somatic cells to function like embryonic stem cells through gene transfer).[1]

There has been so much activity in this area of biological research; and most of the new developments have occurred within the last ten years. In 1997, Ian Wilmut and colleagues cloned the first mammal, a sheep named Dolly, through somatic cell nuclear transfer (SCNT).[2] In 1998, researchers at the University of Wisconsin isolated a cell line derived from human embryonic stem cells (hESCs).[3] In 2001, the Bush administration restricted federal funding for human embryonic stem cell research to cell lines that already existed.[4] The restriction on federal research money did not preclude funding from private sources (e.g., venture capital) or state-based sources. Thus, in 2004, voters in California approved Proposition 71, which supplied researchers in California, one of the biggest areas of biotech research, state money to conduct hESC research. Other states followed suit by proposing similar funding opportunities.[5] In late 2007 and early 2008, researchers reported two major findings. In one report, researchers demonstrated the successes of applying gene transfer to induce certain characteristics found in embryonic stem cells (called induced pluripotent stem cells, or iPSCs). In another report, researchers demonstrated success of using SCNT with human fibroblasts and oocytes for the first time.[6]

This chapter could be several on its own; however, we have decided to treat these topics together due to how closely related their issues are in analysis. First, we will provide a brief sketch of each technology, focusing on stem cell technology, nuclear transfer technology, and chimera technology. Second, we will survey the ethical issues. Finally, we will conclude by outlining the arguments in the human embryonic stem cell research debate.

# CELL-BASED BIOTECHNOLOGIES

## Stem Cell Research and Technology

There are a variety of stem cells, each with qualities important to its function. There are basic properties, however, that all stem cells share: they can divide and differentiate into different cell types, and they can replicate themselves almost indefinitely in the undifferentiated state.[7] There are numerous sources of stem cells: adult bone marrow and other tissues, umbilical cord tissue and blood, fetal tissue, and embryonic cells. This last source has caused the most controversy.

In addition to their properties and the different sources, the potential of stem cells to differentiate also varies. We will outline three levels of potential here. One, embryonic cells that can differentiate into *any* cell type, including a whole new embryo, are *totipotent.* Typically these cells come from the very early stages of embryonic development before the embryo implants into the woman's uterus; that is, before the blastocyst develops (approximately four days after fertilization).[8] For example, one can obtain a totipotent stem cell by removing a cell (i.e., a blastomere) during the cleavage stage of embryonic development—a process called blastomere separation. This mimics the natural process of twinning. Two, stem cells that can differentiate into *any* cell type in the body but cannot develop into a whole new embryo are *pluripotent*. The early blastocyst consists of two parts: the trophoblast (outer part) and the inner cell mass or embryoblast (inner part). The trophoblast eventually develops into the placenta, amniotic sac, and chorionic villi (see chapter 7, under the subhead "Risks of Harm"). The embryoblast eventually develops into the fetus. The cells of the inner cell mass are pluripotent. Currently, the only way to obtain these cells is to destroy the blastocyst. Lastly, cells that can differentiate into a specific and defined set of cells are *multipotent*. While each of these cells cannot differentiate into all different cell types, they do possess significant plasticity; for example, researchers have induced blood stem cells in adult marrow to become liver cells.[9]

Researchers are interested in stem cells for a variety of reasons; many claim that these special cells hold keys to solving some of the most complex medical problems such as spinal cord injuries, Parkinson's disease, and many others. They have a wide range of applications, however, both inside and outside the clinical setting. These applications include the following: research to understand human development, to identify potentially harmful chemicals in human development, to test for drug toxicity (and efficacy), and to develop therapeutic products in regenerative medicine.[10] In this latter domain, therapies could include treatments for spinal cord and nerve damage, heart disease, diabetes, other neurological diseases, and cancer.

## Nuclear Transfer Cloning

Nuclear transfer cloning is a method scientists use to "copy" an adult organism's genomic DNA into another organism. This is fundamentally different from blastomere separation because the usual source for the nuclei that scientists use are differentiated cells. In other words, the cell providing the genomic DNA and nucleus is at a different developmental stage than the cell that receives the nucleus. As the name suggests, nuclear transfer cloning involves the transfer of a nucleus into an enucleated cell, usually an oocyte. In this case, scientists remove the nucleus from the egg (in mammals, this nucleus would contain half the necessary genomic information—it is haploid—before fertilization). They would obtain a diploid nucleus from a differentiated somatic cell (hence, *somatic* cell nuclear transfer). Then, scientists microinject the somatic cell's nucleus and apply a series of treatments (e.g., electric shock and a special cell culture mixture to imitate an embryonic environment) to the newly nucleated egg. In combination, these factors trigger the transferred nucleus and entire cell to function as if they were newly fertilized. Another way one could understand this phenomenon is to think of the series of treatments as "resetting" the genomic DNA; the somatic cell's DNA would basically "reboot" to the embryonic stage. Thus, the resulting cloned cell develops in a similar pattern to an embryo.

Scientists initially developed nuclear cloning to address agricultural problems with maintaining good breeding lines in livestock.[11] Researchers are now, however, using nuclear transfer techniques to develop a variety of potential human applications. There are two basic paradigms: scientific cloning and reproductive cloning. On the one hand, in scientific cloning, scientists use nuclear transfer cloning to research human diseases and to develop therapeutic products. Some commentators note that using SCNT could result in the availability of replacement organs derived from a patient's own cells, which is another expression of personalized medicine. But due to manufacturing and other financial constraints on using the technology for individualized care, commercial developers may use SCNT to develop a neutral set of products that any patient can use. This would be comparable to using blood from a universal donor with blood type O negative. On the other hand, in reproductive cloning, scientists aim to use SCNT as another available procedure in assisted reproductive technology where one could have a genetically related child. Here, a woman could clone herself without the need of any male partner. A man, however, could only clone himself if he had access to (a) an enucleated egg and (b) a woman's womb.

## Chimera Technology

In mythology, the word *chimera* denotes a monster resulting from a combination of different animals. Thus, the centaur (half man, half horse) and the griffin (part eagle, part lion) are examples of chimeras in Western myths. In modern science, chimera technology can include transgenic experiments where scientists use genes from one species in another species. Additionally, organ transplantation is also a form of chimera technology: it is the combination of animal parts (one body and an organ) from members of the same or different species. Indeed, in H. G. Well's *The Island of Dr. Moreau*, the mad scientist uses vivisection to create chimeras—the beast folk. In this chapter, however, we will focus on cellular forms of chimera technology. In these cellular forms, scientists can create chimeras by introducing embryonic cells from one species to the cells of another species through various techniques at various stages of development.[12] As the entity develops, the cells connect and grow together. The result is an animal that possesses cells from each species, yet the genes of each species never mix. Two examples of this kind include a quail and a chicken chimera as well as a goat and a sheep chimera—known as a "geep."[13] Scientists can also create chimeras by surgically grafting tissues from one animal into another.[14] For example, many current experiments involve the placing of human brain cells in mice or other primates.

Again, researchers pursue chimera technology for a variety of reasons. For one, chimeras can function as interesting research tools and objects of study. Scientists can learn a great deal about biological development as well as the progression of disease through chimeras. Two, scientists can use chimeras as animal models of human disease. Thus, chimeras can perform an important preclinical function in the testing of biotech, pharmaceutical, and medical device products in health care.

# ETHICAL ISSUES OF CELL-BASED BIOTECHNOLOGIES

## *Destruction of Embryos and the Sanctity of Life*

As we have seen in the topics of abortion and reproductive technologies, the destruction of embryos is a major ethical issue, especially in how it potentially violates the sanctity of life. In stem cell research, scientists use embryos as objects of study, not as potential human persons. Yet one should recognize that the main cells that scientists use are embryonic *stem* cells derived from the inner cell mass of a blastocyst. These cells do not have the potential to develop into a human being, even if one transfers them to a woman's uterus: the hESCs are pluripotent. Nevertheless, in order to get hESCs, scientists need to acquire and destroy human embryos. Many of these embryos come from discarded embryos at fertility clinics; they are "leftover" from IVF procedures (i.e., they would be destroyed or they would be cryopreserved indefinitely; in either case, the woman does not intend to have the embryos transferred to her uterus). Other sources of embryos include embryos derived from eggs and sperm donated explicitly for the purpose of hESC research. Another source of hESC includes certain fetal tissues, which one can obtain from discarded fetuses after abortions.

In 2005, the President's Council on Bioethics published a white paper outlining four alternative sources of pluripotent stem cells; they are as follows:[15]

1. *From organismically dead embryos*: Researchers would obtain these pluripotent embryonic stem cells in a fashion comparable to obtaining organs from a cadaveric organ donor—that is, from dead embryos. In this case, a scientist determines that the embryo is dead when he or she observes irreversible cessation of cell division.

2. *From extracted blastomeres of living embryos*: Researchers would perform an embryo biopsy or blastomere separation (also done for preimplantation genetic diag-

nosis—see chapter 7). It is currently not clear, however, whether these separated blastomeres (depending on when the researcher separates them) are totipotent or pluripotent; and it is also uncertain whether such a procedure harms the developing embryo.

3. *From biological artifacts*: Here, researchers use gene transfer technology to induce or create pluripotent stem cells. One technique, *altered nuclear transfer*, utilizes gene transfer to prevent the cloned cell from becoming totipotent. The researchers induce these cells to bypass the totipotent stage and immediately go into the pluripotent stage. Another source of pluripotent stem cells in this category is the use of parthenotes. Parthenogenesis is the process by which an unfertilized egg begins to divide as if it were fertilized; a parthenote is one of these dividing cells. Some parthenotes demonstrate characteristics similar to stem cells, but it remains unclear (a) how similar they are and (b) whether they can develop into another human being.

4. *From somatic cell dedifferentiation*: Similar to the use of biological artifacts, researchers use gene transfer technology in this source, too. Here, however, the researchers reprogram differentiated cells to function like undifferentiated, pluripotent stem cells; researchers create induced pluripotent stem cells (iPSCs).

The recent research on induced pluripotent stem cells is promising in this regard because it seems to address many of the ethical concerns about destroying embryos. However, induced pluripotency is a new technique, and scientists have yet to produce conclusive evidence that iPSCs are equivalent to ESCs in scientifically, clinically, commercially, and morally relevant ways.

Notwithstanding the potential for alternative sources, proponents and opponents to hESC research will continue to see this ethical issue differently. On the one hand, opponents see the use and destruction of early human life as a direct and horrid violation of the sanctity of life. On the other hand, proponents see the use and destruction of early human life as a necessary means to the end of treating currently intractable diseases. Although it has been difficult for philosophers, theologians, and scientists to agree to the precise time or moment when an individual human life (or person) begins his or her journey on Earth, some have argued that it may be helpful to think of human embryos as growing into full moral respect.[16] Thus, while we cannot accord full personhood status to a blastocyst, it is still a form of human life and worthy of some form of respect proportionate to its stage of development. Indeed, as we discussed in the chapter on abortion, a key question here is *What* is a person? Though one could phrase the question in this debate as, *When* is an organism a person with full moral status? To be sure, this is not a complete argument in support or in opposition to hESC research. In the very least, it is a call to be more reflective about the way in which we conduct this research. Furthermore, even if this line of reasoning leads one to conclude that the sanctity of human life is not violated by destroying blastocysts, there are still strong counter-arguments not based on this principle that proponents need to address, as we will see below.[17]

## Human Dignity

Many commentators critically draw on the notion of human dignity in the debates over stem cell research, cloning, and chimera technology. To begin, opponents to hESC research argue that such science not only violates the sanctity of life but also violates human dignity by using human embryos and embryonic stem cells as objects of scientific inquiry or for commercial exploitation. Proponents of the research argue, however, that *not performing* the research and seeking this available avenue of knowledge is a violation of the dignity of those persons who suffer the diseases that stem cell research might one day be able to treat.

Similar to the argument against hESC research, opponents to nuclear transfer cloning argue that such a technique violates human dignity. First, the one who, for reproductive reasons, provides the genetic material for cloning may be disrespected by having a genetically identical person created. Additionally, the clone itself may be disrespected by being the genetic copy of an already-existing person. These arguments may be difficult to uphold. Why would a clone have any less dignity than a twin? Perhaps it is not the fact that the cloned and the clone share identical genomic DNA but rather that one uses a clone for a particular reason. Here, the cloner uses a clone as a means to an end. Perhaps someone cloned a person in order to obtain organs from the clone so that there would be a direct match. Again, we may disrespect the dignity of early human life by using such life-forms as means to the ends of obtaining therapeutic products or gaining a greater understanding of human disease.

Finally, one may disrespect human dignity by mixing human cells with nonhuman cells. First, this follows the notion that each species should maintain an integrity and separateness of its cells and biological material. Second, this reflects a speciesism and a belief that human beings are the "highest" animals on the planet. Disrespecting human dignity occurs when human cells integrate with "lower" life-forms.[18]

Interestingly, if chimeras start displaying human characteristics, then what is our obligation to treat them as human? For example, if a chimeric chimpanzee has human brain tissues, and displays humanlike behaviors, then should we continue to treat it as an object of biological research? In what sense, if any, should we consider it a *human* subject of research? In this context, if we continue to treat the humanlike chimera simply as another animal, we may be disrespecting human dignity.

## Benefits of Therapies

One of the main reasons why proponents support hESC research and nuclear transfer cloning is the potential benefits of therapies that the technologies could one day provide. In the area of regenerative medicine, hESC technology and nuclear transfer technology may one day lead us to tremendous breakthrough therapies for serious conditions like spinal cord injuries, Alzheimer's disease, Parkinson's disease, damaged heart tissue following a heart attack, new pancreatic tissue for diabetic patients, and more. In fact, these technologies may one day be able to supply each patient who needs an organ with either a personalized replacement organ grown from their own genetic information or a "neutral" replacement organ that would never be rejected by the patient's immune system. In the area of reproductive medicine, nuclear transfer technology may allow couples or individuals the opportunity to have a genetically or biologically related child when other forms of assisted reproductive technology may not be clinically appropriate.

A key aspect to this issue is that much of it is still an "in principle" argument: there have been no therapies developed to date with hESC technology or nuclear transfer cloning.[19] While it may be true that the basic idea that these technologies *could* provide us with therapies, there are currently none. Most of the clinical success has occurred in adult stem cell research.

## Risks of Therapies

In contrast to the potential benefits of the therapies, one must also consider the issues involving the risks and potential harms of the therapies to patients. Like any major procedure, there will likely need to be a proportion of benefit to burden. Will the procedures be clinically safe *and* effective? Some commentators worry that by inducing stem cells to grow at accelerated rates, we may accidentally trigger cancer. In addition, like gene therapy, there are risks to being among the first human beings in which researchers test these therapies. Thus, an adequate informed consent process will be necessary to ensure that patients are willing to take on the potential risks.

## Benefits of Research

All of the technologies in this chapter function both as tools for research and as possible precursors to therapy. Research utilizing stem cell technology, nuclear transfer, and chimeras provides tools to further the research enterprise, and they function as sources of new knowledge themselves. With cloning and stem cell technology, scientists can perform preclinical testing for drug tox-icity and can rule out drug candidates that will likely not work in human beings by testing them on living human cells *in vitro*. Likewise, scientists can use the technology to continue basic bio-medical research in human embryology and pathology. With chimera technology, humans can gain a significant amount of knowledge about biology in general and about specific animal biology in particular. Furthermore, chimera technology can also pave the way for better disease models in animals, which also sup-ports preclinical testing of drugs, biologics, and medical devices before researchers test them in humans.

## Integrity of Species and Animal Welfare

Chimera technology forces us to probe another set of ethical issues: the integrity of species and animal welfare. Here, one rec-ognizes that there are certain boundaries between species that prevent the "intermingling" of organisms, organs, or cells from different species. These boundaries can serve both a biological function—they distinguish one species from another—and a moral function—they show us limits to what we should do with interspecies technology such as creating chimeras. Here, the bio-logical boundary between species also takes on a normative dimension. The value of species integrity derives from the unique roles each species plays in an ecosystem and from the internal bal-ance of the organism resulting from the process of natural selec-tion; disrupting those aspects could have serious ecological and physiological consequences. Likewise, there is a sense of speciesism at work that affirms some intrinsic worth to the uniqueness of individual species.

Related to the question of integrity of species is animal wel-fare. In this context, the issue is whether chimera technology harms the animals involved in any way. Does the geep suffer because it does not fully belong to either the sheep or the goat families? Since some animals are certainly more social than oth-ers, does this genetic isolation cause any pain for the animal? Does the anatomy and physiology of the chimeric animal inter-fere with the animal's ability to thrive? (Alternatively, a chimera could possess enhanced characteristics that give it competitive advantages over its natural relatives.) In addition, we have concern for animals because they can feel pain—they are sentient. However, with the introduction of human tissue, one may wonder if we may reach the point where a chimera with human brain tissue becomes sapient. If this hypothetical situation becomes true, it may also become a reality that the chimera not only would feel pain but would suffer in a similar way to humans, too.

## Fairness in Research and Development

Similar to human gene transfer, many are concerned with fairness in research and development of these technologies. For one, the development of high-tech medicine may unfairly benefit only those who can afford such technology. This may further exacerbate the disparity between those who can afford health care and those who have no access even to a decent minimum level of health care. Two, the patents of cell lines could create obstacles for noncommercial research as well as erect unfair barriers to competition. Three, the appropriation of federal money to any social program is, in part, a moral decision. Thus, the decision to fund hESC research is a moral decision as much as is the decision not to fund the research. Both positions reflect certain ideologies: some religious, some capitalist, some scientistic. Four, decisions to allocate federal money to social programs need to balance the needs and goods of those programs against one another; each of them competes for the same finite amount of money, as we discussed in the last chapter. So, in the American context, which social goods that the government provides are greater priorities— natural resources and energy, national and homeland security, civil infrastructure, education, or health care?

# THE HUMAN EMBRYONIC STEM CELL RESEARCH DEBATE

The debate over human embryonic stem cell research has been one of the more contested and heated public debates in bioethics. The stakes are high: potential cures for previously incurable diseases, large amounts of money from the government and from private sources, a brain drain where the brightest scientists move abroad because they cannot carry out their research in the United States, and the lives of human embryos. Like most debates, there are shades of gray between two polar positions. But, for the sake of laying out a map of the debate, it is helpful to see either end of the spectrum. To that end, we present both sides of the hESC research debate.

## Arguments for Human Embryonic Stem Cell Research

1. Physicians have an obligation to pursue and use the best available treatments for human diseases; hESC technology is (or holds the greatest potential to be) the best available treatment.
2. Human embryonic stem cells hold potential for learning more about human development and for providing the foundation for breakthroughs in regenerative medicine and tissue engineering.
3. Human embryonic stem cells are pluripotent and are not embryos themselves; their moral status is distinct and not morally equivalent to human embryos or human persons.
4. One can derive human embryonic stem cells from multiple sources:
   a. Discarded embryos following completed ART cycles (left over from IVF-ET);
   b. Discarded fetal tissue; and
   c. Donated gametes used in IVF for research purposes.
5. The lives of those who suffer from the diseases that hESC technology may one day treat are of greater value than the embryos destroyed to acquire embryonic stem cells.

## *Arguments against Human Embryonic Stem Cell Research*

1. Society has an obligation to protect those who are most vulnerable; hESC research and technology threaten those who have no voice and who are most vulnerable: human embryos.

2. While hESC research does hold significant potential for expanding human knowledge and for developing new cures, current research methods require violation of life's fundamental moral principles: respect for the sanctity of life and for human dignity.

3. While hESC research is primarily on pluripotent stem cells, the derivation of those cells and their cell lines requires the destruction of embryos or totipotent stem cells (e.g., separated blastomeres). Therefore, hESC research should not continue unless other methods or sources are used.

4. Although one cannot say conclusively that human embryos are human persons per se, human embryos do have certain moral worth that should not be discounted outright—they deserve at least a minimum amount of respect. This would preclude hESC research. Alternatively, because one cannot say with certitude that human embryos are *not* human persons, we should treat them *as if* they are human persons with full moral status and (therefore) respect. This, too, would preclude hESC research.

5. Using embryos from sources such as IVF-ET or abortion would constitute complacency and possibly illicit moral cooperation with the practices of ART or abortion, which are also morally problematic.

6. One cannot compare the worth of the lives of those who suffer diseases with the worth of the lives of human embryos—such worthiness is incommensurable.

7. There are other social goods to which federal money should be devoted: public education, preventative health and basic health care, and so on.

# CONCLUSION

Contemporary biotechnology continues to push the boundaries of our knowledge and of our moral senses. Often, when we get caught up in the glamour of high-tech medicine, we may fail to see that others in our global community suffer from conditions that could easily be prevented by supplying those local communities with sanitation, clean water, and other basic social goods. The debates about embryonic stem cells, cloning, and chimera research are debates of the developed world; they virtually ignore the overwhelming suffering of many more around the world.

Yet, where is the balance between spurring innovation, responsible research, and promoting health at the basic and at the advanced stages of medicine? How should we grapple with the implications of social justice when we contextualize the debate over stem cell research with end-of-life decision making and other public health initiatives? Should we continue to strive for high-priced, high-tech medicine when the U.S. health care system is broken? In an era of globalization, what sorts of obligations do citizens, corporations, and governments have to developing nations that are in need?

A more basic question applies to all forms of medical technology and care. In the words of Daniel Callahan, What kind of life do we want? Is there a kind of life that we *should* want? The answers to these questions inform the balance of innovation and of access to basic health care. They inform the general orientation we have to medicine and health care in general; they provide us with a backdrop against which we can evaluate the alchemy of stem cell science, the magic of genetic engineering, and the wizardry of modern health care. As we look to the future of biotechnology, nanotechnology, and other biomedical technologies, we must continue to ask ourselves, Toward what kind of life are we headed?

# DISCUSSION QUESTIONS

1. Do you think scientists should use discarded embryos from fertility clinics to conduct embryonic stem cell research? Do you think this source of embryos addresses the concerns of those who do not want to see embryos destroyed for research purposes?

2. Do you think somatic cell nuclear transfer should be used as a treatment for infertility?

3. Do you think we should have more respect for a chimeric mouse with human brain cells than a nonchimeric mouse?

4. Which do you think is the highest priority for the federal government in the United States: health care, education, or national security and defense? Which do you think *should be* the highest priority? Why?

5. From a global perspective, do you think that public money should go to fund embryonic stem cell research when some communities do not have access to proper sanitation and clean water?

# NOTES

1. Kazutoshi Takahashi et al., "Induction of Pluripotent Stem Cells from Adult Human Fibroblasts by Defined Factors," *Cell* 131 (November 30, 2007): 1–12. See also President's Council on Bioethics (PCB), *Alternative Sources of Human Pluripotent Stem Cells: A White Paper*, http://www.bioethics.gov/reports/white _paper/alternative_sources_white_paper.pdf, published May 2005, accessed March 19, 2008, 36–49.

2. Ian Wilmut et al., "Viable Offspring Derived from Fetal and Adult Mammalian Cells," *Nature* 385, no. 6619 (February 27, 1997): 810–13; see also Ian Wilmut et al., "Somatic Cell Nuclear Transfer," *Nature* 419, no. 6907 (October 10, 2002): 583–86.

3. James A. Thomson et al., "Embryonic Stem Cell Lines Derived from Human Blastocysts," *Science* 282, no. 5391

(November 6, 1998): 1145–47. See also C. Holden, "U.S. Patent Office Casts Doubt on Wisconsin Stem Cell Patents," *Science* 316, no. 5822 (April 13, 2007): 182.

4. PCB, *Alternative Sources*, xvii.

5. See "Proposition 71," http://www.cirm.ca.gov/pdf/ prop71.pdf, accessed March 19, 2008; Pam Belluck, "Massachusetts Proposes Stem Cell Research Grants," *New York Times*, http:// www.nytimes.com/2007/05/09/us/09stem.html, published May 9, 2007, accessed March 19, 2008.

6. See Takahashi et al., "Induction of Pluripotent Stem Cells"; Andrew J. French et al., "Development of Human Cloned Blastocysts Following Somatic Cell Nuclear Transfer (SCNT) with Adult Fibroblasts," *Stem Cells*, http://stemcells.alphamedpress. org/cgi/reprint/2007–0252v1.pdf, published January 17, 2008, accessed March 19, 2008, 1–22.

7. Thomas B. Okarma, "Human Embryonic Stem Cells: A Primer on the Technology and Its Medical Applications," in *The Human Embryonic Stem Cell Debate: Science, Ethics, and Public Policy*, ed. Suzanne Holland, Karen Lebacqz, and Laurie Zoloth (Cambridge, MA: MIT Press, 2001), 4–5.

8. President's Council on Bioethics, *Monitoring Stem Cell Research*, http://www.bioethics.gov/reports/stemcell/pcbe_final _version_monitoring_stem_cell_research.pdf, published January 2004, accessed March 19, 2008, 180.

9. R. E. Schwartz et al., "Multipotent Adult Progenitor Cells from Bone Marrow Differentiate into Functional Hepatocyte-like Cells," *Journal of Clinical Investigation* 109, no. 10 (May 2002): 1291–1302.

10. Okarma, "Human Embryonic Stem Cells," 5–10.

11. See Alan Dove, "Milking the Genome for Profit," *Nature Biotechnology* 18 (October 2000): 1045–48.

12. For example, Keith Schneider, "New Animal Forms Will Be Patented," *New York Times*, April 17, 1987, A1.

13. M. Naito et al., "Production of Quail-Chick Chimaeras by Blastoderm Cell Transfer," *British Poultry Science* 32, no. 1 (March 1991): 79–86; C. B. Fehilly et al., "Interspecific Chimaerism between Sheep and Goat," *Nature* 307, no. 5952 (February 16–22, 1984): 634–36.

14. For example, see J. Fontaine-Pérus and Y. Chéraud, "Mouse-Chick Neural Chimeras," *International Journal of Developmental Biology* 49, nos. 2–3 (2005): 349–53.

15. PCB, *Alternative Sources*, 8–23, 24–35, 36–50, 50–54.

16. For a discussion of moral status and embryonic development, see Thomas A. Shannon and Allan B. Wolter, "Reflections on the Moral Status of the Preembryo," in *The New Genetic Medicine: Theological and Ethical Reflections*, ed. Thomas A. Shannon and James J. Walter (Lanham, MD: Rowman & Littlefield, 2003), 41–63.

17. For example, see Thomas A. Shannon, "From the Micro to the Macro," in Holland et al., *Human Embryonic Stem Cell Debate*, 177–84.

18. For an interesting critique of this view of nature and seeing humans as the pinnacle of evolutionary progress, see Stephen J. Gould, *Full House: The Spread of Excellence from Plato to Darwin* (New York: Three Rivers Press, 1996).

19. See Bruce Jaspen, "Market for Adult Stem Cells Multiplies: Progress Made, Sales Rising Away from Political Spotlight," *Chicago Tribune*, http://archives.chicagotribune.com/2008/mar/16/business/chi-sun-stemcell-osiris-stemcyclmar16, published March 16, 2008, accessed March 19, 2008, for a discussion of the successes of adult stem cells versus embryonic stem cells.

## BIBLIOGRAPHY

Belluck, Pam. "Massachusetts Proposes Stem Cell Research Grants." *New York Times*. http://www.nytimes.com/2007/05/09/us/09stem.html. Published May 9, 2007. Accessed March 19, 2008.

Cahill, Lisa Sowle, ed. *Genetics, Theology, and Ethics: An Interdisciplinary Conversation*. New York: Herder & Herder, 2005.

Dove, Alan. "Milking the Genome for Profit." *Nature Biotechnology* 18 (October 2000): 1045–48.

Fehilly, C. B., et al. "Interspecific Chimaerism between Sheep and Goat." *Nature* 307, no. 5952 (February 16–22, 1984): 634–36.

Fontaine-Pérus, J., and Y. Chéraud. "Mouse-Chick Neural Chimeras." *International Journal of Developmental Biology* 49, nos. 2–3 (2005): 349–53.

French, Andrew J., et al. "Development of Human Cloned Blastocysts Following Somatic Cell Nuclear Transfer (SCNT) with Adult Fibroblasts." *Stem Cells.* http://stemcells.alphamedpress.org/cgi/reprint/2007–0252v1.pdf. Published January 17, 2008. Accessed March 19, 2008, 1–22.

Gould, Stephen J. *Full House: The Spread of Excellence from Plato to Darwin.* New York: Three Rivers Press, 1996.

Holden, C. "U.S. Patent Office Casts Doubt on Wisconsin Stem Cell Patents." *Science* 316, no. 5822 (April 13, 2007): 182.

Holland, Suzanne, Karen Lebacqz, and Laurie Zoloth, eds. *The Human Embryonic Stem Cell Debate: Science, Ethics, and Public Policy.* Cambridge, MA: MIT Press, 2001.

Mitchell, C. Ben, Edmund D. Pellegrino, Jean Bethke Elshtain, John F. Kilner, and Scott B. Rae. *Biotechnology and the Human Good.* Washington, DC: Georgetown University Press, 2007.

Naito, M., et al. "Production of Quail-Chick Chimaeras by Blastoderm Cell Transfer." *British Poultry Science* 32, no. 1 (March 1991): 79–86.

President's Council on Bioethics. *Alternative Sources of Human Pluripotent Stem Cells: A White Paper.* http://www.bioethics.gov/reports/white_paper/alternative_sources_white_paper.pdf. Published May 2005. Accessed March 19, 2008.

————. *Monitoring Stem Cell Research.* http://www.bioethics.gov/reports/stemcell/pcbe_final_version_monitoring_stem_cell_research.pdf. Published January 2004. Accessed March 19, 2008.

"Proposition 71." http://www.cirm.ca.gov/pdf/prop71.pdf. *California Institute for Regenerative Medicine.* Accessed March 19, 2008.

Schneider, Keith. "New Animal Forms Will Be Patented." *New York Times.* April 17, 1987, A1.

Schwartz, R. E., et al. "Multipotent Adult Progenitor Cells from Bone Marrow Differentiate into Functional Hepatocyte-like Cells." *Journal of Clinical Investigation* 109, no. 10 (May 2002): 1291–1302.

Shannon, Thomas A., and James J. Walter. *The New Genetic Medicine: Theological and Ethical Reflections.* Lanham, MD: Rowman & Littlefield, 2003.

Takahashi, Kazutoshi, et al. "Induction of Pluripotent Stem Cells from Adult Human Fibroblasts by Defined Factors." *Cell* 131 (November 30, 2007): 1–12.

Thomson, James A., et al. "Embryonic Stem Cell Lines Derived from Human Blastocysts." *Science* 282, no. 5391 (November 6, 1998): 1145–47.

Waters, Brent, and Ronald Cole-Turner, eds. *God and the Embryo: Religious Voices on Stem Cells and Cloning.* Washington, DC: Georgetown University Press, 2003.

Wilmut, Ian, et al. "Somatic Cell Nuclear Transfer." *Nature* 419, no. 6907 (October 10, 2002): 583–86.

———. "Viable Offspring Derived from Fetal and Adult Mammalian Cells." *Nature* 385, no. 6619 (February 27, 1997): 810–13.

*PART V*

---

# OTHER SPECIFIC PROBLEMS

*Chapter 15*

# ORGAN AND TISSUE TRANSPLANTATION

## INTRODUCTION

The field of transplant medicine continues to develop and produce interesting and exciting breakthroughs. Clinicians first used the kidney dialysis machine in Boston in 1948, and the first successful kidney transplant from one human to another occurred in 1954. In the latter case, because the donor and recipient were identical twins, doctors bypassed the problem of the rejection of tissue but did not solve it. In 1959, drug makers began to develop immunosuppressive drugs that were first used in humans in 1961. "By 1965, 1–year survival rates of allografted kidneys from living related donors approached 80% and survival rates of kidneys from cadavers approached 65%."[1] Breakthrough followed breakthrough as organ transplantation became another major success story of modern medicine. Today, organ and tissue transplantation is widespread, and transplant agencies have established practice guidelines and standards of care.

Although we have yet to achieve all the developments presented in science fiction such as *RoboCop, The Terminator, Blade Runner, The Six Million Dollar Man,* and *The Bionic Woman* of an earlier generation and the *Sarah Connor Chronicles* or *Star Trek* Borgs of today, the following replacements are possible from head to toe: eyes and corneas; ear lobes; cochlear implants; hearts and heart valves; lungs; liver and liver lobes; kidneys; pancreas; intestines; hips and other prostheses for arms, legs, and joints; vascular tissue; skin, bone, and tendons. Work continues on developing an artificial heart and other vital organs, improving immunosuppressant

273

drugs to prevent rejection, and using biotechnologies to put genes for the human immune system in animals so that human recipients of animal organs will not be as prone to reject them. In addition, scientists and clinicians are exploring applications of biotechnology, especially stem cell technology, in the field of regenerative medicine, as we saw in chapter 14. Some day, we might be able to build or to grow whole new organs as replacement parts. In fact, one idea is to use inkjet printer technology and combine biotechnology and biomedical engineering: that is, we may one day be able to build and grow a three-dimensional organ in a matter of hours or days.[2]

Yet, in spite of all this progress, most people are aware of the difficulties surrounding organ and tissue transplants. Some of the problems are financial: the cost of the procedure is well beyond the means of some people. Other problems are clinical: examples include the rate of rejection as well as the side effects of the drugs used to prevent rejection. But the problems that receive the most attention continue to be (1) the shortage of organs for transplantation and (2) appropriate criteria in deciding who gets those organs. In spite of media blitzes, public education campaigns, and legislation making such donations easier, people do not donate nearly enough organs to meet the increasing demand. In 1991, for example, "Nearly 24,000 patients [were] awaiting organ transplantation in the United States."[3] Over the past seventeen years, these numbers have grown dramatically. The United Network for Organ Sharing (UNOS) reported in February 2008 that there were 98,059 waiting list candidates in the United States. As of February 8, 2008, 26,022 transplants were reported as occurring between January and November 2007, while only 13,224 donors were reported for the same time period.[4] With this scarcity problem come perceptions of inequities in getting on the list for organs as well as access to them. When, in 1993, the then governor of Pennsylvania received a heart and liver within a very short time of needing one, people commented on how quickly he received them and grew suspicious. Likewise, when the baseball legend Mickey Mantle received a liver transplant, people made two sorts of comments: Should recovering alcoholics ever receive liver transplants? and Should individuals with cancer receive them? In both cases, the assumption people frequently made was that the recipients' social status launched them to the top of the list. Although UNOS explicitly rejects celebrity status as being a factor in receiving anatomical gifts, perceptions such as these circulate as unresolved problems and add another layer of complexity to this important topic.

## Notes on Terms

Often, commentators, clinicians, and bioethicists use *organ donation* as an umbrella term for this topic. However, this can be misleading for several reasons. For one, someone may donate (or procure) organs *and* tissues. That is, the available procedures involve more than just whole vital organs. Two, although the main part of the paradigm we see in the United States is one of charity—organ and tissue transplantation involves someone *donating* or *giving* a part of his or her body (i.e., an anatomical gift)—this is not the only paradigm, as we will see below. Three, *organ donation* seems to oversimplify the complexity of the topic. For example, procuring organs from animals and transplanting them into a human person cannot be, strictly speaking, organ *donation*, either.

Instead, we use the terms *allografting* and *xenografting* to refer to all forms of organ and tissue transplantation. This excludes the use of artificial organs, machines, and other "replacement" organs grown or built outside of a living thing. As technology develops, however, biotechnology and nanotechnology increasingly blur the lines between organ and machine or between natural and artificial. These blurred boundaries bring us into other topics we have already covered in this book: forgoing a life-saving technology may mean forgoing hemodialysis, an allografted kidney, or an artificially grown kidney. *Allografting* refers to transplantation of someone else's organ(s) or tissue(s) into a recipient. Allografting is organ and tissue transplantation between two different members of the same species. *Xenografting* refers to transplantation (that is, xenotransplantation) of an animal's (typically a pig's) organ(s) or tissue(s) into a human recipient. Xenografting is organ and tissue transplantation between two members of different species.

# ETHICAL ISSUES IN ALLOGRAFTING

## *Acceptability of Transplantations*

Such is the nature of modern medicine and medical progress that transplantation progressed from being a highly experimental procedure essentially limited to genetically identical twins who had no problems of tissue incompatibility to being a rather routine set of procedures. The major ethical issues in this transition were twofold. The first issue was the research dimension: the move from drug and surgical trials on animals to the use of these drugs and procedures on humans. Generally, the terminal condition of the patients provided the motivation for them to enter these trials. Transplantation was an option of last resort. The second problem was more unusual: "the ethical decision concerning the removal of a healthy organ from a normal person for the benefit of someone else. For the first time in surgical history, a normal, healthy person was to be subjected to a major surgical operation for someone else's benefit."[5] Proponents resolved this problem by arguing for the primacy of love or charity over the value of the physical integrity of the body with the proviso that the donor gave consent freely. We no longer saw transplant surgery as a mutilation but as a donation—an act of giving life to another.

Now tissue can be matched relatively well between donor and recipient. A new generation of immunosuppressant drugs is available to prevent the rejection mechanism. A new problem has emerged, however: there is a kind of sense of entitlement to a transplant. Within several decades, the ethical question has shifted from justifying whether one could be an organ donor to justifying a highly experimental treatment to securing informed consent for a complex, but routine, medical procedure.

## *Sources of Allografts*

There are two major sources of allografts: the living and the dead. Each source has ethical problems specific to it. With respect to the living, a key issue is consent. If the recipient is a close relative and in critical condition, qualified donors may feel a great deal of pressure or coercion with respect to being a donor. They may not want to be a donor, but they may be under an enormous amount of pressure to donate and may be exposed to a significant sense of guilt if they choose not to. Thus, care must be taken to ensure that potential recipients and health care providers, especially organ procurement coordinators, give prospective donors the psychological and ethical space necessary for a free choice. Related to the consent process is another key ethical issue: preventing harm (nonmaleficence). While many living donors may be able to function normally after the surgery, the transplant surgery is a very risky procedure for donor and recipient alike. Therefore, one must be sure that a potential donor is fully aware of the potential complications of, for example, living kidney donation.

The other source of donors is the dead. The key ethical issue here, in addition to securing consent from relatives, is to guarantee that the individual is dead before surgeons harvest the organs. Bioethicists and clinicians know this as the "dead donor rule." The reason for this type of concern is the conflict of interest between the needs of the recipient—who may be dying—and the rights of the donor who, while dying, is not yet dead. This conflict may manifest as a conflict of interest in the health care team. One can address this conflict of interest by mandating that the physician who pronounces the patient dead has no contact with—let alone be a member of— the transplant team. Other problems are possible, however, and we will discuss these later in this chapter.

## Scarcity and Supply of Allografts

A critical question is what motivates the continued appeals for organ donors? One response, surely, is the desire to help individuals who are dying because of, for example, kidney, liver, or heart failure. Increasing the number of donors would help alleviate the scarcity of organs and provide relief for many patients and families. But another motive could be a desire to have the transplantation field grow. As financial pressures increase, more hospitals may seek to provide facilities that are also good sources of income. An organ transplantation center could do this. Yet, would this not exacerbate the shortage problem by expanding the pool of candidate recipients without increasing the organ supply? Furthermore, manufacturers of drugs have a financial interest in seeing such centers develop because they provide a new market for their drugs. While the motivations for developing new transplantation centers are typically not as crass as these questions suggest, we nevertheless must be aware that such mixed motivations and potential conflicts of interest between patient well-being and financial gains are a part of the transplantation field.

Of all the issues connected with transplantation, supply continues to be the most problematic—need always outstrips supply. While people continually affirm that they are either not opposed to organ donation or that they are willing to be donors, most do not take the steps necessary to be an organ donor, and many families refuse permission for a deceased relative to be a donor. Thus, the primary vehicle for obtaining organs—donation—has not provided the number of organs needed on a daily basis.

## Allograft Procurement

Between the scarcity and supply issues and the allocation issues lies the procurement problem. It is here where the tension between need for, distribution of, and choices regarding allograft procurement collide. There are four main models for allograft procurement. By using the term *procurement*, we are attempting to describe, generally, any process to obtain an allograft.

The first model reflects a voluntary and charitable act on the part of the donor. Here, a person is truly *giving* an anatomical gift; patients, or recipients, are receiving the allograft. Generally speaking, organ and tissue donation in this model is nondirected; that is, the donor does not give the allograft(s) to an identified person ahead of time. Transplant centers allocate organs and tissues based on a scoring system (e.g., based on medical need) to the next patient on the list. Living donors, however, often direct their donation to a particular person, usually a family member in need of a kidney.

In addition to donation, two quasi-voluntary models have been proposed: the opt-out and the mandatory request models. In the opt-out proposal, society presumes that every person who has died is an organ donor unless he or she has explicitly stated otherwise. In order not to be a donor, one would have to take explicit steps to opt out of the procurement process. In effect, society, through transplant surgeons, would harvest or salvage organs and tissues. Here, organ donation does not involve *giving*; it involves *taking*.

The other quasi-voluntary model is the mandatory request. In this proposal, regulatory agencies require health care providers to ask all parties—patients and relatives—if they would consider being a donor. Proponents devised this system in part because of reports that some people said they had not considered organ donation because no one had asked them. This approach, widely in use in the United States, is more respectful of the individual and his or her choices; it also avoids giving the impression that individuals are the property of the state, which can do with them as it pleases. Additionally, this model preserves a sense of charity about the act: someone must still decide to give organs or tissues.

A fourth model is the proposal to commodify allografts and allow market dynamics to encourage the exchange of organs and tissues. The assumption is that market forces would eventually set a fair price for allografts and that many individuals would come forward to sell a particular body part, thus resolving the supply problem. Currently, no country officially permits such a practice, though to be sure there is an underground market in body parts. Again, this model is not donation proper. Here, one is neither giving nor receiving: "donors" are *selling* and patients are *buying*. Two primary concerns are that the policy would further jeopardize the already marginal status of those to whom such a policy might most appeal—the poor—and that pricing of the body and body parts would contribute to the alienation, objectification, and overall commodification of the person, resulting in a loss of human dignity.

## Allograft Allocation

In principle, the issue of allograft allocation deals with both organs and tissues; however, most commentators have whole organ allocation in mind. This issue is mainly about distributive justice and identifying the material principles of justice for allocating allografts and identifying candidate recipients. Who should receive the available organs? There are national registries of

organs that report organ availability. These organs are made available on the basis of medical need in relation to biological compatibility. For example, UNOS relies on "a complex point system
based on blood and tissue compatibility, waiting time, medical
urgency and distance between donor, transplant center and recipient." The University of Pittsburgh, a major transplant center, has
two sets of criteria for liver transplantation: (1) problems that
always rule out a transplant—"active infection, metastatic cancer,
advanced heart and lung disease, and AIDS"; and (2) problems
that nearly always rule out a transplant—"advanced kidney disease, age greater than 60 years, active hepatitis and previous liver
surgery...[make] transplantation technically not feasible."[6]

The 1985 Massachusetts Task Force on Organ Transplantation suggested another approach, which was a combination of
various allocation methods. First, there must be an initial screening based exclusively on medical criteria, including length of survival and capacity for rehabilitation. Second, there should be
sensitivity to the fact that the poor are frequently worse off medically because of their poverty and that their after-transplant
needs will be different than those of people with insurance plans
or plans with more inclusive coverage. Candidates are then to be
selected from this pool based on a first come, first served lottery.
A candidate can move to the top of the list if a review panel thinks
this individual is in danger of death and the originally scheduled
candidate can survive until another organ can be obtained.[7]

In spite of efforts to rationalize the organ distribution system
and make it equitable, issues of discrimination do arise. In 1989,
for example, three major reports showed that "white men received
a greatly disproportionate share of the nation's transplanted kidneys compared with women and blacks of both sexes."[8] In
another example from that year, white males received "79.2% of
hearts transplanted last year, 60.6% of kidneys and 56.4% of pan-
creases."[9] Such disparity is part of a common pattern in which
blacks frequently receive fewer coronary bypass surgeries, participate less in clinical trials, and generally have less access to health
care. In the area of kidney dialysis, the disparity in care is more
striking for two reasons: blacks have three times the rate of kidney
failure than do whites, and since 1972 the federal government has

paid the bulk of the cost for transplants. One can easily understand why such data, as well as broader beliefs and experiences
about racism and discrimination, would lead blacks to be less
willing and able to participate in organ donation.

The death of baseball legend Mickey Mantle in 1995 also
raised the specific problem of whether someone with cirrhosis of
the liver caused by alcoholism should receive a liver transplant.
Mantle was not the first person in such a situation to receive a
liver. In 1988 "alcoholic cirrhosis accounted for 138 of the 1680
liver transplants."[10] In 2001, researchers noted that alcoholic liver
disease had become a primary indication for liver transplantation
in spite of concerns over the behavior of alcohol abuse.[11]
Interestingly, many individuals who have heart disease because of
smoking need heart transplants, and these individuals are not
subject to the same moral scrutiny. The success rates for transplantation due to cirrhosis are getting better, and the primary dis-
qualifications seem to be damage to the brain, heart, and blood
systems. This question is part of a broader discussion of what
kinds of behavior, if any, could disqualify a person from insurance, health care, or other forms of social service. This would be a
form of a merit-based distribution: here, patients would get access
based on what transplant agencies judge they deserve or would be
denied access. A complicating issue in this discussion is whether
one considers alcoholism a disease over which a person has some
control or a form of moral weakness.

Another issue is that even though many people will eventually reap what they sow, does that mean the community is to shun
them and refuse medical care? While personal responsibility is an
important part of the ethical debate over access to health care, we
must also remember that not all victims are self-made. One's
social, economic, and educational background contributes significantly to one's perception of health as well as to access to basic
primary care.

A final question is how many transplants a single individual
should receive. Should each candidate receive one organ only, or
should the patient continue to receive them until the procedure is
successful? Or, as an intermediary position, should transplant
agencies limit an individual to a fixed number of attempts, for

example, three? Here, if the third attempt at transplantation fails, then no further attempts would be made.

# SPECIFIC ETHICAL ISSUES IN TRANSPLANT MEDICINE

## *Donation after Cardiac Death*

In 1993, the University of Pittsburgh initiated a protocol using non–heart-beating cadavers as sources of organs.[12] The protocol was this: If an individual was on a life-support system and dying and elected to have the life-support system removed, then that individual could elect to be an organ donor, too. This donor was taken to the operating room and prepared for the surgery to remove the organs. Then the life-support system was removed. The harvesting team waited for the heart to stop beating. They then waited an additional two minutes. If the heart did not spontaneously resume beating within the two-minute period, physicians declared the patient dead, and the team removed the organs.

Needless to say, this protocol generated no small amount of controversy. On the one hand, the university did very careful studies of the families of the patients who participated in such protocols. The families reported no negative experiences with the procedure and were satisfied that everyone was treated properly. On the other hand, individuals such as Renee Fox, who has reported on organ transplantation since its beginnings, was utterly appalled by the procedure, basically describing it as a form of cannibalism.

Since 1993, the controversy has continued. Bioethicists now refer to this as *donation after cardiac death* (versus after brain death—see chapter 8) and as "going back to the future." This is because before brain death criteria donors were declared dead by cardiopulmonary criteria. After brain death criteria became established, patients tended to become donors only after they were declared dead by these neurological criteria. In addition to the major question of whether the donor who is declared dead by cardiac criteria is really dead, several other questions emerge.[13] Are we using these persons merely as a means to the end of increasing the organ supply? Do they fit the Uniform Determination of Death Act criteria? For example, if we are able (however remote the probability of success may be) to apply cardiopulmonary resuscitation and start the heart again, then technically the patient's heart has not *irreversibly* stopped.

Moreover, several procedural issues exist. One, how long should one wait to be sure that the donor's heart has really stopped? Two values are in tension here. On the one hand, we want to be sure the patient is dead to respect that person and not to kill him or her. On the other hand, the longer the transplant team waits the less viable or useful the organs will be. An additional issue here is that medicines used before death to protect the organs from deteriorating might also hasten death. There are actually two important time intervals: (a) the time between the withdrawal of life support and the cessation of heart function and (b) the time from the cessation of heart function to the initiation of organ procurement. The Pittsburgh protocol set (b) at two minutes. Now, most protocols range from four to five minutes. There are few data available on how long it is possible for a patient to resuscitate spontaneously without the aid of others.

Two, how can we keep the decision to withdraw life support separate from the decision to donate organs? Here, we are primarily concerned with preserving the rationale for forgoing or withdrawing medical treatment—a benefits-burdens comparison and respect for human dignity. If the two decisions become mixed, this might be a subtle way to manipulate unfairly the decision to withdraw life-sustaining treatment to favor the potential recipient's situation.

Three, how can we minimize the potential for conflicts of interest in the health care team? In this situation, a health care provider who has an interest in obtaining the patient's organs may be more prone to make the determination of death more quickly. One solution is to separate the transplant team from the care-giving team. In addition, the person who declares the patient dead ought not to have prior connection with the patient or be a person who is affiliated with the transplant team.

## *Xenotransplantation*

One of many responses to the supply problem has been the use of xenografts: organs and tissues from other species. To this point the attempts have focused on using such organs—a baboon's heart or liver, for example—together with vast quantities of immunosuppressant drugs. Now another attempt is being reported. The body can detect a stranger in its midst, so to speak, and begins a twofold defensive reaction: recognition of the foreign tissue and rejection (or attack) of it.[14] "That reaction is now apparently the other great barrier to transplanting livers, hearts, kidneys and other organs from pigs to humans." Scientists are responding to this problem by inserting human immune system genes into pig embryos so that the pigs' organs possess human proteins.[15] In this way, the human immune system would then recognize the transplanted porcine organ as its own (human) and would not mount the immune defense.

While there is no suggestion at all that such a transgenic pig would be thought of as human or quasi-human because of the presence of a particular gene, nonetheless the technology does reveal the potential for interspecies gene transfer, putting genes where no genes have gone before. In addition, as we saw in chapter 14, chimera technology also raises these questions of interspecies relationships. This type of research forces the animal welfare and rights questions because scientists would engineer, breed, and kill such transgenic animals solely for human well-being. The use of such xenografts could also raise new questions about human identity and the integrity of the body. Members of certain religions that prohibit the use of pork, such as Judaism and Islam, could raise additional questions. While it is the case that pig arteries have typically been used in repairs to the human heart without objection, a more intimate mingling of human being and pig may be problematic.

We can summarize the major ethical issues as follows.[16] First, as with increasing the supply of allografts, the issue of the need for organs and tissues provokes research into xenografts. Thus, proponents claim xenografts may be an efficacious way to address the need for organs and other tissues and support that claim with the principle of beneficence. Second, as mentioned above, one must ask whether the human need for organs and tissues outweighs the issues of animal rights and welfare. In addition, there is the issue of species integrity. How should we protect both the human species and the animal species we use for xenotransplantation? Third, as with allografting, the issue of safety is of major concern. In appealing to the principles of nonmaleficence and autonomy, bioethicists identify the risks of immunosuppression and susceptibility to animal viruses and other contagions. This latter risk poses a public health concern if those viruses mutate and become infectious for all humans, not just those with xenografts. To address this risk, proponents suggest that a recipient must be made fully aware of the complications and risks in an informed consent process if xenografting is to be acceptable.

# CONCLUSION

The development of new methods of procuring allografts and the use of biotechnology to make animal organs available for human beings have generated a new set of controversies within the field of organ transplantation. These will serve to further complicate the already difficult questions of availability and access.

While it is clear that allografting is a routine part of medical treatment, it is also clear that the availability of allografts (and xenografts) is also a problem. One wonders if the kinds of expectations about receiving an organ and the pressures to obtain them will not produce a kind of backlash that will cause people to become even less willing to donate them. We may wind up in an ironic situation: as great technical progress is made in organ transplantation, the social acceptability of donating organs may decrease. Publicity about technological advances and how transplant professionals treat donors and their families will contribute much to the future of organ and tissue transplantation in this country.

# DISCUSSION QUESTIONS

1. What problems, if any, do you see with organ donations from living donors, for example, parent to child, sibling to sibling, cousin to cousin?
2. Do you think individuals with high social status receive preferential treatment for organ transplantations? If so, is this fair or unfair?
3. An individual who filled out an organ donor form (expressing her desire to donate) dies. Her relatives object to her being a donor. Whose wishes should be followed?
4. What is your reaction to the practice of donation after cardiac death (DCD)? Are those donors really dead? Should they be given treatments to protect organs even if that hastens their deaths?
5. Does using animals as a source for human organ transplants raise any problems for you?

# NOTES

1. Joseph E. Murray, "Human Organ Transplantation: Background and Consequences," *Science* 256, no. 5062 (June 5, 1992): 1414. The term *allografted* refers to the transplantation of one human being's organs or tissues into another human being's body.

2. Tao Xu, Joyce Jin, Cassie Gregory, James J. Hickman, and Thomas Boland, "Inkjet Printing of Viable Mammalian Cells," *Biomaterials* 26 (2005): 93–99.

3. Aaron Spital, "The Shortage of Organs for Transplantation: Where Do We Go from Here?" *New England Journal of Medicine* 325 (October 24, 1991): 1243.

4. United Network for Organ Sharing, "United Network for Organ Sharing: Organ Donation and Transplantation—Data," http://www.unos.org/, accessed February 14, 2008.

5. Murray, "Human Organ Transplantation," 1413.

6. Lawrence K. Altman, "A Question of Ethics: Should Alcoholics Get Transplanted Livers?" *New York Times*, April 3, 1990, C3.

7. "Report of the Massachusetts Task Force on Organ Transplantation," *Law, Medicine, and Health Care* 13 (1985): 8–26.

8. Sandra Blakeslee, "Studies Find Unequal Access to Kidney Transplants," *New York Times*, January 24, 1989, C1.

9. "Transplants Mostly Involve White Men," *Worcester Telegram and Gazette*, May 30, 1989, A6.

10. Altman, "Question of Ethics," C3.

11. C. O. Bellany, A. M. DiMartini, K. Ruppert, A. Jain, F. Dodson, M. Torbenson, T. E. Starzl, J. J. Fung, and A. J. Demetris, "Liver Transplantation for Alcoholic Cirrhosis: Long Term Follow-up and Impact of Disease Recurrence," *Transplantation* 72, no. 4 (August 27, 2001): 619–26.

12. M. A. DeVita, J. V. Snyder, and A. Grenvik, "History of Organ Donation by Patients with Cardiac Death," *Kennedy Institute of Ethics Journal* 3, no. 2 (June 1993): 113–29. This entire issue of the *Kennedy Institute of Ethics Journal* was devoted to this topic.

13. J. L. Bernat et al., "Report of a National Conference on Donation after Cardiac Death," *American Journal of Transplantation* 6 (2006): 281–91.

14. Ibid.

15. Philip J. Hilts, "Gene Transfers Offer New Hope for Interspecies Organ Transplants," *New York Times*, October 19, 1993, C3.

16. See Michael J. Reiss, "The Ethics of Xenotransplantation," *Journal of Applied Philosophy* 17, no. 3 (2000): 253–62; and Helena Melo, Cristina Brandão, Guilhermina Rego, and Rui Nunes, "Ethical and Legal Issues in Xenotransplantation," *Bioethics* 15, nos. 5 and 6 (2001): 427–42.

# BIBLIOGRAPHY

Altman, Lawrence K. "A Question of Ethics: Should Alcoholics Get Transplanted Livers?" *New York Times*. April 3, 1990, C3.

Bellany, C. O., A. M. DiMartini, K. Ruppert, A. Jain, F. Dodson, M. Torbenson, T. E. Starzl, J. J. Fung, and A. J. Demetris. "Liver Transplantation for Alcoholic Cirrhosis: Long Term Follow-up and Impact of Disease Recurrence." *Transplantation* 72, no. 4 (August 27, 2001): 619–26.

Bernat, J. L., et al. "Report of a National Conference on Donation after Cardiac Death." *American Journal of Transplantation* 6 (2006): 281–91.

Blakeslee, Sandra. "Studies Find Unequal Access to Kidney Transplants." *New York Times*. January 24, 1989, C1.

DeVita, M. A., J. V. Snyder, and A. Grenvik. "History of Organ Donation by Patients with Cardiac Death." *Kennedy Institute of Ethics Journal* 3, no. 2 (June 1993): 113–29.

Hilts, Philip J. "Gene Transfers Offer New Hope for Interspecies Organ Transplants." *New York Times*. October 19, 1993, C3.

Melo, Helena, Cristina Brandão, Guilhermina Rego, and Rui Nunes. "Ethical and Legal Issues in Xenotransplantation." *Bioethics* 15, nos. 5 and 6 (2001): 427–42.

Murray, Joseph E. "Human Organ Transplantation: Background and Consequences." *Science* 256, no. 5062 (June 5, 1992): 1411–16.

Reiss, Michael J. "The Ethics of Xenotransplantation." *Journal of Applied Philosophy* 17, no. 3 (2000): 253–62.

"Report of the Massachusetts Task Force on Organ Transplantation." *Law, Medicine, and Health Care* 13 (1985): 8–26.

Spital, Aaron. "The Shortage of Organs for Transplantation: Where Do We Go from Here?" *New England Journal of Medicine* 325, no. 17 (October 24, 1991): 1243–46.

"Transplants Mostly Involve White Men." *Worcester Telegram and Gazette*. May 30, 1989, A6.

United Network for Organ Sharing. "United Network for Organ Sharing: Organ Donation and Transplantation—Data." http://www.unos.org/. Accessed February 14, 2008.

Veatch, Robert M. *Transplantation Ethics*. Washington, DC: Georgetown University Press, 2000.

Xu, Tao, Joyce Jin, Cassie Gregory, James J. Hickman, and Thomas Boland. "Inkjet Printing of Viable Mammalian Cells." *Biomaterials* 26 (2005): 93–99.

*Chapter 16*

# RESEARCH ON HUMAN SUBJECTS

## INTRODUCTION

Although medical researchers carry out most of their work in the laboratory, unknown and unobserved by the public, probably no feature of modern medicine has had as dramatic an effect on so many people as research. By careful design and countless hours of running experiments, scientists have succeeded in identifying the causes of many diseases, designing vaccines to prevent them, and developing drugs and devices to treat them. The medical and public health communities have virtually eliminated smallpox, polio, most childhood diseases, and other sources of human illness because of research into their causes. Officials and professionals are marshaling these same efforts against the major diseases of our day: cancer, HIV/AIDS, and heart disease.

Yet, these benefits notwithstanding, some problems have been associated with research, especially in the last few decades. Several well-publicized cases involving the involuntary infection of children with hepatitis, injection of live cancer cells into nursing home residents, and omission of treatment of diagnosed syphilis so that researchers could observe the natural course of the disease raised problems about consent. The experiments conducted by Nazi physicians in the concentration camps produced questions about the motives of the physicians and the value of the knowledge gained. More recently, publicized cases of fraud through data faking, either by inventing patients or by falsifying experiments, revealed the dangers of a too highly competitive atmosphere in the lab.

Concerns such as these as well as the desire to ensure the traditionally high standards of research and the integrity of the scientists led to a long national—and, more recently, global—process of examining the ethics of research on human subjects. In this chapter, we will highlight some of the ethical and legal elements of that process.

# ETHICAL ISSUES IN RESEARCH ON HUMAN SUBJECTS

## *Consent*

The key issue in research is consent.[1] First, consent protects the patient's autonomy. By consenting (or not consenting) to the research, the patient exercises control over his or her life. Second, consent protects human dignity. A researcher recognizes the patient as a center of value that one cannot use as a mere object. Third, consent is functional in that it reassures the public that investigators do not manipulate or deceive research subjects. Fourth, consent promotes trust between a physician-investigator and a research subject. Finally, consent can help the person become a better subject. By knowing more about the research project, the subject can perhaps provide better information, be more cooperative, and be more diligent in fulfilling the requirements of the study. This last element is particularly important because some studies can last several months or even years. Thus, for ethical, practical, and scientific reasons, consent is important.

In a rather dramatic move, the Food and Drug Administration (FDA) made a critical exception to the consent requirement. When neither a patient with a life-threatening condition nor a relative of the patient can consent, and if investigators notify the community about the FDA-approved study, then one can enroll that patient in a research protocol without consent. The problem this seeks to resolve is the inability to perform research on critically ill patients, such as heart attack or stroke victims, for whom no one is available to consent but for whom time is critical. The problem that the new rule creates is precisely what the tradition of medical ethics since the Nuremberg Code seeks to prevent: namely, research on patients without their consent. While patients may benefit in the long term from such research, the fear is that in the short term we may compromise the well-being of particular patients, especially when pharmaceutical, biotechnology, and medical device companies have a substantive interest in seeing biomedical research move forward.[2]

## Selection of Research Subjects

In an old but classic article, Hans Jonas identified four categories of possible research subjects.[3] The first category includes *the best educated, most highly motivated members of society*, who are represented by the researcher-scientists themselves. The tradition of self-experimentation has had an honored place in science, and many researchers still participate in the research protocol, at least to know what the subjects are experiencing. The second category contains *the most marginal people in society*: the defenseless, the poor, and the powerless. These people would not be able to resist the power of the scientific or medical establishment and would ensure a type of captive audience. The third category consists of *those willing to sell their services*. This method of recruitment is in the spirit of free enterprise so valued by our American society. The critical issue is whether the price is right for the subject. Finally, the fourth category of possible research subjects includes *members of the public at large selected by lottery*. Since all have benefited from advances in medicine, all would repay this benefit by participating in research. Also, this is a type of public service that could be an expression of one's sense of civic responsibility. Although never used before, this seems a fair way to obtain research subjects.

There is, though, another way of recruiting subjects that is probably the most typical. Physicians frequently ask their patients to participate in research by trying a new drug, a new procedure, or a new device. While this option provides the *possibility* of a direct benefit to the subject as well as advances in knowledge, it has the disadvantage of blurring the distinction between physician and researcher and between clinical practice and biomedical research.

On the one hand, some have suggested that a sense of fair play would require that all be willing to participate in research. Because we have benefited from others who have been research subjects, we *should* participate in research so that future generations can benefit as we have. This reason for participation in research stresses the utilitarian dimension. People should participate because of the valuable knowledge and other benefits that society can gain from research. That is, there may be *an obligation to participate* in research.

On the other hand, altruism also can be a motivation for participation in research. Altruism focuses on the benefits to society and the good to be received by those in need. Such generosity of spirit can motivate others to participate and help create bonds of community between the ill and the healthy. Altruism can translate into a spirit of *voluntarism* in biomedical research.

The issue behind all these schemes is fairness. The concern is to ensure that researchers do not single out one population for continual use in research or place that population at risk because of an inability to resist requests to participate.

## Conflicts of Interest

Biomedical research contains potential for several conflicts of interest. For one, it may confuse clinical practice and biomedical research, which have different goals: benefiting the patient and expanding human knowledge, respectively.[4] This can put stress on the physician-patient relationship when both players take on added roles. Thus, the physician is also the clinical investigator and the patient is also a research subject. In some cases, continuing with a research project may be harmful to the patient even if investigators can gain valuable knowledge. Moreover, some investigators may have financial interests tied to the success of a particular research project. How much do these interests cloud their clinical judgment of what's in the best interests of the patients?

Likewise, recent history suggests that a growing source of biomedical research funding is the private commercial sector. Here, the conflicts of interest may be experienced by scientists. They are situated between the scientific enterprise of research and the commercial enterprise of product development. Financial gains and prestige challenge a scientist's commitment to discovering truth and professionalism in science. In fact, prestige alone in the highly competitive scientific community may be enough to tempt scientists to conduct dishonest research.

## *Distribution of Burdens and Benefits*

The issues of justice concerning the distribution of burdens and benefits relate directly to the issues of consent and selection of research participants. There are two levels to this issue: justice in the research protocol itself and justice in the results of the research. First, several commentators discuss the need for fairness in research protocols. This includes a variety of factors: how do scientists assign patient-subjects to different cohorts, how do scientists choose treatment and control groups, and so on? A major question here is whether researchers can use placebos (fake treatments) when other effective treatments are available. Similarly, even if researchers choose not to use placebos, how should they select alternative treatments and assign patients to the different treatment groups? The technical term used to describe the standard is *clinical equipoise*. Ashcroft describes the problem as follows:

> Suppose we have two treatments, and a patient in a certain condition, and a physician (or other healthcare worker) trying to decide what to prescribe. The physician has a decision problem, which is to choose the better treatment for this patient. He or she is ignorant as to which of the two treatments is superior. In this situation we can say that he or she is in *equipoise* regarding the two options.[5]

In other words, a researcher should be genuinely uncertain about the differences in effectiveness of each treatment option. Basically, this standard means that researchers must be in clinical equipoise about the treatments in a study in order for a clinical trial (or clinical research) to be fair and ethical. However, this standard and the concept of clinical equipoise are controversial.[6] In general, one is concerned with distributing the possible benefits and burdens of research fairly *within the research project itself.*

Second, bioethicists call for justice in access to the benefits and in sharing burdens (risks) of a research project. This is related to the larger question of access to health care in general. Likewise, it is related to the fairness in selecting research participants. One group (e.g., the poor, marginalized, or vulnerable) should not have a disproportionate share of the burdens of research while only few (e.g., the wealthy) benefit from their sacrifices.

## The Meaning of Public Funding

The stem cell debate in the United States calls attention to the meaning of public funding. That is, arguments on both sides of the issue connect the morality of embryonic stem cell research to the moral implications of funding (or not funding) that research. On the one hand, opponents claim that because embryonic stem cell research is immoral (e.g., because it requires the destruction of human embryos), public funds should not be used because many Americans share that moral view. On the other hand, proponents claim that because embryonic stem cell research is moral, and the goals of the research are noble, not using public funds is an atrocity. Additionally, proponents argue that using moral arguments to prevent such research is a form of moral imposition and reflects intolerance in a pluralistic society. What many proponents fail to recognize, however, is that their position is just as imbued with moral imposition as the opponents' position. Nevertheless, we ought to be prudent about the use of public money to finance research, and we ought to recognize the moral reasons for and against the use of such money. This has implications for public policy and appropriations bills when Congress sets the budgets for research agencies like the National Institutes of Health.

## Privacy and Confidentiality

Another major issue in research on human subjects is the protection of privacy and confidentiality. In the course of conducting research, investigators may discover sensitive information about patients. Protection of this information is essential to guard the patient's dignity against stigmatization and discrimination as well as to minimize limitations on the person's autonomy (e.g., access to employment opportunities). Of course, the issue of confidentiality is related to the physician-patient relationship. Given the potential for conflicts of interest, and the different roles doctors and patients play in research, one wonders whether the patient's trust in and the therapeutic intent of physicians can be preserved.

## Commercial Interests and Proprietary Natural Resources

The rise of commercial involvement in biomedical research has raised several issues. The first is the nature of ownership and property of biological material. At one level, should a company compensate an individual from whose cells a successful commercial product was developed? In what sense does a human subject "own" his or her cells, tissues, or organs after investigators remove them from the subject's body? In the 1990 California case, *Moore v. Regents of the University of California*, a physician-investigator developed a commercially valuable cell line from cells he obtained from a patient of his. Although, the California Supreme Court held that the patient (Moore) did not have property rights to his "discarded" cells (and therefore no right to compensation), the physician did have an obligation to disclose his financial interests in obtaining the patient's cells. This disclosure should have occurred during the informed consent process.

At another level, should companies compensate entire nations, villages, or communities in whose geographic region the company obtained commercially valuable material? Here, many are concerned with the exploitation of indigenous peoples and their knowledge. Many drugs derive from certain (usually tropical) plants, which may grow exclusively in one part of the world. Often, knowledge about the medicinal effects of plants leads to research aimed at isolating the active chemical. After researchers isolate the chemical, drug makers can tweak it to be clinically safe and effective for human use. Do drug makers owe anything to those who gave them the knowledge about the plants? Or to those who gave them access to the plants themselves? Here, one is concerned about commutative justice on a global or international scale.

# THE PUBLIC CONDUCTING OF RESEARCH

Because of the publicity given to problems in the conducting of research, a lengthy public debate was held about how scientists conduct research. The primary forums for this debate were a presidential commission and discussion by the Department of Health and Human Services. One result of the discussions held in these forums was the creation of a set of federal regulations on how investigators ought to conduct human research (Code of Federal Regulations, title 45, part 46).[7] These regulations primarily do two things. First, they clearly define informed consent. This is the knowing consent of an individual, or his or her legally authorized representative, so as to be able to exercise free power of choice, without undue inducement or any element of force, fraud, deceit, duress, or other form of constraint or coercion. While this standard is rather high, it highlights the value of autonomy and sets the standard high to maximize protection of the research subjects.

Second, the regulations spell out the information that must be given to the research subject in the process of informed consent. This information includes the following:

- An explanation of the procedures and their purposes, making sure the subject knows they are experimental;
- An identification of the risks and side effects that can be reasonably expected;
- A description of possible benefits;
- An indication of alternative therapies, if any, that are available;
- An offer to answer any questions the subject has; and
- An affirmation that the subject may withdraw from the experiment at any time without penalty.

Regulatory officials implement these regulations through specific means: the institutional review board (IRB). The regulations do not explicitly establish an IRB, but they certainly presume its existence. Thus, many commentators argue that the authority of the IRB comes from the institution that it represents, so it has as much (or as little) power as the institution gives it. An IRB can review human research that is supported only by federal funding, or it can review all of the research conducted by the institution, regardless of the funding source.

The IRB's tasks are basically twofold. First, the IRB reviews and monitors research conducted at its home institution. A particular issue of concern is ensuring the intelligibility of the consent form that the research subject will eventually read and sign. Second, it evaluates the balance between risk and benefit in particular research protocols to ensure the acceptability of the risk-benefit ratio for the research subjects. This evaluation both protects autonomy, by making the ultimate decision of whether or not to participate the subject's, and ensures that investigators provide relevant information about the protocol and its risks and benefits so that this autonomous choice is also an informed one.

While IRBs do add another layer of bureaucracy and paperwork between the research and the investigator, research appears to continue at its normal pace. Rather than reject proposals, most IRBs seem to prefer to resolve differences by negotiation. Sometimes, as in the case of the first use of the artificial heart, these negotiations are lengthy; and sometimes, as in the case of the first transplantation of an animal heart into a human, they are highly criticized. Even though problems remain at the margins of the research enterprise, a reasonable and responsible system is in place that serves to balance the rights of research subjects without disrupting legitimate research projects.

# CONCLUSION

Not all scientific progress is true human progress. While the scientific enterprise is an important one in society, the ethics of conducting research in general, including research on human subjects in particular, should involve an honest discussion of how research and development will be just and will truly attend to the authentic needs of human persons. What goods do research projects explore? To what technological solutions do they lead? What kind of society are we building? Research is a human activity grounded in curiosity and concern for human well-being; it is also a reflection of our values. If we exploit our neighbors to fulfill our needs, is that the kind of society in which we want to live?

## DISCUSSION QUESTIONS

1. Why is consent so important in research?
2. How do you think research subjects should be selected?
3. Do you think research subjects should be paid for participating in research?
4. Should research subjects have to pay for tests, medications, or other costs associated with the research? Should their insurance company pay for these expenses? Should the hospital pay for them? Should the company sponsoring the research pay for them?
5. Do you think you would be willing to participate in a research project?
6. Selection procedures typically exclude pregnant women from research projects. This means that when a new drug is released, no one knows the effects, if any, of it on the fetus. Is there a way to resolve this problem?
7. Should public money be used for research that a minority of people believes to be immoral? Why or why not?

# NOTES

1. See K. Getz and D. Borfitz, *Informed Consent: A Guide to Risks and Benefits of Volunteering for Clinical Trials* (Boston: Thomson CenterWatch, 2003).

2. Gina Kolata, "Ban on Medical Experiments without Consent Is Relaxed," *New York Times*, November 5, 1996, A1.

3. Hans Jonas, "Philosophical Reflections on Experimenting with Human Subjects," *Daedalus* 98, no. 2 (Spring 1969): 219–47.

4. For example, see Paul Litton and Franklin G. Miller, "A Normative Justification for Distinguishing the Ethics of Clinical Research from the Ethics of Medical Care," *Journal of Law, Medicine and Ethics* (Fall 2005): 566–74.

5. Richard Ashcroft, "Equipoise, Knowledge and Ethics in Clinical Research and Practice," *Bioethics* 13, no. 3/4 (1999): 314–15.

6. See, for example, Franklin G. Miller and Howard Brody, "A Critique of Clinical Equipoise: Therapeutic Misconception in the Ethics of Clinical Trials," *Hastings Center Report* 33, no. 3 (May–June 2003): 19–28.

7. See Office of Human Research Protections, Department of Health and Human Services, at http://www.hhs.gov/ohrp/, accessed March 4, 2008.

# BIBLIOGRAPHY

Ashcroft, Richard. "Equipoise, Knowledge and Ethics in Clinical Research and Practice." *Bioethics* 13, no. 3/4 (1999): 314–15.

Eaton, Margaret L., and Donald Kennedy. *Innovation in Medical Technology: Ethical Issues and Challenges.* Baltimore: Johns Hopkins University Press, 2007.

Getz, K., and D. Borfitz. *Informed Consent: A Guide to Risks and Benefits of Volunteering for Clinical Trials.* Boston: Thomson CenterWatch, 2003.

Jonas, Hans. "Philosophical Reflections on Experimenting with Human Subjects." *Daedalus* 98, no. 2 (Spring 1969): 219–47.

Kolata, Gina. "Ban on Medical Experiments without Consent Is Relaxed." *New York Times*. November 5, 1996, A1.

Levin Penslar, Robin, ed. *Research Ethics: Cases and Materials.* Bloomington: Indiana University Press, 1995.

Litton, Paul, and Franklin G. Miller. "A Normative Justification for Distinguishing the Ethics of Clinical Research from the Ethics of Medical Care." *Journal of Law, Medicine and Ethics* (Fall 2005): 566–74.

Loue, Sana. *Textbook of Research Ethics: Theory and Practice.* New York: Kluwer Academic, 2000.

Miller, Franklin G., and Howard Brody. "A Critique of Clinical Equipoise: Therapeutic Misconception in the Ethics of Clinical Trials." *Hastings Center Report* 33, no. 3 (May–June 2003): 19–28.

Murphy, Timothy F. *Case Studies in Biomedical Research Ethics.* Cambridge, MA: MIT Press, 2004.

*Chapter 17*

---

# A WHOLE EARTH ETHIC

## INTRODUCTION

Hovering at the edges of many of the questions we have discussed are several broader issues. These issues lead us beyond health care and the physician-patient relationship into a wider discussion of problems that are primarily social in nature, even though individuals are involved. We have already discussed some aspects of these problems: for example, the allocation of resources in organ transplantation; the obligations for future generations in reproduction, genetic diagnosis, and genetic engineering; and the tension between social and individual priorities in research.

The reason for titling this chapter as we did is that we address the problems we discuss here from the perspective of the whole Earth. The concerns and implications of the problems are that great. Yet, while some of these problems may also have an individual dimension—for all ethical concerns ultimately descend upon the individual—the impact of individual and social actions has profound and long-lasting results.

These problems are important to consider, in a preliminary fashion, to round out our discussion of the other bioethical problems discussed in this book. In the rest of this chapter, we will describe several of these problems.

# PROBLEMS OF A WHOLE EARTH ETHIC

## *Population Control*

If there is one thing that is true about the human species, it is that it is not an endangered species. We have so successfully reproduced that we encounter the opposite problem—overpopulation. While we have not reached the point of licensing space or issuing permits for reproduction, as some commentators predicted would happen, we are in the beginnings of a population crisis.

In fact, the ethical issues of population control deal with issues we have already discussed in this book. For example, considerations of assisted reproductive technologies (ARTs) influence how one sees the issue of population control. How one sees the issues in the abortion debate also influences judgments on population control more broadly. Related to reproductive technology and abortion are the issues of contraception and sterilization. All of these topics bridge the gap between the individual and personal decisions in human reproduction and the social dimensions and consequences of human reproduction.

In 2000, the world's population was estimated to be about six billion people; the United Nations Commission on Population and Development estimates that by 2050 it will be nine billion people.[1] We know that the population of China is more than 1.3 billion, and the population of India is rapidly approaching that same number. Birthrates are increasing in Latin America and in other developing countries. Thus, in terms of absolute numbers, the population is increasing dramatically in some parts of the world. While some countries are responding severely—China with its one-child-per-family policy,[2] for example—others do not have population control as a major priority.

One needs to consider several issues here. First, and in some ways most important, is the issue of perspective. Is Latin America's population growth a problem because it might mean that North America's standard of living will have to change? That is, is the population problem a problem because of the rate of growth, which is an *intra*-national justice problem? Or is it a problem because the consumption and growth patterns of other countries prevent equitable distribution of resources, which is a global justice problem? For example, while the United States might have a smaller population with respect to numbers, the average child in the United States consumes 20 percent more resources than children in developing countries. Problems are always problems for someone, and it is important to determine who defines the problem and on what basis.

A second, related issue is the imposition of values by one nation on another.[3] Many of the developed nations provide funding for population control programs in developing nations. The problem is that while the developed nation may see population control as a good in itself, such programs may violate a particular culture's social and/or religious values about reproduction or children. Such funding of population control programs may simply be another form of colonialism—economic and moral rather than political. Of course, this is related to the larger philosophical issue of moral relativism, especially when one considers differences in cultural views on the morality of birth control, ARTs, and abortion. The intensity of this problem is only heightened in the era of globalization.

A third issue is the tension between an individual's reproductive liberty and the good of a particular society. The right to reproduce is often seen as a basic human right and part of the concepts of human dignity and sanctity of life. Yet, there are pressing social needs and limited resources that, even if distributed fairly, can stretch only so far. China, for example, has made remarkable strides in solving the malnutrition problems that plagued it for centuries. But now, in part because of population growth, famine is again a possibility in parts of China. The reaction has been a stringent population control policy of one child per family. The policy is enforced through advocating delayed marriages, use of contraceptives, social pressure, negative economic incentives, and abortion. The policy asks individual Chinese to reverse one of their deepest cultural values—children—for the social good.

## Food and Malnutrition

One of the dominant media images of the last few decades is that of starving children. While we may have become hardened or grown numb with continual exposure to the problem, the images of the devastation from famine still disturb us. This is especially true because we know that there is a surplus of food in the world. We know that grain rots in American storage bins. Annually, we read of record harvests, especially in the United States. Yet, people die of starvation and of diseases to which individuals have a lower resistance because of malnutrition.

First, a major problem with the global experience of malnutrition is distribution. The surplus mentioned above is the reason that many suggest that the first food-related problem is not one of quantity (or production) but one of distribution. Political relations (or lack thereof) between nations, fears of control, imperialism, and the domestic political implications of a nation's failure to provide for its own citizens complicate the problems of distribution.

Second, while distribution can account for a significant amount of malnutrition, another problem is the quantity of food. Much of the success of the record harvests in the United States is the result of the heavy use of fertilizers. These fertilizers are expensive and require high capital investments. Also, the harvests require the mechanization of farming. The traditional family farm will probably not be able to feed the population levels in many developing nations. This has caused a shift to agribusiness, which has its own social, economic, and environmental implications. With the rise of agricultural biotechnology and genetically modified organisms (GMOs), many claimed that this would alleviate shortages of food, would increase yields in desert or high-salt conditions, and would add nutritional and medicinal value. Others criticized GMOs for being unsafe, for creating dependency on seed and fertilizer companies, and for further perpetuating the financial debts of developing nations.[4] Finally, many of the grains are hybrids; while they can produce more bushels per acre, these grains are not hardy and are vulnerable to many blights. Thus, observing the new grains' failure to thrive, or even survive, in natural environments dashed many hopes of the green revolution, which was not as dependent on the use of chemical fertilizers.

Third, the relation between food production and population growth also poses a problem for addressing malnutrition. Assuming that one has solved the distribution problem and that there has been a transition to contemporary agricultural methods, the question still remains whether supply can keep up with demand. A country may be producing as much food as it can and still not be able to keep pace with the population growth. There is a vicious circle operating here: the better fed a population is, the lower the infant mortality rate; the lower the infant mortality rate, the more people survive and the larger the population becomes. In turn, this can cause problems of malnutrition if the supply does not keep up with the demand.

Fourth, food aid may perpetuate dependence on foreign help, which prevents countries from being accountable for self-sufficiency in food production and addressing nutritional concerns. In other words, what does providing food aid do for a country? In the short run, aid feeds people and relieves starvation; thus, consciences are satisfied. But what happens in the long run? Providing food alone does not address the problem of the underlying causes of the famine. These may be overpopulation, poor or inadequate agriculture practices, inefficient or corrupt infrastructure, or other consequences of distribution problems. A whole Earth ethic would differentiate between episodic relief because of crop failure due to drought or some other natural disaster and relief that merely prolongs a nation's coming to terms with domestic policy problems. Thus, some would justify withholding aid to force nations into resolving their problems. In this perspective, aid simply prolongs the agony of a nation and allows it to continue its irresponsibility at the expense of those nations who would benefit from such aid while they make the transition to self-sufficiency and responsibility.

Finally, taking the previous point in a different direction, food can be a weapon of war. In an analogy to the old strategy of laying siege to a castle, one nation can attempt to starve another nation into political submission. The issue is not promoting self-sufficiency but rather leading to conquest. Populations are not hostage to internal development policies but captive to international policies. While death occurs in war, those who die are usually soldiers. Here the victims are whole populations.

## The Environment and Sustainable Development

One of the major shifts in consciousness of the last several decades is the awareness of the interconnectedness of our environment. This ecological mind-set has emerged as a consequence not of sensitivity to the environment but of several centuries of insensitivity to it. Our careless disposal of chemicals, for example, has returned to haunt us through increased levels of cancer and water unfit to drink. Our wasteful consumption habits have caused the near depletion of many nonrenewable resources. More recently, this shift in consciousness has led to a "green" movement. Former vice president and presidential candidate Al Gore's documentary, *An Inconvenient Truth*, sheds light on the problems as well as on the urgency of global warming (or "climate change") and other environmental concerns. Gore's voice is one of many in this green movement.

One issue is natural resource use or conservation. One author has proposed four ways of thinking about this concern.[5]

1. *Resource conservation*. The purpose of this viewpoint is to curtail the thoughtless exploitation of forests, wildlife, farmland, and so forth. The intent is to preserve nature for the good of the many rather than for the profit of the few. The prime issue is avoiding the exploitation of the environment while encouraging minimal use of available resources.
2. *Wilderness preservation*. This perspective focuses on preserving the environment for its own sake. In this view, the environment—e.g., forests, wilderness areas, rivers, the Grand Canyon—is valuable in and of itself, regardless of whether or not human beings appreciate it. Thus, nature is a sort of sacred place, a sanctuary that we should not violate.

3. *Moral extensionism* or *natural moralism.* This position
   argues that humans have duties to natural entities
   and that some intrinsically valuable characteristic of
   the entities forms the basis for the rights on which
   these duties are founded. Thus, human beings
   should protect dolphins because they are intelligent.
   Rain forests are valuable because of their contribution to ecology. The important feature of this perspective is that it breaks with the tradition of seeing
   the environment as valuable only because of its relation to human beings. The environment has more
   than instrumental value: it is valuable in and of
   itself.
4. *Ecological sensibility.* This orientation involves three
   perspectives. One, there is a respect owed to anything
   that has an end of its own or some capacity for internal self-regulation. Two, there is an understanding of
   reality that takes into account the importance of relationships and systems, as well as human beings.
   Third, there is an ethic that is oriented in the direction of peaceful cohabitation with nature, which
   involves a restrained and respectful use of it.

All of these ways of thinking about the environment imply, first,
a very respectful attitude toward nature and, second, varying
degrees of permissibility of intervention. To obtain the full import
of these attitudes, one should compare them to various models of
nature in chapter 2. One should especially consider the view of
nature in the plastic model for this seems to be the basic attitude
operative in Western societies.

In addition to resource conservation, another major debate
is over not whether one can intervene in nature but rather to what
extent one can do this as well as to what ends. The model of ecological sensibility does not prohibit interventions in nature, but it
certainly would severely critique many of the ways we have gone
about intervening. Although the most liberal of the four models,
it still runs contrary to dominant Western cultural values. One can
evaluate the four models more adequately by determining how

one would assess the following problems through each of them: acid rain, hazardous waste disposal sites, depletion of nonrenewable resources, strip-mining, development of more national and/or state parks, the status of rain forests, and GMOs.

An ethic of resource conservation, or an ethic of the responsible use of resources, provides an interesting standpoint from which to evaluate many of the problems we have discussed in this book and opens the door to different national and international perspectives. The debate about the wise and responsible use of our resources and how they relate to our food and energy needs is an especially important one. Our resolution of that debate will determine what world we leave to our descendants.

## Animal Rights and Welfare

The animal rights movement is, first, a logical extension of an environmental ethic that is respectful of the environment and its inhabitants. Second, it is a response to the ways in which human beings have historically used animals in some experiments. The animal rights movement is not of recent vintage, however. The antivivisection movement in England and the United States antedates the animal rights movement and has kept the issue of the irresponsible, or morally problematic, use of animals in experiments before the eyes of the public.

There are two basic orientations to animal rights. The first orientation is the more strict movement, which argues that animals and human beings are on the same moral level with respect to how individuals can treat them. The basis for ascribing rights, or at least interests, to animals is their capacity to feel pain, that is, because they are sentient. This orientation is combined with a rejection of speciesism: the conferring of privileged status on the human species simply because it is "our" species and can exert power over all other species. These two orientations combine to ground an ethic that rejects any human use of animals. As a sign of their consistency, members of the animal rights movement are typically vegetarians.

The second orientation is more utilitarian in nature; it sees animals as at the disposal of human beings but defines limits on their uses. Here, the ethical standard mandates that human beings treat animals in such a way that the human beings do not become desensitized to pain or brutalized by the treatment of animals. Thus, this ethic focuses not on the rights or interests of animals, but on what effects treating animals in a particular way will have on human beings.

On the one hand, the first orientation in the animal rights movement, originally in England but now, too, in the United States, includes a growing and continuing activism. Activists raid labs, liberate animals, issue injunctions, and terminate research. Clearly, these activities have focused attention on the conditions in which scientists house animals in labs, the worthiness of the experiments to which scientists subject them, and the pain animals undergo. As such, the movement has been responsible for initiating regulations and monitoring systems with respect to the treatment of animals in research as well as higher standards of cleanliness, feeding, and care in the labs themselves.

On the other hand, the second orientation accepts the subjugation of animals to humans, their use in experiments, and their function as a major food source. While this orientation would seek to accomplish these goals as humanely as possible, many will continue to inflict pain on animals, and many will continue to eat them without consideration of the sacrifices made. Furthermore, the use of animals as a source of organs for humans, whether transplanted directly or genetically engineered so they are less likely to be rejected, will continue to raise more complex questions.

## CONCLUSION

This chapter has introduced problems that are exceptionally complex. They have much to do with the traditional problem of resolving the tension between individual behavior and the common good. But they also raise problems concerning national and international policies. For example, one nation alone cannot solve the problem of acid rain. The same is true with respect to resolving energy issues and toxic waste disposal. How we use land

and other resources says a good deal about us, but the issues transcend individual and national behavior. They even transcend our time in history by calling attention to our obligations to future generations. Each individual can be responsible in terms of conservation, food habits, and waste disposal, but the country as a whole will still generate waste and will still consume nonrenewable resources to generate energy.

The difficulty of the problems and the complexity of their resolution do not excuse our not debating them. In fact, their very difficulty should motivate us to debate the issues immediately and to seek to resolve them.

## DISCUSSION QUESTIONS

1. What elements are involved in defining "the population problem"?
2. Should one country use food as a bargaining chip in international policy?
3. Do you think objects in the environment such as trees or mountains or forests have moral standing? Or, to ask the same question in a different way, do you think they have rights?
4. Do you think animals have similar rights as human beings do?
5. Do individual actions really have any significant impact on preserving the environment?

## NOTES

1. Nils Blythe, "India's Big Population Challenge," *BBC News*, http://news.bbc.co.uk/2/hi/business/7261458.stm, published February 24, 2008, accessed March 5, 2008.

2. "China Warns of Population Growth," *BBC News*, http://news.bbc.co.uk/2/hi/asia-pacific/6631471.stm, published May 7, 2007, accessed March 5, 2008.

3. For example, see Lisa Sowle Cahill, "Toward Global Ethics," *Theological Studies* 63, no. 2 (June 2002): 324–44; and Jean Porter, "The Search for a Global Ethic," *Theological Studies* 62, no. 1 (March 2001): 105–21.

4. For example, see Lisa Sowle Cahill, "Bioethics, Theology and Social Change," *Journal of Religious Ethics* 31 (2003): 386–91.

5. John Rodman, "Four Forms of Ecological Consciousness Reconsidered," in *Ethics and the Environment*, ed. Donald Scherer and Thomas Attig (Englewood Cliffs, NJ: Prentice Hall, 1983), 82–92.

# BIBLIOGRAPHY

Blythe, Nils. "India's Big Population Challenge." *BBC News.* http://news.bbc.co.uk/2/hi/business/7261458.stm. Published February 24, 2008. Accessed March 5, 2008.

Cahill, Lisa Sowle. "Bioethics, Theology and Social Change." *Journal of Religious Ethics* 31 (2003): 386–91.

———. "Toward Global Ethics." *Theological Studies* 63, no. 2 (June 2002): 324–44.

"China Warns of Population Growth." *BBC News.* http://news.bbc.co.uk/2/hi/asia-pacific/6631471.stm. Published May 7, 2007. Accessed March 5, 2008.

Farmer, Paul. *Pathologies of Power: Health, Human Rights, and the New War on the Poor.* Berkeley: University of California Press, 2005.

Porter, Jean. "The Search for a Global Ethic." *Theological Studies* 62, no. 1 (March 2001): 105–21.

Sachs, Jeffrey D. *Common Wealth: Economics for a Crowded Planet.* New York: Penguin Press, 2008.

Scherer, Donald, and Thomas Attig. *Ethics and the Environment.* Englewood Cliffs, NJ: Prentice Hall, 1983.

green
press
INITIATIVE

Paulist Press is committed to preserving ancient forests and natural resources. We elected to print this title on 30% post consumer recycled paper, processed chlorine free. As a result, for this printing, we have saved:

12 Trees (40' tall and 6-8" diameter)
5 Million BTUs of Total Energy
1,244 Pounds of Greenhouse Gases
5,608 Gallons of Wastewater
356 Pounds of Solid Waste

Paulist Press made this paper choice because our printer, Thomson-Shore, Inc., is a member of Green Press Initiative, a nonprofit program dedicated to supporting authors, publishers, and suppliers in their efforts to reduce their use of fiber obtained from endangered forests.

For more information, visit www.greenpressinitiative.org

Environmental impact estimates were made using the Environmental Defense Paper Calculator. For more information visit: www.papercalculator.org.